MUSIC IN ENGLISH RENAISSANCE DRAMA

MUSIC IN ENGLISH RENAISSANCE DRAMA

CONTRIBUTORS

Nan Cooke Carpenter

Ernest Brennecke

Ian Spink

R. W. Ingram

MacDonald Emslie

Willa McClung Evans

Vincent Duckles

EDITED BY

John H. Long

University of Kentucky Press
Lexington 1968

Printed in the United States
Library of Congress Catalog
Card No. 68-12969

INTRODUCTION

It is the purpose of this volume to present some significant examples of the use of music in English dramatic and semidramatic works composed and presented between the years 1550 and 1650, a span of a century which for this limited purpose shall serve as a temporal definition of the English Renaissance. The bulk of scholarship devoted to the subject in the past has been limited largely to the works of one playwright, Shakespeare, and to one semidramatic form, the court masque. Monumental as Shakespeare was and is, and magnificent as the court masques were, they did not encompass completely the versatility with which music was employed for dramatic purposes during the period, in the works of lesser playwrights or in the elaborate "entertainments," the interludes, the pageants, the folk-plays, and other more-or-less dramatic productions that, in intent and practice, merged one into another to defy formal categorization. It is not the aim of this symposium to explore all of these areas, but by means of a series of selected essays to call attention to the important influences of comparatively minor dramatic writers and less-known works on the mainstream of Renaissance drama and music in England, and to emphasize the richness of these areas as subjects for future study. Therefore, the essays treat as representative authors John Lyly, Thomas Campion, John Fletcher,

John Milton, and William Cartwright; types of dramas include the medieval mystery plays, the "entertainment," the "entertainment-masque," the familiar Elizabethan-Jacobean drama as written by Fletcher, and the Cavalier drama of Cartwright. The order is chronological.

The musical theory of the English Renaissance was a synthesis of classical and Christian concepts. Pythagoras, Plato, Aristotle, Boethius, and the later Polydore Virgil are some of the major contributors to an accumulation of myth, philosophy, religious exegesis, and numerology that developed throughout the classical and medieval centuries and presented the poets and dramatists of the sixteenth and seventeenth centuries a wealth of associations, similes, and metaphors. In general, Renaissance musical theory had four divisions–*divine music,* which exists as an archetype in the divine Intellect and which takes as its subject all harmonic proportions; *created music,* which depends upon divine music and takes as its subject the order and harmonic proportions of the created universe and each individual form; *mundane music,* or the harmony of creatures, elements, and forces of which the world is composed; and *human music,* or the association of musical harmony with the humors of the human body or microcosm. Divine music is incomprehensible by the human mind and is therefore beyond speculation. Created music may be described by the Pythagorean concept of "the music of the spheres" as expressed in *The Praise of Musicke,* published by Joseph Barnes in 1586:

> Pithagoras and his sectatours, thought that the world did not consist without musical proportion and concent. And therefore both he & the best philosophers ascribe unto every Celestial sphere, one *Goddess* or Muse, which is the governes & ruler thereof: & because there are eight of those spheres, the seven planets, and the eight which is called the firmament, therefore they made 8. peculiar Muses, attributing to *Luna* the muse *Clio*: to *Mercurius, Euterpe*: to *Venus, Thalia*: to *Sol, Melpomene*: to *Mars, Terpsichore*: to *Jupiter, Erato:* to *Saturne, Polymnia,* to the firmamēt or *coelum stellarum, Urania*: and because of eight particular sounds or voices, keeping due proportion and time, must needs arise an harmony or concent, which is made of them all, therefore that sound which all these make is called *Calliope.* And hence is that pleasant harmony of the celestial globes caused, which *Pythagoras* so much speaketh

> of. If then both Gods and men, and unreasonable creatures of what kind soever, be allured and mitigated with musicke, we may safely conclude that this proceedeth from that hidden virtue, which is between our soules and musicke: and be bold with *Pindarus* to affirme, that . . . Al those things that *Jupiter* doth not love, do only contemne the songs of the Muses.

Spenser shows us what a poet can do with the concept of mundane music as he describes the beauties of the Bower of Acrasia in *The Faerie Queene,* Book II, Cantos 70 and 71:

> Eftsoons they heard a most melodious sound
> Of all that mote delight a dainty ear,
> Such as at once might not on living ground,
> Save in this paradise, be heard elsewhere.
> Right hard it was for wight which did it hear
> To read what manner music that mote be,
> For all that pleasing is to living ear
> Was there consorted in one harmony—
> Birds, voices, instruments, winds, waters, all agree.
>
> The joyous birds, shrouded in cheerful shade,
> Their notes unto the voice attempered sweet;
> Th'angelical soft trembling voices made
> To th'instruments divine respondence meet;
> The silver sounding instruments did meet
> With the base murmur of the water's fall;
> The water's fall with difference discreet,
> Now soft, now loud, unto the wind did call;
> The gentle warbling wind low answered to all.

Human music is that physical and mental harmony attained by man when he acquires a proper balance of the four humors—body fluids. He is then in tune with his world and his universe; he is "good-humored" or "good-tempered." When mentally or physically unbalanced he becomes "bad-tempered" or "ill-humored." The harmony of sweet music brought to the ears of the distraught or melancholy man can heal him by sympathetically harmonizing his unbalanced humors. Conversely, harsh or discordant music can destroy the harmony of the four humors and make men mad. Shakespeare directs that soft music be played to help return the mad King Lear to sanity, and he has Cerimon, in *Pericles,* use music to restore life to the seemingly dead Marina. On the other hand, the incoherent bits of ballads sung by Ophelia and Hamlet reveal the disorder in the minds of these characters. Webster, we recall, has Ferdinand use a group of singing madmen to attack the sanity of the Duchess of Malfi.

The key term in Renaissance musical theory is "harmony." All of the concepts that can be defined by or associated with any kind of harmony—harmony within the individual, between man and man, man and woman, man and the state, man and nature, man and God—can also be expressed by music or associated with music. Therefore, performed music—*musica practica*—could be used by dramatists to suggest or to emphasize in characterization ethical, moral, and religious modes of thought or emotional states; it could be used to establish atmospheric (good or evil) settings and political and social contexts; it could be used as a rhetorical device to ornament or underscore set speeches by means of the emotional effects of the music on the audience; it could be used to make tangible various forces, both natural and supernatural. The flourish of trumpets that announces the entrance of an actor-king not only commands the attention of the spectators but is also a musical symbol of his authority and the harmony of the state which he personifies. Shakespeare is not simply theatrical when he directs that harmonious music be sounding as Prince Hal, *2 Henry IV,* picks up the crown from the bed of his dying father, places it on his own head, and claims it by rightful succession. By his legal succession to the throne he restores harmony to the state; the music marks this new political condition.

This brief sketch of Renaissance musical theory gives at least a glimpse of the main concepts that underlie the practice of music and allusions to music in the drama and poetry of the period. Certain habitual practices based upon this theory appear in the earliest English drama; they are established by the time Marlowe and Peele write their plays and, for the most part, are merely varied or extended by the later dramatists.

In the performance of the medieval mystery plays, beginning with the chanted *Quem quaeritis* trope and for centuries thereafter, music and drama were inseparable. Following Scriptural authority in dramatic materials and drawing upon the familiar corpus of church music, the mystery plays proclaimed the glory of God in both words and music—music both vocal and instrumental, sacred and secular. When Elizabeth began her reign in 1558, the mystery plays were still being performed, and for about two decades they would share the Elizabethan public's interest in drama and make their impress upon the emerging secular stage. Nan Cooke Carpenter, in "Music in the English Cycle Plays," traces the development of several musico-dramatic practices as they originate in particular mystery plays. The patterns she demonstrates are the prototypes for some of the conventional practices of the later Elizabethan and Jacobean dramatists; her survey thus provides an appropriate introduction to the essays that follow it.

Coincident with the rapid development of secular drama in the hands of Marlowe, Greene, Peele, and others, the spectacular court progresses and "entertainments"—a blending of classical learning and adulation of royalty in various semidramatic forms—replaced the dramatic glorification of God found in the mystery plays with an exaltation of the Vicar of God in the person of the English monarch, who was both temporal and spiritual ruler of the realm. The intent of the entertainment was to praise a spiritual ruler, but the content reflected the humanistic learning that flourished under the patronage of the Queen. Ernest Brennecke reconstructs the historical setting, the events, and the music performed during the course of the lavish entertainment given Queen Elizabeth at Elvetham in 1591. The music and its performance emphasize the classical quality of the Renaissance musical theory.

In the summer of 1617, King James was given a royal entertainment on the occasion of his visit to Brougham Castle. This event, for which Thomas Campion may have been largely responsible, differed from the Elvetham entertainment mentioned above. Although it was an entertainment in that it consisted of a series of musical and semidramatic performances extending over several days, it also included a well-defined masque. The court masque had earlier reached its peak of formal development at the hands of Ben Jonson. Since the formal masque was the most successful attempt of its time to achieve an art form which combined, in more-or-less equal proportions, the arts of poetry, song, instrumental music, dance, and scenic design (all within a semidramatic method of presentation), the proper matching of music to dramatic or declamatory text in conformity with the musical theory outlined earlier posed a new problem for composers of songs for the masque. Ian Spink, in the course of his description of "Campion's Entertainment at Brougham Castle, 1617," discusses the solution of this problem by the creation of a new kind of song, the recitative or declamatory song. A few years later Henry Lawes would be acclaimed for his skill in composing this type of song.

In "Patterns of Music and Action in Fletcherian Drama," R. W. Ingram explores Fletcher's use of music to evoke emotional or psychological responses in the audience; in other words, his is a study of the "rhetoric" of music. The "rhetoric" of music, of course, would have been understood by Fletcher and his contemporaries in terms of that theoretical part of music called *musica humana,* the effect of music on the body's humors.

One of the most familiar commendations of the musical settings of Henry Lawes is Milton's Sonnet XIII, "To My Friend, Mr. Henry Lawes, On His Airs." MacDonald Emslie in his "Milton on Lawes: The Trinity MS Revisions" considers the changes made by Milton in composing his sonnet—changes designed to identify the declamatory ayre as the type he had in mind when praising Lawes' success in setting the songs for *Comus.* Milton as both musician and poet was of course familiar with the musical theory of his age; he could hardly be surpassed as a critic of the new declamatory style.

The declamatory air, apparently originating in dramatic performances, continues this association in the Cavalier drama, as Willa M. Evans notes in her essay, "Cartwright's Debt to Lawes." In the conclusion of *The Royal Slave,* the declamatory song is a part of the music and ritual, which are a paganized version of the Christian sacrament of the Eucharist. Thus, in one of the last dramas of the English Renaissance are summed up many of the influences that combined to make its music and drama golden—the religious music and ritual of the medieval mystery plays, the rhetorical pomp and musical pageantry of the entertainments and masques, the poetry and emotional appeal of Fletcher's verse and music, and the merging of poetry, drama, and music in the declamatory songs of Lawes.

Sustained and thorough study of the music in English Renaissance drama is comparatively recent, and some of the requisite tools are still experimental or inadequate. The bibliography of the subject, for example, is scattered and unorganized. Vincent Duckles helps to remedy this weakness by providing a listing of the musical settings for the lyrics in early seventeenth-century English drama, the primary sources. More general than the specialized compilations of Murray Lefkowitz, Willa M. Evans, John Cutts, Ian Spink, MacDonald Emslie, and others, Duckles' listing permits immediate reference to the music for the texts of dramas and masques composed between 1603 and 1662. It may also serve as an accurate quantitative measure of the importance of music and song in English Renaissance drama after the death of Queen Elizabeth.

Taken together, the essays in this volume illuminate each other and collectively reveal the scope of the subject and the range of investigative techniques used in treating its topics. Here the scholar may almost at a glance survey the field of study and observe both the results of careful research and the dim outlines of areas yet to be explored. The hiatus between our knowledge of the music in medieval drama and that in the Elizabethan drama suggests the need for more study of the music in early-Tudor plays; the attention given to the entertainments and masques also serves to accentuate our ignorance of the musical performances in the Lord Mayors' pageants and similar semidramatic shows. Underlying and linking the apparently disparate essays in this symposium are a unifying theory and traditional practices that this collection may place in sharper focus as general principles are followed by practical applications. Even so, many of the particulars remain obscure.

None of the authors treated herein, excepting Milton, may be numbered among the great English poets and playwrights; none of the musicians can equal a Bach or Beethoven; none of the semidramatic works, and few of those dramatic, will probably be again presented on the stage. Yet, without some knowledge of them our understanding of the Renaissance man and his art is defective. And, as it is the blending of poetry, drama, and music in accord with a comprehensive musical theory that is especially characteristic of Renaissance drama, it is well that these three components be studied as they were used, that is, as organic parts of single works of art. In our time it is not easy to find scholars equipped to observe intelligently and simultaneously all three components and their relationships. Fortunately, I was able to call upon these scholars, each eminently qualified to deal with the three areas described. For their willing and generous contributions to this volume I am grateful.

JOHN H. LONG
Greensboro College
March 22, 1967

CONTENTS

CONTENTS

ILLUSTRATIONS

MUSIC IN THE ENGLISH MYSTERY PLAYS

Nan Cooke Carpenter

MUSIC in the medieval drama is a subject that has been barely touched upon by historians of either literature or music.[1] And yet liturgical drama was actually musical drama; the words were sung throughout, often to the accompaniment of musical instruments.

Modern drama was, in fact, born of music. Its earliest beginning was as an organic part of the sung Mass—a form of worship that has rightly been called a vast drama in itself, celebrating and symbolizing in words and music the life, suffering, and resurrection of Our Lord. When some anonymous tropist perceptively inserted a few lines of peripheral dialogue into the Introit of the Mass for Easter—simple question-and-answer amplification of the Easter story, to be sung antiphonally—he opened the way for the birth of medieval drama. And when this simple dialogue, the so-called *Quem quaeritis* trope, was moved from the Roman Mass to the celebration of Matins in the Canonical Office a few hours after midnight, with singers impersonating the angel and the three Marys, the *Quem quaeritis* play became an actuality, the ovum from which modern drama was born.[2]

The earliest extant manuscript of the *Quem quaeritis* play dates from the mid-tenth century and comes from the monastery of St. Gall in what is now Switzerland. This monastery was especially famous for its cultural activities during the Carolingian Renaissance and counted among its membership several monks who were distinguished composers of tropes and sequences. Pictures of the St. Gall manuscript and other early examples of the *Quem quaeritis* trope are often found in histories of the drama. These show words written beneath staffless neumes and also give stage directions specifically stating that the lines are to be sung and the dialogue acted out with proper costumes.

As time went on, dramatic tropes for other occasions were added to the liturgy. For example, the Christmas trope imitated the one for Easter, with "Whom seek ye in the manger?" replacing the Easter query "Whom seek ye in the tomb?" Eventually there came to be a number of short plays associated with the *Sepulchrum* (Easter play) and the *Pastores* (Nativity play), dramatic amplifications of incidents from the Bible or the apocryphal writings. The Canonical Hour of Matins—with its three services called nocturnes at nine o'clock, midnight, and three in the morning—seems to have been a favorite spot for these dramatic insertions, which were placed between the third responsory and the *Te Deum* closing the service. The inclusion of the *Te Deum* at the end of a play, in fact, relates it quite specifically to Matins. Vespers was another service much favored for short plays; and here the ending of a play with the *Magnificat* effectively brought it back to the regular order of worship.

Along with these plays that branched off organically from the ecclesiastical chant of the Mass or Office, there grew up also an enormous body of plays inspired by non-Biblical characters. These are nowadays referred to as miracle plays, for they commemorate the life of a saint, characterized generally by the performance of miracles. These dramatized saints' legends became a part of the Office on the appropriate feast day. Again, the origin of this type of play is the sung liturgy of Mass and Office, including sequences and antiphons amplifying and embellishing the original plainchant.[3] By far, the most popular of such plays was the St. Nicholas play, emphasizing the saint's kindness to children, one or more of whom are usually restored to life after having been cruelly murdered. Such plays, in verse and set to music, generally end with the *Te Deum* or an antiphon *(O Christi pietas)* attached to the *Magnificat*, bringing the performance back to the ordinary procedure of Matins or Vespers.[4]

Although musical notation appears in manuscripts of the early *Sepulchra, Pastores,* and other liturgical plays from the Old and New Testaments, this notation is in the form of chironomic or staffless neumes. The notation is such, in other words, that one can get no clear indication of pitch from it—as in the great English collection of music from the eleventh century called the *Winchester Troper.*[5] The famous collection of songs from the same century called the *Carmina Burana* contains a Christmas play—"truly comprehensive," as Professor Young observes, "uniting all the dramatic themes of Christmas"—noted in staffless neumes.[6]

With the introduction of lines to indicate pitch, however, the musical setting to plays from later times can be more accurately determined and the music transcribed into modern notation. A miracle play on a New Testament theme, the conversion of St. Paul, in the French manuscript from the twelfth century called the *Fleury Playbook,* is noted on a four-line staff.[7] A final rubric here relates the play to Matins: "Omnes Apostoli incipiant Te Deum laudamus. Sic finiatur." Other such plays are discussed and the texts given in Karl Young's volumes. One of these, the Beauvais play of Daniel, has been most successfully revived at the Cloisters in New York in very recent times. Gorgeously mounted, the play is sung throughout by soloists and chorus. There are charming musical interludes, and various characters are distinguished by the same instruments each time they appear—the Queen, for instance, by little bells. Some of the rubrics give specific musical directions, and the chorus of princes before King Darius sings of praising him with drums, lutes, and organs:

> Simul omnes gratulemur; resonent et tympana;
> Cythariste tangent cordas; musicorum organa
> resonent ad eius preconia.[8]

The enthusiastic reception that the play has received is convincing proof of the great effectiveness of this type of music drama. Indeed, listening to the recording alone, with none of the colorful spectacle of the actual performance, one will be amazed at the beauty and vitality of it all.[9]

During the high and later Middle Ages (roughly, between 1200 and 1325), the plays underwent a gradual transition from the church with its readymade body of professional musicians to the town laity and, at the same time, changed from Latin to the vernacular.[10] Establishment of the feast of Corpus Christi in 1311 by Pope Clement V and the procession characteristically associated with that event seem to have given great impetus to the production of Biblical plays by the craft guilds in England.[11] As part of this celebration, the Corpus Christi play—"a dramatic species in cosmic form," as it has been described—was set up, "probably on the model of an inclusive dramatic form invented on the Continent, about the end of the first quarter of the 14th century, and probably in the north of England, spreading from there to other parts of the country."[12]

The Corpus Christi cycle of plays dramatized Biblical episodes from the Fall of Man in the Garden of Eden to the Last Judgment. Of the many such plays known to have been in existence, four complete cycles are extant today, as well as a number of separate plays. It has long been thought that these plays were, for the most part, performed on wagons that moved from one place to another, each play being succeeded by the next one in the cycle.[13] And even although the plays, now out of the church, no longer had a highly trained clergy to act and sing in them, nonetheless the centuries-old tradition of music in the medieval plays seems to have carried over to a large extent, as these plays became the exclusive property of town artisans and master craftsmen, all members of the trade guilds.

Generally agreed to be the oldest of the four extant cycles of plays are the Chester plays.[14] Consisting of twenty-five plays from the *Fall of Lucifer* to *Doomsday,* this cycle is thought to have originated in the late thirteenth or early fourteenth century. Largest of all the cycles is the set of plays from York—forty-eight plays, dating from 1340-1350.[15] This cycle was a strong influence upon the Wakefield Corpus Christi plays (also called Towneley plays, after the family who once owned the manuscript). In fact, it is now believed that at one time the York and Wakefield plays were one and the same, that late in the fourteenth century the York cycle was borrowed and set up at nearby Wakefield, and that thereafter each cycle underwent its own line of development.[16] The Wakefield cycle, apparently, was revised a number of times—once at the hands of the so-called Wakefield Master, an unidentified cleric with a strong sense of humor (and a strong musical sense!) who lived around the middle of the fifteenth century.

The fourth cycle differs markedly, in certain respects, from the

Chester, York, and Wakefield plays. These forty-two pageants, called by the cycle's first editor *Ludus Coventriae,* have nothing to do with the city of Coventry (which had its own cycle of plays, of which two remain) and are preferably referred to as the Hegge plays, from the name of a former owner of the manuscript.[17] Compared to the other three complete cycles, these plays are chiefly distinguished by the importance given to the Virgin Mary and to her mother, St. Anne. It is now thought that the plays were given in the city of Lincoln, dedicated from ancient times to the worship of Mary and the honoring of St. Anne. The manuscript containing the *Ludus Coventriae* dates from around 1468, but, like other cycles, this one undoubtedly developed over a long period of time.

Music plays a most important and often exciting role in all the cycles. One notices, first of all, that it is consistently associated with angelic beings. Archangels acknowledge God's presence and glory with "a songe *Dignus Dei*" in the opening play *(The Fall of Lucifer)* of the Chester cycle:

> hym for to thanke with somp solace
> A songe now let us singe in feare.[18]

And angels sing again later, as God withdraws.[19] Similarly, in the York play of the Creation, God speaks of his greatness and of the nine orders of angels, who praise him everlastingly. This is immediately dramatized, as the angels do actually sing the *Te Deum.*[20] And in the same play, after God exalts Lucifer, the angelic choir underline God's power by singing the *Sanctus* from the Mass: "*Tunc cantant angeli, Sanctus sanctus sanctus, dominus deus sabaoth.*"[21] Almost identical here is the musical usage in the parallel Hegge play, where God describes Heaven in terms of angelic singing:

> In hevyn I bylde angelle fful bryth,
> My servauntes to be, and for my sake
> With merth and melody worchepe my myth.
> . . . . .
> Aungelle in hevyn evyrmore xal be
> . . . . .
> With myrthe and song to worchip me,
> Of joys thei may not mys.[22]

As God ceases to speak, his words come alive—for angels in Heaven, according to the stage directions, sing the *Sanctus.*[23]

Angelic singing heightens the scene of the Salutation or Annunciation in two or perhaps three of the cycles. The Chester play of the Salutation has Gabriel make the wonderful announcement to Mary in lines that could be either spoken or sung, beginning, "Haile be thou, Mary, maiden free."[24] In the York play, this important scene is altogether musical.[25] Stage directions bid the angel Gabriel sing *("Tunc cantat angelus")* as he makes his announcement, beginning with the familiar greeting "Hayle! Marie! full of grace and blysse." And Gabriel reassures Mary with song *("Tunc cantat angelus, Ne timeas Maria")* as she questions him in wonderment at the strange news. The antiphon *Ne timeas, Maria* follows the *Ave Maria* at Second Vespers on March 25, the Annunciation of the Blessed Virgin Mary. Mary's singing of the *Magnificat* (always sung at Vespers) closes the scene in the York play.

Even more elaborate, musically speaking, is the parallel scene in the Hegge plays.[26] Here, after a brief morality play in which Truth, Mercy, Justice, and Peace converse with the Father and Son, God sends the angel Gabriel to tell Mary that she is to bear God's son to redeem the world. Gabriel agrees to go immediately ("I take my flyth and byde nowth"), after which appear the words of the beloved antiphon in honor of Mary sung in many a Mass and Office, always as Gabriel's salutation—*"Ave Maria gratia plena, Dominus tecum!"* Perhaps these words are chanted by a choir to mark the quick transition of Gabriel from Heaven to earth: "It xal be do with a thought," the angel has just said to the Father. Gabriel at once greets Mary, paraphrasing in English and explaining the Latin words: "Heyl, fful of grace, God is with the. . . ." At the end of the play, as Gabriel prepares to return to Heaven, he says,

> And as I began, I ende with an Ave new,
> Enjonyd hefne and erthe with that I ascende.

Then the angels sing the sequence in honor of the Virgin *("Angeli cantando istam sequenciam"):*

> Ave Maria gratia plena!
> Dominus tecum, virgo serena!

In each of the Nativity plays in the four cycles, the angel's *Gloria in excelsis* is the high point, prompting the listening shepherds to discuss the music in a lively manner and to imitate the celestial singing. This *Gloria* is actually from the first respond at Matins on Christmas Day and is therefore a significant reminder of the beginnings of drama in the expansion of the liturgy of the Office at important times in the church year. It is a musical angel, too, in the Chester *Slaying of the Innocents* who warns the Holy Family to flee into Egypt, with the promise:

> that men of Egipt Gods can call,
> at your coming downe shall fall,
> when I begin to singe.[27]

This promise is dramatically carried out, for according to the stage direction, statues and images are to come crashing down as the angel sings an antiphon. After the death of Herod, the angel bids the Holy Family return to Judea, promising protection with music:

> And I will make a melody,
> and singe here in your company. . . .[28]

The words of the plainsong follow: "Ex Agipto vocavi filium meum, ut Salvum faciet populum meum"—appropriately enough, the antiphon for Vespers on Friday in the first week of Advent. In the parallel play of the Wakefield cycle, the angel's warning is also sung —Joseph wonders aloud at the "sweet tune" of the angel who has just warned him to flee into Egypt:

> A ! myghtfull god,
> what euer this ment,
> so swete of toyn?[29]

In the Wakefield *Purification of Mary,* angels sing *("Angeli cantant")* —obviously, the *Nunc dimittis,* although the song is not specified— after Simeon has received the Child in the Temple.[30] And in the Chester dramatization of Christ's descent into Hell, the archangel Michael leads Adam and the good souls to Paradise, all singing the *Te Deum.*[31] Michael figures also in the Chester play of Antichrist, when, after having slain Antichrist, the angel leads Enoch and Elijah to Heaven singing a joyful strain: "Gaudete Iusti in Domino,"[32] which is the verse from the *Alleluia* for the Mass of St. Thomas (December 21).

When two angels are specifically called for, the chances are that the music introduced is a two-part setting of the appropriate plainsong. After John has baptized Jesus in the York play of the Baptism, two angels sing the hymn *Veni creator spiritus.*[33] This tune, traditionally sung at Terce on Whitsunday,[34] is an old Gregorian hymn, a great favorite with medieval composers as a basis for polyphonic settings. The beautiful Gregorian melody may be found in the *Liber Usualis* at Second Vespers for Whitsunday. This same hymn, sung by angels, enhances the spirituality of the scene in the next play in the York cycle, *The Temptation of Jesus,* as Jesus resists the devil.[35] The Hegge plays also include a scene of the Temptation, in which angels sing "Gloria tibi, Domine!" as they minister to Jesus after he has successfully resisted Satan.[36]

In three of the cycles, the Resurrection is solemnized with angelic singing, and each time the music specified is the Easter processional antiphon celebrating Christ's rising from the dead, *Christus resurgens.*[37] In the Chester play, two angels sing "Christus resurgens a mortuis" as Jesus rises from the tomb, watched over by the soldiers.[38] In the York play, one angel sings of the event *("tunc angelus cantat Resurgens")* as Jesus rises; and later, in telling of this marvel, a soldier speaks in wonderment of the music:

> We herde never sen we were borne,
> Nor all oure faderes vs be-forne,
> Suche melodie, mydday ne morne,
> As was made there.[39]

In the Wakefield play, the scene unfolds exactly as in the Chester pageant: soldiers sleep, Jesus rises, and the angels sing *Christus resurgens.*[40]

Another especially solemn moment in each cycle, the Ascension, is invariably accompanied by angelic singing; and in each cycle the antiphon sung at Lauds of the Ascension of Our Lord is the focal point: *Ascendo ad patrem meum.* The scene in the Chester cycle is apparently sung throughout, for the words *"cantat"* or *"cantet"* are carefully noted for each speaker. According to a stage direction, Jesus sings the antiphon *Ascendo;* and when the song is finished, Jesus appears upon a cloud amid a chorus of angels, as the lines of the scene are sung antiphonally between Jesus, two angels, and a chorus.[41] The Latin plainsong is immediately paraphrased in English verse. As Jesus ascends out of sight, the angelic choir sing praises and hallelujahs.[42] Following this, angels are directed to descend and to sing "Viri Galilei quid aspicitis in Coelum?" which is both Introit for the Mass of the Ascension and antiphon for Second Vespers.[43] This is also paraphrased in English verse, either spoken or sung.

In the York play of the Ascension, the dialogue may be spoken, but again angels sing as Jesus rises to Heaven, for a marginal note reads "Ascendo ad patrem meum. Tunc cantent angeli."[44] So, too, in the Wakefield play, Jesus ascends to the Father as an angelic chorus sing the antiphon *Ascendo*.[45] Finally, in the Hegge play, celestial music is heard as Jesus rises to Heaven before the eyes of the disciples.[46] Although the song is not specified, there can be no doubt as to what form the music takes. Jesus' last words on this occasion, in fact, refer to this music:

> With myrthe, and melody, and aungelle songe,
> Now I stey streyte ffro zow to hevyn.

Two of the cycles, Chester and York, contain a *Descent of the Holy Ghost* after the Ascension, and both are embellished by the music of angels. The Chester play calls for Peter and the Apostles to sing the beautiful hymn already discussed, *Veni creator spiritus*.[47] An elaborate stage direction then shows how the Father's promise to send his "ghost" to strengthen the Apostles in their work is to be carried out to music. For as God sends the Holy Spirit in the form of fire, two angels are to sing the antiphon for Lauds on Whitsunday, *Accipite spiritum sanctum,* and while singing, they are to spread the fire upon the Apostles.[48] Quite similar to this is the parallel scene in the York cycle, where an angel sings the Pentecostal hymn and the Apostles comment upon the angelic music:

> In thare sigging saide thei thus,
> And tolde ther talis be-twene them two,
> *Veni creator spiritus,*
> *mentes tuorum visita.*[49]

It is interesting to note here that the Apostles refer to the singing of two angels, showing us that stage directions (here specifying an angel) appear to be the simplest of indications, allowing for expansion at will.

Mary's ascension into Heaven in the York cycle takes place to celestial singing, for Jesus sends a chorus of angels to fetch his mother ("bringe me my modir to the highest of heuene, / With mirthe and with melody hir mode for to mende").[50] "A semely song latte vs sing," suggests an angel, after which the singing angels honor the Virgin with *Ave regina celorum,* one of the four antiphons of the Virgin, sung at Vespers from Purification until Easter. The unique play in which Our Lady appears in a vision to Thomas (the famous York 46) gives us many interesting sidelights on musical usage in the plays. To Thomas, asleep in the Vale of Jehoshaphat, Mary appears, with angels singing before her: *"Surge proxima mea columba mea tabernaculum glorie vasculum vite templum celeste."*[51] Each of twelve angels then addresses Mary, in English, the sixth one paraphrasing the words (reminiscent of the Song of Songs) of the opening song: "Rise, turtour, tabernacle, and tempull full trewe." The angels then sing a verse from Solomon's Song (IV, 8): *"Veni de libano sponsa veni coronaberis,"* which evokes a response in Thomas: "But this mirthe and this melody mengis my mode." The vision vanishes amid singing a *versus alleluiaticus* for the Feast of a Virgin and Martyr and other services for women: *"Veni electa mea et ponam in te tronum meum Quia concupiuit rex speciem tuam";* and Thomas returns to the other disciples, as he has been bidden to do, taking with him the Virgin's girdle, given him as a token. The music for all these songs was thought important enough by the copyist to be included in the manuscript of the play, and the pieces are noted in a sophisticated setting of two parts—basically note-against-note, a plainchant melody with a discant written above. The pieces are written out twice, in fact, for they occur again at the end of the play in a slightly more elaborate version.

The last play in which Mary figures in the York cycle—*The Assumption and Coronation*—is again marked throughout by angelic singing. The angels sing *("Cantando")* as Mary rises from the grave and as the sixth angel tells of the joys of Heaven:

> Alle heuene and erthe schall worschippe the,
>
> . . . . . .
>
> Thy joie schall euere incressid be,
> Of solas sere than schall thou synge.[52]

And as Jesus places the crown on Mary's head, he bids the angels sing again:

> Myne aungellis bright, a songe ȝe singe,
> In the honnoure of my modir dere.

In a list of plays to be performed at York, 1415, with guilds responsible for each, there is the item: "Hostilers—Maria, Jesus coronans eam, cum turba angelorum cantans."[53] Here is another indication that the choir of angels was an indispensable part of this pageant.

Mariolatry is particularly strong in the York plays, but the Hegge cycle is unique in laying great stress upon both Mary and her mother, St. Anne. Angelic singing is a regular part of the scenes dramatizing episodes in the lives of these ladies. Just before the annunciation in *The Barrenness of Anna,* we find the direction:

> *Here the aungel descendith the hefne syngyng,*
> *"Exultet cœlum laudibus!*
> *Resultet terra gaudiis!*
> *Archangelorum gloria*
> *Sacra canunt solemnia."*[54]

The hymn is regularly sung at Lauds for the Common of Apostles.[55] Joachim, Anna's husband, reacts strongly to the celestial music, asking:

> Qwhat art thou, in Goddys name, that makyst me adrad?
> It is as lyth abowt me as al the werd were fere.

Continuing the story of Anna and her daughter, the play *Mary in the Temple* follows. Here angels constantly attend the young girl, to the accompaniment of celestial harmonies. We read, for example, *"Here the aungel bryngyth manna in a cowpe of gold lyke to confeccions, the hefne syngynge."*[56] And a bit later, more specific heavenly singing is called for: *"Here xal comyn alwey an aungel with dyvers presentes, goynge and comynge, and in the tyme thei xal synge in hefne this hympne, 'Jhesu corona virginum.'"* The hymn is a regular part of Vespers of the Common of Virgins.

From the point of view of music, perhaps the high point of all the Hegge plays is the last play dramatizing scenes from the life of the Virgin, *The Assumption of Mary.* For here the full panoply of voices and instruments is called into play—including, of course, the angelic chorus. As Mary kneels in prayer in the Temple, two angels appear. The First Angel descends to speak to Mary, while both angels play on their harps.[57] Later, the Lord Jesus descends with all the heavenly court and speaks to his mother, saying that he is here "Wyth the hefnely quer yowre dirige to rede"; the *organa* play (organ or instruments or both), Mary's soul leaves her body, and the entire celestial court bursts into song.[58] The disciples bear Mary's corporeal remains to the tomb while the angels sweetly sing in heaven *Allelujah!*[59] A Bishop who is present is overwhelmed at the angelic *Allelujah* and wonders what it means:

> The erthe and eyer is ful of melodye;
> I herde never er sweche a noyse now i-wys:
> Con ye outh say what they signefye?[60]

And a Prince comments on the wondrous noise:

> . . . sweche another noyse herd I never er;
> Myn herte gynnyth ogyl and quake for fer.

The Lord Jesus bids his angels and "alle this court celestyalle" to descend to earth to bring Mary to Heaven. The angels respond with music: "Ya, for yowre hye mercy, Lord, all hefne makyth melodé."[61] And as Mary rises to Heaven, the musicians play and the entire chorus sings the antiphon for Vespers of the Assumption of the Blessed Virgin Mary (August 15): "Assumpta est Maria in caelum: gaudent Angeli, Laudantes benedicunt Dominum."[62]

Angelic singing, finally, accompanies the good souls on their journey to Heaven in the final plays in each cycle. In the Chester play of the Last Judgment, Jesus descends in a cloud, his presence enhanced by the angelic chorus. As these angels bring up to Jesus "those Soules that bene withouten Sinne," they are directed to sing an antiphon of rejoicing or the hymn *Salvator mundi.*[63] Similarly, in the parallel York play, God descends to judge the dead, accompanied by a chorus of angels, who sing as the good and bad go off to reward or punishment.[64] In the Wakefield play, everyone sings the *Te Deum,* as the good souls climb toward Heaven.[65] And in the Doomsday play of the Hegge cycle, one may assume that celestial music again embellishes the passage of the blessed souls to God's right hand, for Peter says to these souls:

> Com on, and sytt on Goddys ryght syde,
> Where myrthe and melody nevyr may mys.[66]

The largest amount of singing, then, in the pageants seems to have been on the part of the angels—either solo, duo, or chorus—

invariably accompanying and underlining scenes of great spiritual significance or scenes of great joy. Occasionally, however, other highly placed participants act as soloists. We have noticed Jesus' participation in antiphonal singing with a chorus of angels as his ascension is dramatized. Jesus sings antiphonally with the Apostles in Latin and in English in the play *Thomas of India* in the Wakefield cycle.[67]

In the Chester and York cycles, Mary sings the *Magnificat*—the canticle of the Blessed Virgin regularly sung at Vespers—after Gabriel's announcement about the birth of Jesus.[68] And in the Hegge play, a whole scene is devoted to this canticle: *The Visit of Elizabeth* consists largely of antiphonal recitation of the verses of this chant—either spoken or sung—as Mary gives each verse in English and Elizabeth responds with the Latin equivalent. At the conclusion of this, Mary comments:

> This psalme of prophesye seyd betwen us tweyn,
> In hefne it is wretyn with aungellys hond,
> Evyr to be songe and also to be seyn,
> Every day amonge us at our evesong.[69]

The canticle *Benedictus* occupies a place at Lauds similar to that of the *Magnificat* at Vespers. Thus, a bit later in the same scene, the *Benedictus* is explained as the special song of Elizabeth and Zachary:

> He [zakarye] and Elizabeth prophesyed as thus,
> They mad *Benedictus* them beforn;
> And so *Magnificat*, and *Benedictus*,
> ffyrst in that place ther made worn.[70]

At the end of the scene, all the players sing the well-known antiphon to the Virgin:

> With Ave we begunne, and Ave is our conclusyon,
> *Ave regina cœlorum* to oure Lady we synge.

In the Wakefield Prophet play, David sings a long prophecy of the coming of Jesus, accompanying himself on his harp.[71] And three of the cycles contain a Purification scene in which the *Nunc dimittis* is sung after Simeon receives the Child in the Temple. (A regular part of the Office of Compline, this chant is generally sung antiphonally by cantor and choir.) In the Chester play, Simeon sings the chant; in the Wakefield play, angels sing; and in the Hegge play, Simeon or perhaps a choir—or both—sing the canticle.[72]

There are many other occasions when large choruses of non-angelic characters participate in the singing. This happens in two of the Noah plays. In the Chester play, the assembled company sing praises to God after everyone is safely aboard.[73] In the Hegge play, Noah and his company come aboard the ark singing *("statim intrat Noe cum navi cantantes")*.[74] And after the dove returns with an olive branch, Noah suggests a song in praise of God:

> ffor joye of this tokyn ryght hertyly we tende
> Our lord God to worchep, a songe let us synge.

The play ends as the company sing Latin plainsong verses appropriate to the occasion, glorifying God for having caused the waters to recede:

> Mare vidit et fugit,
> Jordanis conversus est retrorsum,
> Non nobis, Domine, non nobis,
> Sed nomini tuo da gloriam.

The stage direction immediately preceding these verses *("Hic decantent hos versus")* probably refers to singing in discant style—in two-part or three-part harmony.

The York cycle contains a play, *The Departure of the Israelites into Egypt,* which calls for a song of praise by the assembled players. After the Egyptians are drowned in the Red Sea, a boy suggests,

> Now ar we wonne, fra waa, and saued oute of the see.
> Cantemus domino, to god a sange synge wee.[75]

The song of gratitude is not indicated, being left to the discretion of the singers. Priests and worshipers in the Temple furnish a good deal of choral music in the St. Anne plays of the Hegge cycle. For example, *"There they xal synge this sequens, 'Benedicta sit beata Trinitas,'"* we read, as Anna and her husband are sacrificing in the Temple; and antiphonal singing follows, between Bishop and chorus.[76] In *Mary's Betrothment,* a bit later in the cycle, the Bishop announces the singing of the hymn *Veni creator spiritus:*

> Mekely eche man ffalle downe on kne,
> And we xal begynne *Veni Creator spiritus.*[77]

The assembled company sing the hymn *("Et hic cantent 'Veni Creator' ")* and during the actual betrothal repeat the sequence sung earlier—*Benedicta sit beata Trinitas.*[78] The ceremony over, the Bishop speaks of singing to record "this solempn ded":

> Here is the holyest matremony that evyr was in this werd,
> The hyz names of oure lord we wole now syng hy,
> We alle wole this solempn ded recorde
> Devowtly. Alma chorus Domini nunc pangat nomina Summi![79]

Triumphal singing on the part of the multitude is a part of the drama in three of the cycles as Jesus rides into Jerusalem. The Chester play contains an elaborate note directing a choir of boys bearing palm branches and citizens spreading clothing on the road to sing *Hosanna in excelsis.*[80] In the York play, the importance of the music is underlined by a conversation about it between a blind man (Cecus) and a poor man (Pauper).[81] The former asks, "What noyse is this that makis me gladde?" And in explaining the coming of Jesus to his sightless companion, the poor man speaks of the singing:

> And all the cetezens thay are bowne
> Gose hym to mete with melodye.

At the end of the scene, there is more singing *("tunc cantant").* Although the music is not specified here, it was obviously the processional antiphon for Palm Sunday, *Hosanna in excelsis*—still sung as hymn or anthem in many orthodox congregations on Palm Sunday. For in the play *Jesus Before Pilate,* a Beadle, sent to fetch Jesus, bows to him and observes,

> They worshipped the full holy on hy,
> And with solempnite sange Osanna till.[82]

A bit later the Beadle describes the entry into Jerusalem, remarking once again on the music:

> Osanna thei sange, the sone of dauid
>
> . . . . .
>
> And made myrthe and melody this man for to mete.

There is no play of the triumphal entry in the Wakefield cycle, but in the Hegge play, a chorus of children sing praises: *"Here Cryst passyth forth, ther metyth with hym a serteyn of chylderyn with flowers, and cast beforn hym, and they synggyn 'Gloria Laus.'* "[83]

Very rarely does one find secular music called for in the plays. The "Song of the Good Gossips" in the Chester Noah play is a unique interpolation. Here for the first time in any play, as far as we know, is a vernacular song used for specifically dramatic purposes. Traditionally, there is discord between Noah and his wife—comedy that strongly marks the impingement of British humor on the religious drama. In the Chester play, Mrs. Noah refuses to board the ark without her "good gossips." These cronies sing with her a drinking song at the height of the argument:

> Heare is a pottill full of Malmsine good and stronge;
> Itt will rejoyce bouth harte and tonge;
> Though Noye thinke us never so longe,
> Heare we will drinke alike.[84]

Once Mrs. Noah is on board, there is no more comedy, and the subsequent singing is limited, as we have seen, to psalms in praise of God.

The shepherds invariably sing in the various Nativity plays, and at least some of their music is secular, possibly in the form of carols. In the Chester cycle, stage directions state that the shepherds (and supporting players) sing a merry song as they set off for Bethlehem.[85] In fact, several manuscripts of this play direct, "Sing troly-loly troly loe"—surely a merry song from the vernacular. After having presented their gifts to the Christ Child, the shepherds go off singing: "brethren, let us all three / Singing walke homewardes," says the Second Shepherd.[86] And at the end of the play, the Third Shepherd directs, perhaps to all on stage: "Amen all singe ye." A prolonged, elaborate *Amen,* set for many voices, would make a most effective close to the pageant. In the York play, one of the shepherds suggests that they go to seek the Child with music ("And make myrthe and melody, / with sange to seke oure savyour"), but no hint is given as to what they sing *("Et tunc cantant").*[87] After presenting their gifts, the herdsmen sing as they go off—"And go we hame agayne, / And make mirthe as we gange," says the Third Shepherd—and thus the play ends with music.[88]

The Wakefield cycle is unique in containing not one but two Nativity plays, in each of which there are three very musical shepherds whose singing and musical conversation highlight the plays. In the first play, after eating and drinking on the moor, the three herdsmen sing what is obviously a catch or round, led by the one who can best "raise the tune":

> Who so can best syng
> Shall haue the begynnyng.[89]

They are pleased with their singing, for the First Shepherd comments after the song, "We haue done oure parte / and songyn right weyll."[90] After the *Gloria* of the angel, the shepherds engage in a lively discussion of the music, which they wish to imitate; and before setting out for Bethlehem, they do sing another song. We know that this is a three-part song because the Third Shepherd, who has been eager to sing, is taunted by his fellows: "Brek outt youre voce / let se as ye yelp," to which he replies, "I may not for the pose / bot I haue help."[91] Having presented their gifts to the Child, the shepherds end their pageant with another song and an *Amen.* Closing lines spoken by the First Shepherd refer not only to their song but to the discant style of this composition—improvisation at sight:

> Amen, to that worde / syng we therto
> On hight.
>
> . . . . .
>
> To the lawde of this lam
> Syng we in syght.[92]

The words "Syng we in syght" are especially significant, for they evidently refer to English discant style—a type of improvisation at sight in parallel sixth chords upon a given tenor. To be complete and fully sonorous, the music must consist of all three parts; hence the remarks of the eager shepherd that he cannot sing alone, but needs the help of the other two.

The *Second Shepherds Play* of the Wakefield cycle is regarded as the gem of the entire collection, as the first genuine English comedy, and as a brilliant example of the Wakefield Master's gift for imposing native British realism (with its characteristic humor) upon serious religious drama. The larger portion of the play is a clever farce centering upon the sheep-stealing Scotsman Mak and climaxing symbolically in the discovery of the stolen sheep in a child's cradle. Only at the end is there a brief Bethlehem scene. The play is permeated with music, for the three shepherds talk about music a great deal and never miss an opportunity to burst into song. As they settle down on the moor at the beginning of the pageant, the First Shepherd suggests a song ("thyse nyghtys ar long, / yit I wold, or we yode / oone gaf vs a song") and the men decide on the parts:

primus pastor. lett me syng the tenory.
ijus pastor. And I the tryble so hye.
iijus pastor. Then the meyne fallys to me;
lett se how ye chauntt.[93]

Again, the song is obviously in discant style, with a given tenor and parallel sixth chords. This song (the title not indicated) marks the end of the first division of the play, just as the *Gloria* of the angel marks the end of the next division—the farce about the stolen sheep. Like their counterparts in the *First Shepherds Play,* these musical herdsmen comment most intelligently upon the wondrous music and wish to imitate it. The First Shepherd's "Hark after, than!" is the cue for another song: "Be mery and not sad / of myrth is oure sang," remarks the Third Shepherd, as the men set out for Bethlehem.[94] Having presented their gifts, the three men, singing once more, leave Bethlehem, as the Third Shepherd calls for more music:

To syng ar we bun:
let take on loft.[95]

The Adoration of the Shepherds in the Hegge cycle is quite similar to the parallel Chester play. Here, again, the men are inspired by the heavenly *Gloria* to sing joyfully as they set out to seek the Babe. The Second Shepherd suggests,

Lete us go fforthe fast on hye,
And honowre that babe wurthylye,
With merthe, songe, and melodye;
Have do! this song begynne![96]

The name of the song is given in the manuscript: *Stella coeli extirpavit.* This chant was a votive antiphon in honor of the Blessed Virgin, with words not found in liturgical books but in *Books of Hours* for private devotion; and so it lies in the realm of sacred rather than secular song.

There was no lack of instrumental music, apparently, when the plays were performed. In fact, probably many more musical instruments were used in performance than are actually specified in the various manuscripts, since characters in the plays often speak of instruments when stage directions make no mention of any. In the Banns to the Chester cycle, for example, the guild of smiths, playing Jesus among the doctors in the Temple, are told: "To set out in playe comely yt shalbe your parte, / get mynstrilles to that shewe, pipe, tabarte, and flute."[97] And yet when we find the boy Jesus among the doctors *(The Purification),* there is no mention of either music or musical instruments, only the direction for singing the *Nunc dimittis* in the earlier part of this pageant when Simeon receives the Child. A list of payments made by the Smiths in 1554 to various people who helped mount their pageant (reckoned to total about $6,000 in mid-twentieth-century terms) does indeed include payments to angels, to minstrels, and to a music master and singers.

Instrumental music is emphasized, however, in the Chester *Creation and Fall,* for three times there appears the stage direction *"Mynstrilles playinge":* first, when "the Creator bringeth Adam into Paradice, before the tree of knowledge"; again, when God speaks to Adam and Eve after they have eaten the forbidden fruit; and still later, as Adam tells of a dream about Heaven.[98] The purpose of the music was obviously to enhance the power and glory of God. The music of trumpets marked the appearance of royalty in the Chester play *Balaam,* for a *"fluryshe"* is called for as *"Balacke Rex"* enters and introduces himself as "kinge of Mobe land."[99] In the Nativity play, the First Shepherd seems to be a virtuoso on some sort of horn, for he speaks of summoning the lad Gartius—

> with this horne I shall make a "howe"
> that he and all heaven shall heare,
> yonder lad that sittes on a lowe
> the lowt of this horne he shall heare—

after which comes the stage direction *"Tunc cantabit."*[100] At the manger scene in this play, four boys join the shepherds. One of these offers his treasured pipe as a gift, possibly giving a sample of his expert performance as he comments:

> Were I in the rockes or in,
> I coulde make this pippe,
> That all this woode shoulde ringe,
> And quiver.[101]

In the play of the Three Kings, according to stage directions, *"the mynstrilles muste plaie"* as the royal trio are presented to Herod.[102] And *The Last Judgment* opens to the blare of trumpets. God directs the ubiquitous angels to waken everyone: "my Angells, fayre and bright, / looke that you wake eche wordly wight."[103] The Second Angel agrees enthusiastically: "Take we our Beames, and fast Blow." According to stage directions, the angels blow their trumpets and the dead arise from their graves—a scene that lends itself to all manner of dramatic possibilities.

When a musicians' guild was formed at York in 1561, *The Coming of the Three Kings to Herod* was taken from the Masons and assigned to the "Mynstrells."[104] Although there are no specific directions for music in this pageant, one cannot reasonably doubt that the musicians lavishly employed their talents here, just as in the parallel Chester play. Indeed, stage directions would be utterly superfluous, with the musicians themselves in charge. The York *Judgment Day* opens, like the Chester play, with a great blowing of trumpets.[105] Even the dialogue is similar, as God commands the angels to call up all creatures ("Aungellis! blawes your bemys belyue! / Ilke a creatoure for to call") and an angel responds vigorously ("Thy will schall be fulfillid in haste, / That heuene and erthe and helle schalle here").

The Prophet play in the Wakefield cycle makes much of King David, who is distinguished by his harp and his psalm-singing.[106] Bearing his harp when he enters, David promises,

> As god of heuen has gyffyn me wit,
> shall I now syng you a fytt,
> With my mynstrelsy.

David then sings a prophecy of the coming of Jesus:

> Myrth I make till all men,
> with my harp and fyngers ten
> . . . . .
> ffor god will that his son down send
> . . . . .
> ffor that I harp, and myrth make.

When David's long song is over, he concludes,

> Now haue I songen you a fytt;
> loke in mynd that ye haue it.

In the *Second Shepherds Play* of the Wakefield cycle, the entrance of the Third Shepherd is heralded by the sound of his flute ("hard I hym blaw," says the Second Shepherd; "he commys here at hand").[107] In the Purification play, stage directions call for the ringing of bells *("Tunc pulsabunt")* as Simeon prepares to meet the child Jesus in the Temple:

> A, dere god! what may this be?
> Oure bellys ryng so solemply.[108]

As the Holy Family appears, Simeon realizes that the bells are ringing without human help: "Oure bellys ryng by thare oone," he remarks. Finally, the Wakefield Judgment is characterized by much trumpet music.[109] In fact, trumpet blasts are apparently blown between speeches throughout the play, for several lively demons and four lost sinners refer continually to the trumpets' rousing everyone. "Alas, I harde that horne / that callys vs to the dome," says the Secundus Malus as the pageant begins; and there is much talk of the powerful effects of the trumpet as the play unfolds. After the good and bad have been judged by Jesus, Tutivillus (the devil's registrar of souls) bids the trumpets blow a final blast, as the wicked are led off to their doom: "Blaw, wolfys-hede and oute-horne."

In the Hegge play of the Magi, instrumental music again embellishes the presence of royalty, for Herod himself gives the royal command: "ye mynstrelle of myrthe, blowe up a good blast!"[110] After the innocent children have been slaughtered at his order, Herod calls for a banquet, and his seneschal bids the royal trumpeter (s) furnish fanfares for the feasting: "Now blowe up mynstralle with alle your myght!"[111] A bit later, as Herod tells his knights to be merry, he calls for more instrumental music: "minstrelle, rownd abowte / Blowe up a mery fytt." Stage directions immediately following this refer to the fact that several trumpets are blowing as death strikes down Herod *("Hic dum buccinant mors interficiat Herodem")*. Much later in the cycle, the last play to dramatize the life of Mary—*The Assumption of the Virgin*—relies heavily upon instrumental as well as choral music. Angels play on their harps *("ludentibus citharis")* and perhaps the organ is used *("Hic cantabunt org.")* throughout much of this very elaborate scene.[112]

We have already noted a good deal of dialogue in which various characters talk about the music, generally referring to its powerful emotional effects. This is especially evident in all five of the shepherd plays: invariably the shepherds get into a lively discussion of the angel's *Gloria,* which is obviously in a florid, melismatic style quite unlike the syllabic, *nota-contra-notam* discant style that the shepherds are used to singing.[113] In the Chester play, the shepherds discuss the chant syllable by syllable in a lengthy conversation, showing their amazement at the virtuosity of the singer.[114] The lad Gartius, for example, comments,

> Nay, it was "glore, glore glorius,"
> me thought that note went ouer the howse.

The herdsmen here continually emphasize the powerfully moving effects of the angelic music—for instance, the First Shepherd, who associates the singing with Gabriel:

> Naie, on a "glore" and a "glare" and a "gli"
> good Gabriell when he so glored,
> when he sang, I miht not be sory,
> for through my breast-bone bloting he bored.

In the Hegge play, the scene is quite similar to that in the Chester play, as the shepherds discuss with wonder the syllables "gle," "glo," "glory"—obviously a reference to the highly melismatic form of the *Gloria* sung by the angel.[115] In both Wakefield Nativity plays, the shepherds are extremely erudite musically, and their discussion—again, shot through with awe and amazement—becomes quite technical. In the first play, the virtuosity and speed of the angel's music, with its diminution of long-note values, causes strong comment. "It was wonder curiose / with small noytys emang," says one of the men; and another goes into even greater detail:

> Now, by god that me boght / it was a mery song;
> I dar say that he broght / foure & twenty to a long.[116]

In the second play, the dialogue centers upon the same technique, although the critical remarks now become somewhat more conservative:

primus pastor. This was a qwant stevyn / that euer yit I hard

. . . . .

ijus pastor. Say, what was his song? / hard ye not how he crakyd it?
Thre brefes to a long. /

ijus pastor. yee, mary he hakt it,
was no crochett wrong / nor no thyng that lakt it.[117]

In all five Nativity plays, the shepherds are moved to imitate the celestial music, and, as we have seen, actually do so—in their own way.

Amidst the trumpet-blowing of the Doomsday plays, there is much talk of the powerful effects of the trumpet blasts, which do indeed awaken everyone from the sleep of death. In one instance (Wakefield), a demon testifies to the power of the trumpet, even to the breaking of prison bonds:

> Oute, haro, out, out! / harkyn to this horne,
> I was neuer in dowte / or now at this morne;
> So sturdy a showte / sen that I was borne
> hard I neuer here abowte / in ernyst ne in skorne,
>   A wonder!
> I was bonde full fast
> In yrens for to last,
> Bot my bandys thai brast
>   And shoke all in sonder.[118]

We have noticed that music is consistently associated with joy, "myrthe," and gladness in the lines of many speakers—for example, in Peter's characterization of the bliss of Heaven in musical terms, as he says to the blessed ones in the Hegge Doomsday play:

> Com on, and sytt on Goddys ryght syde,
>   Where myrthe and melody nevyr may mys.[119]

From a number of musical metaphors that occur throughout the plays, a certain pattern emerges with regard to sorrow also; that is, deepest sorrow is often promised or announced in musical terms of quite a different sort. Antichrist in the Chester play is carried off to Hell to a musical metaphor: "a sorrowfull songe . . . shall he singe."[120] The author of the York plays, moreover, is consistent in his use of this type of metaphor.[121] An angel says of Adam and Eve being led from the Garden: "of sorowe may yhe synge." And Mary, missing her son Jesus who has remained with the doctors in the Temple, speaks in the same tone: "Of sorowes sere schal be my sang." Finally, God promises the wicked souls at Judgment Day: "Of sorowes sere now schall thei syng." In the Wakefield *Pharoah,* God speaks of impending doom for the Egyptian ruler: "ful soyn hys song shall be 'alas.' "[122] And at the Crucifixion, Mary laments in identical terms: "Alas! may euer be my sang."[123] At the Judgment Day (Wakefield), Jesus speaks of doom for the sinful: "of sorrow may euery synfull syng."[124] The author of the Hegge plays consistently speaks of sorrow and doom in terms of the song "Welaway"—a song mentioned at least twice in the poems of John Skelton.[125] When Herod and his soldiers die at the banquet, the devil receives them in musical terms:

> Of oure myrthis now zal ye se,
> And evyr synge "welaway."[126]

And in *The Council of the Jews,* Satan similarly speaks of his mission: whoever serves him faithfully shall "syng weleaway ever in peynes ffelle."[127] Finally, at Doomsday, "Welaway" characterizes sinners in Hell: "Now may oure songe be, wele away."[128]

Undoubtedly, "singing of sorrow," singing "Welaway," was often more than a metaphor: in certain instances, at least, it must have been actually carried out. A play, *The Fall of Man,* from the fragmentary Norwich cycle does indeed call for the singing of sorrow as the pageant ends.[129] After being driven from the Garden, Adam laments, "O with dolorows sorowe we maye wayle & weepe." And Eve continues,

> With wonderous woo, alas! it cane not be told.
>
> . . . . .
>
> O wretches that we are, so euer we xall be inrollyd;
> Therfor ower handes we may wrynge with most dullful song.

Stage directions follow: *"And so thei xall syng, walkyng together about the place, wryngyng ther handes"*:

> Wythe dolorous sorowe, we maye wayle & wepe
> Both nyght & daye in sory, sythys full depe.

A final stage direction is especially significant: *"N.B. These last 2 lines set to musick twice over and again, for a chorus of 4 parts."*

The importance of music in the presentation of the medieval mystery plays, then, is everywhere paramount and reveals much about the plays and their makers. We have seen similarities among the various plays underlined by the musical usage: for example, all four Ascension plays rely upon the same characteristic antiphon to mark this deeply spiritual moment. And when three Resurrection plays call for *Christus resurgens,* it seems more than likely that the fourth (Hegge) play introduced this processional antiphon also. Musical similarities have also pointed up the influence of the Chester plays—the oldest cycle—upon the others: for example, in the musical dialogue among the shepherds in the Christmas plays. And even although the Wakefield plays contain fewer musical rubrics than do the other plays, certain hymns or antiphons are undoubtedly to be understood because of traditional usage in the Chester or York cycles.[130] In all the cycles, music is constantly associated with joy and "myrth"; consequently, it is not surprising to find that music is entirely lacking in scenes dramatizing the darker episodes in the life of Jesus. Such plays as *The Betrayal, The Passion,* and *The Crucifixion* make no mention whatever of music.

The musical touch of the Wakefield Master is obvious in certain distinct differences between the Wakefield and other cycles. David's singing to his harp is unique here. Fun-loving demons, rather than traditional angels, blast the doomed to judgment with their trumpets in the last scene. And especially in the two Nativity plays do the innate humor and musical interests of the Wakefield Master come to full flowering, with musical criticism on the part of the would-be sophisticated herdsmen unique in the literature of the period. In their comic episodes and realistic human touches, these plays are expanded far beyond parallel plays in any cycle—and music shares largely in this expansion. Comic episodes found in the Chester and Wakefield plays are altogether missing in the York cycle, presented, one recalls, at the site of a great cathedral; and even the shepherds' discussion of the *Gloria* is quite abbreviated. The Hegge plays, too, are deeply serious in tone; and the close parallels between music of the liturgy and music specified in these plays emphasizes this seriousness.

Just what was the music used in the plays, and what was its deeper significance? All that remains today of actual music from the four complete cycles is a bit of plainsong (the angel's *Gloria*) from the Chester Christmas play and three Latin polyphonic songs from the York cycle ("The Appearance of Thomas to Our Lady"). There are also two songs from the plays (only a fragment of the complete cycle) of the true-Coventry group, fortunately transcribed and printed before the manuscript of the plays burned at Birmingham in 1879.[131] Although sometimes the music to be used is not specifically indicated, often rubrics are quite definite and most of the music called for can be identified as hymn, psalm, sequence, canticle, antiphon, or alleluia verse. In other words, by far the largest part of the music performed in these plays was from the liturgy of Mass or Office, carried over bodily from church to guild. These pieces are invariably appropriate, as we have seen, underlining the theme of the scene. Occasionally, indeed, the scene is an actual dramatization of the plainsong text—for instance, the Annunciation play in the York cycle, which follows the service in the *Liber Usualis.* Plainsong chants mentioned in the rubrics in the pageants may still be found in their proper places in service books in Gregorian notation. But from the eleventh century onward, individual parts of the Mass and Office were set polyphonically and would be available to performers in the plays.[132] Often after the appropriate Latin text was sung, there followed an English paraphrase, as in the Chester Ascension play. This is quite in line with the fact that many pieces from the sung liturgy of the church—especially motets or anthems—were set by Renaissance composers to both Latin and English words, as the Reformation spread over the kingdom, and that the change from the Latin ritual to the new order of service was a very slow process.[133] The anthem "Save me, O God," specified in one of the Noah plays (Chester), surely indicates Protestant influence. Traditional pieces from the liturgy are especially important in plays honoring Mary in the York cycle and in the numerous episodes from the lives of both Mary and St. Anne in the Hegge plays. In other words, the more orthodox the doctrine, the more traditional the music.

There are indications that certainly at times singers in the plays were choristers directed by the cathedral singing master.[134] There seems, too, to have been a certain amount of audience participation in the music of the plays. At least, this was the custom on the Continent;[135] and some of the closing scenes in the plays call for music in which the audience might well take part. The familiar hymn *Salvator mundi* called for at the end of the Chester Doomsday play would lend itself admirably to this sort of thing. The same is true for the *Te Deum* that closes the parallel play in the Wakefield cycle (and is called for more often than any one song throughout the cycles). One cannot help being reminded here of Benjamin Britten's wonderfully successful setting of the Chester Noah play, in which the audience participates by singing familiar hymns.

The pattern in all the cycles is that music was predominantly associated with angels—one angel, two angels, or a chorus of angels. A prime dramatic function of this singing was obviously to represent Heaven to the assemblage and to establish the presence of God or of His Son; celestial singing also marked auspicious events or moments of deep spiritual significance in the life of Jesus, his parents, his followers. The representation of Heaven through music is underlined in several instances in the pageants when characters speak of music as being a heavenly quality, as when Gabriel is identified by his heavenly singing. In addition to angels, God himself occasionally sings, Jesus frequently sings his lines, and other highly placed good characters sing—King David, Mary, Elizabeth, Simeon, some priests and bishops. Non-angelic choruses take part from time to time, invariably to sing songs of praise, of gratitude (often the *Te Deum*), or of joy and triumph. The trio of shepherds always sing both before and after worshiping at the manger. It is worth pointing out, too, that no "bad" character ever performs musically in any of the plays.[136] Herod may order his minstrels to "blow up a merry fit," but he takes no part in the music himself. The only exception here is the singing of "Welaway" or some other "song of sorrow" by the doomed souls as they go off to everlasting punishment.

Joyful singing on the part of the angels, then, represents Heaven; and joyful singing on the part of humans signify their response to spiritual events here on earth (as when Noah's company responds with a song of gratitude or the Israelites return thanks to God for their preservation from the waters of the Red Sea). This music—both solo and choral—was, of course, preponderantly sacred. Only rarely is there secular music, but this type also has its dramatic function. Two vernacular songs occur at places of comic relief in the Chester cycle: the drinking song of the Good Gossips in the Noah play and the "Hey troly loly loe" of the shepherds after their clowning on the moor and before they have worshiped at the manger (after which, their attitude becomes subdued, owing largely to the powerful effects of the celestial music they have heard). These Chester herdsmen speak of singing a jolly refrain[137] and the Wakefield shepherds speak of singing at sight—all, obviously, in the simple amateur tradition of singing in parallel thirds and sixths upon a given tenor, in great contrast to some of the more professional solo and choral singing in other parts of the play, especially the elaborate singing of the Christmas *Gloria*. Two secular songs from the true-Coventry cycle support this idea, songs unique because they are the only vernacular songs whose words and music are still extant from the plays.[138] The shepherds sing two stanzas ("As I out rode this enderes night") to the same music, each consisting of three lines and a refrain ("They sange terli terlow; / So mereli the sheppards ther pipes can blow") set for three voices: treble, tenor, and bass. The first stanza comes after the men's decision to find the Babe in Bethlehem, and the second after the presentation of gifts at the manger. Between these lies one of the best known of all medieval songs, the so-called Coventry Carol. The text ("Lully, lulla, thow littell tine child") reflects the sorrow of the women whose children are to become victims of Herod's wrath; and the song, again scored for three parts *("Here the wemen cum in wythe there chyldur, syngyng them"),* occurs just before the entrance of Herod's murderous soldiers. Like the "Song of the Good Gossips," this song is unusual, too, in being the exclusive property of women.

A definite pattern is apparent also with regard to instrumental usage in the plays. Of musical instruments called by name in the rubrics, stringed instruments—the "harp" of the "minstrels"—and organs are consistently associated with angelic harmonies and occasionally with human performance. Trumpets embellish the presence of royalty (the Magi) and blare forth at the death of mortal majesty (Herod). The all-powerful trump of doom, of course, marks the Last Judgment. Minstrels play whenever God appears and "utters his voice" in the Chester Creation, a play so well marked with musical rubrics that one is tempted to see it as a pattern for other scenes in which there are no musical directions. Minstrels also play when the Eastern kings are presented to Herod, augmenting the pomp of the royal court; and we recall that the minstrels' guild itself produced this pageant during the later years of the York cycle. What instruments did these instrumentalists play? Since only the barest of directions occur in the manuscripts of the plays themselves, one must look elsewhere to find what instruments were actually used.[139]

A long tradition of instrumental usage lies behind the mystery plays. Basic to this is a history of musical symbolism, a vast subject that goes back to the patristic writers, many of whom found mystical correspondences between musical instruments and spiritual ideas.[140] The facts of this tradition greatly illuminate instrumental usage in dramatic performance. First of all, like angelic singing, instrumental music represented Heaven. Scenes depicting Heaven in religious drama—on the Continent as well as in England—had for centuries been associated with music, with angelic choirs, both singers and instrumentalists.[141] Soft-sounding *(bas)* instruments, generally played indoors—organs, vièles, harps, psalteries, and lutes—were the ones that customarily represented Heaven; and the performers might be professional musicians who hid behind the angels with their duplicate instruments. Traditionally, certain stringed instruments had long been associated with the figure of Christ,[142] and these accompanied both solo and choral voices when Jesus took part. It is more than likely, then, that a variety of stringed instruments added their celestial overtones to scenes of Heaven, not only when rubrics specifically call for the music of minstrels but in similar scenes where there are no musical directions. The organ had long been the instrument above all others used to symbolize Paradise, to accompany both God and Jesus, to indicate praise of God, and to accompany angelic choirs. We have noticed the use of the organ in the cycle plays in just such scenes, and especially in scenes depicting the heavenly rewards of the Virgin; and surely the organ can be assumed at the center of the celestial instruments in great scenes of Heaven when no rubrics appear.[143]

The pipe in the shepherds' play is, of course, the recorder or its simple ancestor, the reed pipe, associated for centuries with shepherds in Nativity plays, and so represented in art as well as literature.[144] Music to embellish the trappings of royalty, as at Herod's court, was probably the music of loud *(haut)* instruments usually played outdoors—trumpets, buisines, long associated with regal entries. The trumpet fanfare, too, was long considered the prerogative of kings and nobles. And this "king of instruments" together with other loud wind instruments customarily depicted the Last Judgment, arousing fear and terror in the minds of the onlookers: lines in the pageants as well as rubrics in the manuscripts bear out the tradition in the craft cycles. Indeed, the great Doomsday scenes in the pageants would lend themselves admirably to large groups of contrasting instruments—as the angels with their trumpets and other loud instruments awaken the dead, and the celestial choirs, organist, and stringed instrumentalists depict the blessedness of Heaven. Bells, finally, undoubtedly shared in the performances (they are specifically mentioned, we recall, in Purification scenes in several of the cycles), symbolizing, as they had done for centuries, the proclaiming of God's word to the multitude: their use in singing the *Te Deum* was especially widespread.[145]

We may conclude, then, that music in the craft plays served a purpose like that of the plays themselves and of sculpture in the cathedrals—*ad majoram gloriam Dei*—to strengthen the faith of the viewers unable to read the Holy Scriptures. In many of the scenes, the function of the music is clearly dramatic, either realistically or symbolically. The realistic approach is seen in the use of loud, outdoor instruments to indicate royal settings and royal entries. It is seen, too, in the introduction of vernacular song, sometimes for obvious comic relief, an innovation that has its parallel in the typically British introduction of farcical, comical material into the pageants (of which the best-known examples are the sheep-stealing episode in the Wakefield Shepherds' play and the domestic scenes between Noah and his wife in several of the cycles). The symbolical use of music, on the other hand, is seen in the depiction of Heaven by angelic singing and by the sound of soft strings and organ, scenes made especially intimate because of the traditional association of these instruments with indoor performance. These heavenly choirs, moreover, conveyed to the audience a sense of divine order, of cosmic harmony, of which earthly affairs and earthly harmony were only a pallid reflection.[146] And many times, as we have noticed, music marks the juxtaposition of the divine with the human, of divine ordering in the affairs of men —as in the Christmas *Gloria,* the protection of the Holy Family through angelic music, the assumption of the Virgin, the Pentecostal scenes.

Closely connected with these ideas is an idea derived from ancient Greek philosophy that found widespread expression in the music treatises of the Middle Ages, an idea underlying many scenes in the pageants: that of music's powerful effects upon the emotions of man and of man's response.[147] Here we recall the reaction of Thomas to the angelic music in the York play ("But this mirthe and this melody mengis [mend?] my mode"), Anna's husband's (Joachim's) remark that the celestial music fills him with dread, the Prince in the Hegge play who "quakes for fear" at the marvelous "noise" that marks Mary's assumption. A Chester shepherd reacts to the music by resolving,

> vnkind will I never in no case be
> but preach Ever that I can and crye,
> as Gabryell taught by his grace me,
> singing alway hethen will I.[148]

In all the cycles, shepherds comment upon the marvelous effects of the Christmas *Gloria* (the lad Gartius says that the music has "healed my hart")[149] and respond by imitating the heavenly harmonies. The Emperor Augustus, worshiping at the manger (Chester), is so moved by the angelic music that he resolves to build a church to commemorate the spot.[150] And a Wakefield demon who speaks of music's power to break prison bonds gives a hint of the underlying idea of the entire scene of the Last Judgment: the power of the trumpet to arouse the very dead from their graves.

As one observes the dramatic use of music in the pageants to symbolize Heaven and divine harmony, to mark divine intervention in the affairs of men, and to show the psychological power innate in this harmony, one is inevitably reminded of Milton, who, influenced by the same ideas more than a century later, invariably portrayed Heaven as celestial harmony and angelic response to God's commands as ineluctably musical.[151] The absence of music in scenes depicting the suffering of Jesus in all the cycles supports these ideas, for here evil is operating in a material, mortal world far removed from heavenly harmony and order.

The didactic and moral purpose of the music, finally, is everywhere noticeable, especially in the many parallels between the music of the liturgy and the singing in the plays. Traditional character of the hymns, antiphons, and canticles specified in the rubrics underlines the traditional character of the plays generally—plays performed over a large period of time basically unchanged. The traditional character of much of the music, indeed, rooted in the ages-old plainsong of the church, obviously contributed in large measure to maintaining the conservatism of the plays. Thus the music of the plays, except for the few vernacular innovations, is a part of that continuing tradition that characterizes England's great musical heritage in the later Middle Ages and Renaissance.

THE ENTERTAINMENT AT ELVETHAM, 1591

Ernest Brennecke

FOR nearly four days, from Monday afternoon, September 20, to Thursday morning, September 23, 1591, Queen Elizabeth I and her court were the guests of Edward Seymour, Earl of Hertford, at his estate at Elvetham in Hampshire.

This was an event of the utmost importance in the Earl's remarkable and for the most part unfortunate career.[1] When he was thirteen years of age his father, former Lord Protector and Duke of Somerset, had been beheaded. Two months after the accession of Elizabeth, Seymour had been created Earl and was eventually granted his father's confiscated estates, thus becoming one of the wealthiest noblemen in the kingdom. In 1559, however, he had secretly married Lady Catherine Grey, sister of the hapless Lady Jane Grey. It was an act of treason to marry a person of the blood royal without the sovereign's consent. Upon the discovery of the Lady Catherine's pregnancy, both culprits were committed to the Tower, where they managed to produce a second son, and Hertford was fined the crushing sum of £15,000. Elizabeth was eventually contented with a settlement of £1,187; Hertford was released, but his wife (her sons being declared illegitimate) languished under various forms of custody until her death in 1568. He lived in comparative obscurity until 1582, when he married Frances Howard, daughter of one Lord High Admiral and sister of another. The Queen had bestowed her benediction upon this match. But the Earl had a persistent genius for attracting misfortune. His elder son, the young Lord Beauchamp, had followed the parental footsteps by marrying one Honora Rogers without troubling to obtain either his father's or the Queen's consent, and again Seymour was made aware of the royal displeasure.

During the years of his disgrace and banishment from the court —and in spite of them—he amused himself by patronizing a theatrical company. Between 1582 and 1591 "The Earl of Hertford's Men" appeared at Canterbury, Faversham, Newcastle, Leicester, Bath, Marlborough, and Southampton.[2] By the autumn of 1591, therefore, Hertford had at his disposal a group of seasoned men and boy actors.

And now at last Her Majesty seemed inclined toward a genuine reconciliation. Her affairs both public and private had prospered since the God-sent victory over the Armada three years before. This present late-summer Progress of hers, which had cost her hosts thousands of pounds and still further thousands of hours of acute concern, was drawing to a successful close. She had taken the court as far as Southampton[3] and had indicated through her ministers that she would not be averse to a visit at Elvetham as she passed through Hampshire on her return to her winter palaces.[4] Hertford now hoped to rise at last into the royal favor by outdoing all previous entertainments in extravagance and splendor. No effort and no expense were to be spared.

The result was one of the most magnificent events of the kind since the Earl of Leicester's famous Kenilworth entertainment of 1575. There were vast spectacles and pageantry, games, fireworks, dancing, acting, and singing. Above all, there was music of many kinds in great profusion, used for a large variety of purposes and effects. Shakespeare's Polonius might have described it as "martial, pastoral, nautical, rustic, courtly, amorous, panegyrical," with a free intermingling of these types. Nowhere else can we find better illustrations of the ways in which Elizabethan music assumed its place on such dramatic occasions.

We are extremely fortunate in having two groups of material preserved that enable us to construct a fairly detailed account of the proceedings.

First, no fewer than three editions of a little book, *The Honorable Entertainment,* were published almost immediately following the festivities.[5] These quartos supply a picturesque running account of the events, and they contain a complete "libretto" of all the speeches and poems and all the lyrics that were sung. They were reprinted by Nichols[6] and by Bond[7] and do not contain transcripts of any of the music.

Second, a fair amount of the music has happily survived in manuscript and can be readily identified and reproduced. Some portions of it that are not extant can be at least partially supplied by the use of a little scholarship and imagination.

Who devised and supervised this whole entertainment, and who wrote the detailed account for publication? There is no proof in the form of external evidence. Bond[8] gives major credit for both tasks to John Lyly, who was perhaps assisted by one or more of Hertford's confidential secretaries; Bond's assertion has not been seriously disputed. Lyly had won fame and established a fashion with his *Euphues* in 1579. Beginning in 1584, he had written plays for the children's companies connected with the Chapel Royal and St. Paul's, of which latter company he was vice-master. Since 1588 he had held the post of Clerk-Controller in the Revels office and was aspiring (vainly) to the Mastership.[9] Experienced in the courtly drama and ambitious to display his virtuosity, he was a person to whom the Earl might well have turned when seeking an impresario.

At any rate, the artistic preparations for this entertainment engaged the services, in person or by contributions, of an impressive number of poets, actors, dancers, singers, instrumentalists, and composers. In addition to Lyly, the following artists were more or less involved:

1. Thomas Morley, organist and choirmaster at St. Paul's, shortly to become the composer of madrigals (1593 and thereafter), compiler and arranger of *Consort Lessons* (1599), author of *A Plain and Easy Introduction to Practical Music* (1597), composer of ayres for voice and lute (1600 and thereafter), and possibly one of Shakespeare's musical collaborators.[10]
2. William Byrd, Morley's master, already the most revered figure

among Elizabethan composers of both sacred and secular music.

3. John Baldwin, a "singing man of Windsor,"[11] who had only nine days before this entertainment, completed his elegant manuscript of forty-two of Byrd's virginal compositions for Lady Rachel Nevell,[12] and who was soon to become a member of the Royal Chapel.

4. Francis Pilkington, (*ca.* 1563-1638), composer of both ayres and madrigals.

5. Edward Johnson, mentioned in Francis Meres' *Palladis Tamia* (1598) as one of the leading composers of the time, but whose fame rests largely on his two contributions to this Elvetham entertainment.

6. Thomas Watson, swashbuckling university wit, court poet, and friend of Christopher Marlowe, with whom he was involved and imprisoned in the case of the slaying of one William Bradley in a scuffle in Hog Lane in 1589.[13]

7. Nicholas Breton, friend of Lyly and Thomas Nashe, poet and collaborator with John Baldwin. He was a stepson of George Gascoigne, who had been the principal reporter of the entertainment at Kenilworth.

This was a most notable confluence of the leading talents of the time. And it is not unlikely, as we shall see, that among the guests and observers was a young playwright named William Shakespeare.

They were to entertain not only the Queen but also some of the most powerful personages in the realm: Lord Burghley, the Lord Treasurer; the Lord Admiral, the Countess of Hertford's brother; Lord Hunsdon, the Lord Chamberlain, commander of the Queen's bodyguard at the time of the Armada, a patron of Byrd and of Burbage's theatrical company, for which Shakespeare was working; and many others of great note.

"Elvetham House, being scituate in a parke of but two miles in compasse or thereabouts, and of no great receipt, as being none of the Earl's chiefe mansion houses . . . his honor with all expedition set artificers a work, to the number of three hundred, many daies before her Maiestie's arrival, to inlarge his house with newe roomes and offices."[14] The physical preparations were awesome. Two wings and a large, low gallery had been added to the house itself. An upper gallery had been lavishly refurnished as the Queen's private apartment, with tapestries not only on the walls but also on the floor. A new fireplace and chimney had been added, and a room had been set aside for Lord Burghley in which he might attend to his official correspondence.

Beyond the house a huge pond had been constructed in the shape of a half-moon and equipped with a "snail mount," a raft for artillery, a castle, and a model man-of-war. Some two hundred yards beyond this artificial lake, at the base of a wooded hill, more than twenty temporary structures had been built. The largest of these was a "room of estate" for the nobles, the outside covered with boughs and clusters of ripe hazel nuts, the roof with ivy vines, the floor with herbs and fresh rushes. Nearby was a large hall of cruder construction for the lodging of knights, ladies, and gentlemen. Partly hidden by shrubbery was a group of utility houses, all neatly tiled within: a pantry, a ewery for dishes and table linen, a wine cellar, a chaundry for the thousands of candles that would be needed, a larder, and a spicery.

Still other buildings were designed for the Queen's footmen and their friends, for her personal armed guard, for her steward and his helpers, and for the gentlemen in waiting. Finally, there was a large buttery, a pitcher house, a pastry with five new ovens (some of them 14 feet deep), a kitchen with four ranges, two boiling houses for preparing the meat dishes, still another immense kitchen to provide ample cooked food for all comers of whatever degree, a scullery, and lodgings for the cooks. Some of these buildings were of substantial wooden construction, some merely of heavy canvas.

THE FIRST DAY: MONDAY, SEPTEMBER 20, 1591

At nine o'clock in the morning the Earl "drewe all his servants into the chiefe thicket of the parke," where he exhorted them to do their best. Final preparations were completed by dinnertime, and at three o'clock, followed by more than two hundred retainers, "most of them wearing chaines of golde about their neckes, and in their hats yellow and black feathers," he met Her Majesty at Odiham House, three miles away. As the train entered Elvetham Park, a poet (Lyly?) clad in green "to signify the joy of his thoughts at her entrance, a laurel garland on his head, to expresse that Apollo was the patron of his studies; an olive branch in his hand, to declare that continual peace and plentie he did wish her Maiestie: and lastly booted, to

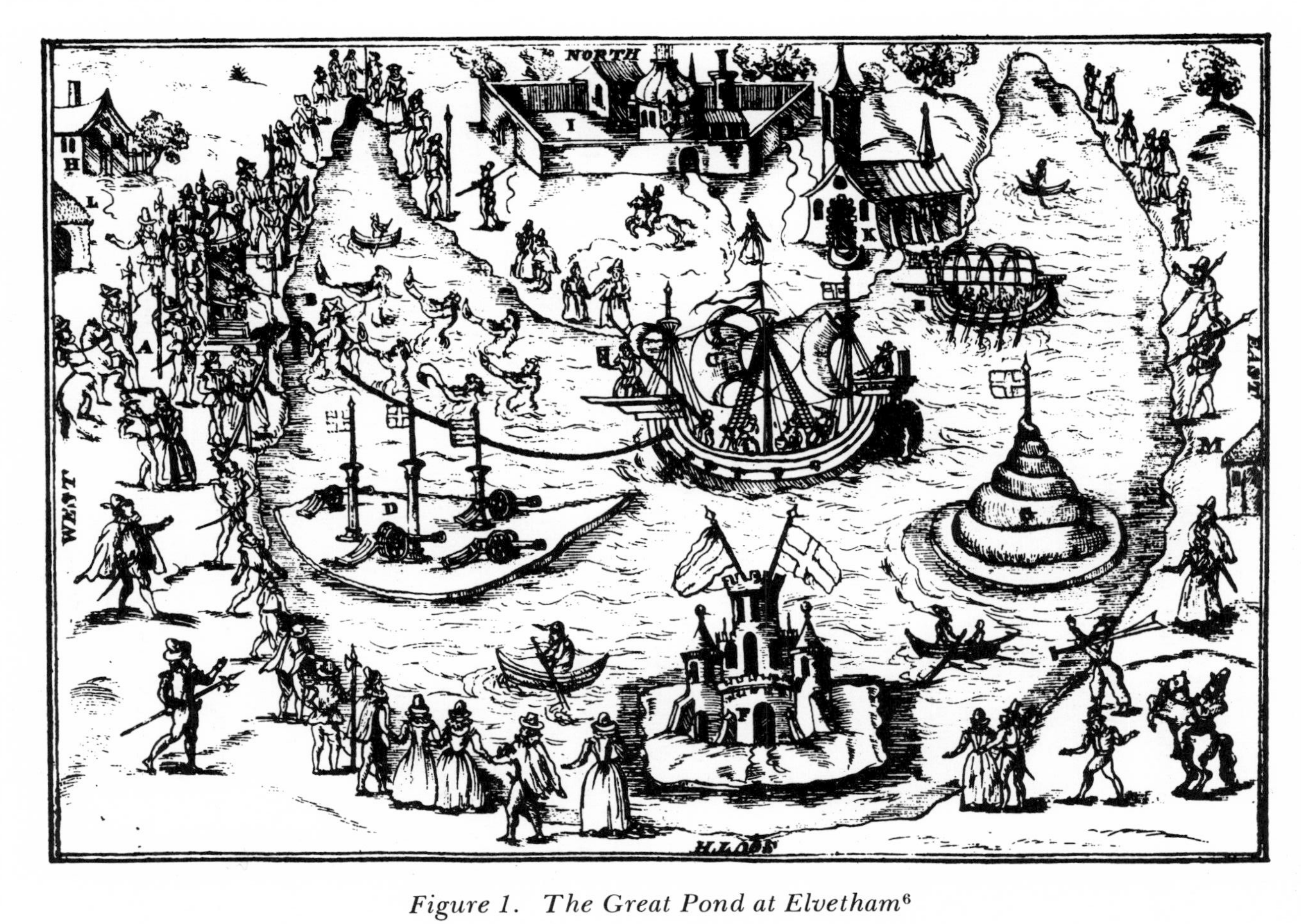

Figure 1. The Great Pond at Elvetham[6]

betoken that he was *vates cothurnatus,*" saluted her with a Latin oration in "heroicall verse."

> The Poet's Boy offered him a cushion at his first kneeling to her Maiestie; but he refused it, saying as followeth:
>
> Non iam puluillis opus est, sed corde sereno:
> Nam plusquam solitis istic aduoluimur aris.
>
> The Poets speach to her Maiestie.
>
> Nuper ad Aonium flexo dum poplite fontem
> Indulci placido. . . .
>
> Because all our Countrymen are not Latinists, I thinke it not amisse to set this downe in English, that all may bee indifferently partakers of the Poets meaning.
>
> Now let us use no cushions, but faire hearts:
> For now we kneel to more than usuall Saints.
>
> While, at the fountaine of the sacred hill,
> Under Apollos lute, I sweetly slept. . . .

The Latin speech went on for sixty-five hexameters, telling the Queen what she never tired of hearing: that she was the English Nymph, the sweet Princess, whom trees, rivers, birds and beasts, heavens and earth saluted; likewise, himself the poor Poet, and "Semer" [Seymour], welcomed her to rest in his "guileless house," etc.

At length the Poet beckoned to six "virgins" who followed him, boys and men representing the three Graces and the three Hours, "all attired in gowns of taffeta sarcenet of divers colors, with flowrie garlands on their heads, and baskets full of sweet herbs and flowers upon their armes." This little choir removed certain blocks, supposedly laid in the roadway by "Envie," and then walked on before her toward the house, "strewing the way with flowers, and singing a sweete song of six parts, to this dittie which followeth."

> With fragrant flowers we strew the way,
> And make this our chiefe holliday:
> For though this clime were blest of yore,
> Yet was it never proud before.
> O beauteous Quene of second Troy,
> Accept of our unfained joy.
>
> Now th'ayre is sweeter than sweet balme,
> And Satyrs daunce about the palme:

Now earth, with verdure newly dight,
Gives perfect signe of her delight.
O beauteous Quene of second Troy,
Accept of our unfained joy.

Now birds record new harmonie,
And trees do whistle melodie:
Now everie thing that nature breeds,
Doth clad itselfe in pleasant weeds.
O beauteous Quene of second Troy,
Accept of our unfained joy.

There can be very little doubt that the words of this six-part madrigal were composed by Thomas Watson. His edition of *The First Sett of Italian Madrigals Englished* was published in 1590[15] and contained the following lyric:

This sweet and merry month of May
While Nature wantons in her prime
And birds do sing, and beasts do play
For pleasure of the joyful time,
I choose the first for holiday
And greet Eliza with a rhyme:
O beauteous Queen of second Troy,
Take well in worth, a simple toy.

These words were set in two madrigals by William Byrd as No. 8 and No. 28 of Watson's collection, the first for four, the second for six voices. Watson's title page contains the remark, "There are also heere inserted two excellent Madrigals of Master William Byrde, composed after the Italian vaine, at the request of the said Thomas Watson." Byrd republished the four-part setting in his *Psalms, Songs, and Sonnets* in 1611.[16] Therefore it has been sometimes assumed that Watson and Byrd altered and shortened the six-part madrigal for the purpose of providing a proper song of welcome at Elvetham, retaining the essence of its most appropriate refrain. The difficulty lies in the fact that no madrigal setting of the Elvetham song has survived, and it is now obviously impossible to reconstruct Byrd's elaborate music for an eight-line stanza to fit a six-line stanza.

The problem becomes more tantalizing when we observe that Francis Pilkington, in his *First Book of Songs or Airs* (for single voice and lute) of 1605, included as No. 20 a setting of "With Fragrant Flowers,"[17] attributing the words to Watson and merely altering the refrain to "O gracious King of second Troy." However,

Pilkington also composed madrigals in three, four, five, and six parts and would have been quite capable of providing the kind of unaccompanied composition *à* 6 for the Elvetham occasion. He perhaps was too young at the time (the date of his birth is not known), for he took his Mus. B. at Oxford in 1595, but the records indicate that he had studied music for sixteen years and that his exercise consisted of a "choral song in six parts."[18]

So what are we to conclude? Watson provided the words for the madrigal of welcome sung by three or four boys and two or three men, without instrumental accompaniment. If Byrd made the setting, we can get an idea of its style by listening to his "This Sweet and Merry Month of May." If Pilkington did it, we can hear his "With Fragrant Flowers" and imagine what he might have produced if he had decided to transform it into a madrigal. And that is as far as our surmises may take us.

> This song ended with her Maiesties entrance into the house: and her Maiestie alighted from horsebacke at the Hall-dore, the Countesse of Hertford, accompanied with divers honourable Ladies and Gentlewomen, moste humbly on hir knees welcomed hir Highnesse to that place: who most graciously imbracing hir, tooke hir up, and kissed hir, using manie comfortable and princely Speeches, as wel to hir, as to the Earl of Hertford standing hard by, to the great rejoysing of manie beholders. And after hir Maiesties entrance, where shee had not rested her a quarter of an houre; but from the Snail-mount and the Ship-Ile in the Pond (both being neare vnder the prospect of her Gallerie windowe) there was a long volley of Chambers discharged. [The Queen dearly loved loud noises.]
>
> After this, supper was serued in, first to her Maiestie, and then to the Nobles and others. . . .
>
> After supper was ended, her Maiestie graciously admitted vnto her presence a notable consort of six Musitions, which my Lord of Hertford had prouided to entertaine her Maiestie withall, at her will and pleasure, and when it should seeme good to her highnesse. Their Musicke so highly pleased her, that in grace and fauour thereof, she gaue a newe name vnto one of their Pauans, made long since by Master *Thomas Morley,* the Organist of Paules Church.

It is indeed a pity that our narrator did not see fit to mention the original title of Master Morley's pavan or the new name bestowed upon it by the Queen. It cannot therefore be identified—if indeed it survives. But at least we know what it was like. A pavan, according to Morley himself, is "the next in grauity and goodness unto this [the fantasie] . . . a kind of staide musicke, ordained for graue dauncing, and most commonlie made of three straines, whereof euerie straine is plaid or sung twice. . . ."[19] Its rhythm was four-square, and it was generally followed by a galliard in a lively triple measure. It was frequently performed on festal occasions. Thoinot Arbeau in 1588 remarked that it "has not disappeared or passed out of fashion, nor do I think it ever will, though it is true that it is not favoured as it was in the past. Our musicians play it when a damsel of good family is taken to Holy Church to be married, or when musicians head a procession of the chaplains, master, and brethren of some notable guild."[20]

As to the "notable consort of six Musitions" employed by Hertford, we can be certain of the instruments used by this little orchestra. They were the treble viol, the flute or recorder, the bass viol, the lute, and two other now obsolete plucked instruments, the cittern and the pandora. In the National Portrait Gallery there is a charming illustration of such a "broken consort" (i.e., of different types of instruments) performing at the wedding of Sir Henry Unton, *ca.* 1596. Morley's *Consort Lessons,* published in 1599, provides twenty-five compositions arranged for this combination.[21] If one hears a typical Morley pavan, such as the one in the *Fitzwilliam Virginal Book*[22] and then imagines it as performed by a consort sextet such as we have described, one can entertain a fairly clear notion of the music that delighted Elizabeth on the evening of her first day at Elvetham. Morley, one imagines, was present, and it may not be too fantastical to imagine that she renamed his pavan as something like "The Queenes Delight." This occasion may have had something to do with Morley's being appointed to the coveted post of Gentleman of the Chapel Royal on July 24th of the following year.[23]

THE SECOND DAY: TUESDAY, SEPTEMBER 21, 1591

The forenoon was wet and stormy, so that nothing in the way of entertainment could be offered to Her Highness except "a faire and rich gift" from the Countess of Hertford, "which greatly pleased and contented her." By dinnertime the weather had cleared, ordnance was discharged, a state banquet was held in the new structure on the hillside above the pond, and "a variety of consorted music" was performed.

At four o'clock the Queen was conducted to a regal seat under a "canopy of estate at the western edge of the pond." It was of green satin, heavily ornamented, and supported by four silver pillars held by four knights. Her Highness expected "the issue of some devise, being advertised that there was some such thing towards."

Close to the opposite bank there was a bower, from which there now emerged a fantastic procession. It was headed by Nereus, "prophet of the sea," attired in red silk. He plunged into the water and headed, wading waist-high and swimming, toward the royal throne. Five Tritons followed him, "all with grislie heades and beardes of diuers colours and fashions, and all fiue cheerefully sounding their Trumpets." Neptune and Oceanus came next, towing with them a gaily bedecked pinnace, in which there were three "virgins, which with their Cornets played Scottish Gigs, made three parts in one."

The jig, as the term was used here, was a lively dance tune, generally in a 6/8 measure, and was popular with instrumentalists, singers, and dancers in England as well as in Ireland and Scotland.[24] Morley, apparently considering it a rather primitive form of composition, remarked that if one meets a would-be musician "who thinketh himself the best discanter of all his neighbors, enjoigne him to make but a scottish Iygge, he will grossly erre in the true nature and qualitie of it."[25] The jigs played by the virgins in the pinnace seem to have been far more sophisticated than the simple dance forms of which we may find many examples and arrangements. "Three parts in one" means that they were in the form of strict three-part canons, rounds, or catches. This writer has never encountered a traditional jig of the period, Scottish, northern, or even Irish, that would lend itself to this sort of treatment without drastic alteration. It would have been child's play, however, for a technician such as Morley to have contrived a series of such arrangements.

What would they have sounded like, as performed by the three virgin-cornetists? To provide a rough idea, there follows here a jig-like tune, "three parts in one," "Now kiss the cup, cousin, with courtesy," published by Thomas Ravenscroft in 1609 in a collection of such popular "old . . . but renewed" compositions.[26]

"There was also in the saide pinnace an other Nymph of the sea,

Figure 2. "Now Kiss the Cup, Cousin, with Courtesy"

named *Neaera,* the old supposed loue of *Syluanus,* a God of the woodes. Neare to her were placed three excellent voices, to sing to one lute, and in two other boats hard by, other lutes and voices to answer by manner of Eccho." The rest of the train followed through the water, "all attired in ouglie marine suites, and euery one armed with a huge wooddin squirt in his hand. . . . The Tritons sounded one halfe of the way, and then they ceasing, the Cornets plaied their Scottish gigs." Meanwhile, the snail mount came to resemble a monster, putting forth horns "full of wild-fire, continually burning."

Nereus, heading the aquacade and approaching the throne, gave a signal to one of his minions on the ship-isle, who somersaulted into the water and handed him a jewel "hidden in a purse of greene rushes." There followed the formal oration of Nereus to "faire Cinthia the wide Oceans Empresse," in thirty-seven lines of completely conventional blank verse, after which he presented the jewel.

The singers and the lutenist in the pinnace then performed the "Sea-nymphs' dittie" with the echo provided by the musicians in another boat, somewhat "a farre off."

> The Song presented by Nereus on the water, sung dialogue-wise, everie fourth verse answered by two Echoes:
>
> 1. *Dem.* How haps it now when prime is done.
> Another spring-time is begun?
> *Resp.* Our happie soile is overrunne,
> With beautie of a second sunne.
> *Eccho.* A second sunne.
>
> . . . . .
>
> 4. *Dem.* O yet devoid of envious blame,
> Thou maist unfold hir sacred name.
> *Resp.* 'Tis dread Eliza, that faire name
> Who filles the golden trump of Fame.
> *Eccho.* Trump of Fame.
>
> 5. *Dem.* O never may so sweete a Quene
> See dismall daies or deadly teene,
> *Resp.* Graunt Heavens hir daies may stil be greene,
> For like to hir was never seene.
> *Eccho.* Was never seene.

This poetic device must have been very effective. Its musical setting, unfortunately, has not survived.

And now, the aquatic deities having had their show, it was proper for the spirits of the woodland to receive their opportunity. They had been concealed in the shrubbery behind the throne, but at a trumpet signal from the Tritons they advanced, led by their god Sylvanus,

> attired, from the middle downewards to the knee, in Kiddes skinnes with the haire on, his legges, bodie and face naked, but died ouer with saffron, and his head hooded with a goates skin, and two littel hornes ouer his forehead, bearing in his right hand an Oliue tree, and in his left a scutchion. . . . His followers were all couered with Iuy-leaues, and bare in their handes bowes made like darts. At their

> approache neare her Maiestie, *Syluanus* spake as followeth, and deliuered vp his scutchion, in grauen with goulden characters, Nereus and his traine still continuing near her Highnesse.

Sylvanus now delivered an oration of twenty lines of fulsome blank verse and handed the scutcheon to the Queen. He was answered by Nereus, who called his attention to Neaera awaiting him in the pinnace and remarked, "On this condition shall she come on shore, / That with thy hand thou plight a solemn vow, / Not to prophane her undefiled state." Sylvanus replied, "Here, take my hand, and therewithall I vowe–," with Nereus, interrupting, "That water will extinguish wanton fire." At this point the concluding horseplay took place, for Nereus seized Sylvanus and threw him head-over-heels into the water. (The Queen meanwhile had perused the scutcheon and its commendatory Latin verses, headed "Detur Dignissimae.")

"After that the sea Gods had sufficiently duckt Sylvanus, they suffered him to creepe to the land, where he no sooner set footing, but crying *Revenge, Revenge,* he and his begunne a skirmish with those of the water, the one side throwing their dartes, and the other vsing their squirtes, and the Tritons sounding a point of warre." At last Nereus pleaded for peace, noting that Her Majesty, being present, was always an enemy of war. Whereupon Sylvanus and his followers retired to the woods.

Neaera now presented Her Majesty a "sea jewel" in the form of a fan and delivered still another oration, which the Queen interrupted by naming the pinnace "The Bonadventure." The actual battleship "Elizabeth Bonadventure" had been Drake's flagship in 1585 and had been commanded by the Earl of Cumberland against the Armada.[27]

And now, with peace and happiness restored, Nereus and his train retired to their bower, to the alternate sounds of trumpets and cornets. The appearance of Nereus was so "ugly" as he ran toward his shelter that he "affrighted a number of the countrey people, that they ran from him for feare, and thereby moved great laughter."

"And here ended the second daies pastime, to the so great liking of her Maiestie, that her gracious approbation thereof, was to the Actors more than a double reward, and yet withall, her Highness bestowed a largesse vppon them the next day after, before shee departed."

THE THIRD DAY: WEDNESDAY, SEPTEMBER 22, 1591

At nine o'clock in the morning the Queen opened a casement of her gallery window and beheld on the lawn beneath her three "excellent Musitians, disguised in auncient countrey attire." They greeted her with a song "Of Coridon and Phyllida," composed in three parts. Both the words and the music so appealed to her that she commanded it to be repeated. The lyric ran as follows.

The Plowmans Song

In the merry moneth of May,
In a morne by breake of day,
Foorth I walked by the Woodside,
When as May was in his pride:
There I spied all alone,
Phillida and *Coridon.*
Much adoo there was God wot,
He would loue, and she would not.
She sayd never man was true,
He sayd, none was false to you.
He sayd, he had lou'd her long,
She sayd, Loue should haue no wrong.
Coridon would kisse her then,
She sayd, Maides must kisse no men,
Till they did for good and all.
Then she made ther Sheepheard call
All the heauens to witnesse truth:
Neuer lou'd a truer youth.
Thus with many a pretty oath,
Yea and nay, and faith and troth,
Such as silly Sheepheards vse,
When they will not Loue abuse;
Loue, which had beene long deluded,
Was with kisses sweete concluded.
And *Phillida* with garlands gay:
Was made the Lady of the May.

About the authorship of these lines there is happily no question. They appeared in 1600 in the miscellany called *England's Helicon*[28] and were signed "N. Breton." It was entirely appropriate that Nicholas Breton, a prolific court poet who was acquainted through his mother with those who had devised and witnessed the Earl of Leicester's Kenilworth festivities sixteen years before, should be chosen to provide at least this one item.

Who, then, composed the music for this "three-men's song"? For some time it was believed that it was Michael East, whose setting of these words for three voices appeared in his *First Set of Madrigals* in 1604.[29] East, however, was only about eleven years old in 1591. Musicologists such as Dr. Fellowes therefore have been compelled to rule him out.[30] Another candidate was the composer Richard Nicholson, whose manuscript setting, written down some time after 1600, survives in the British Museum.[31] Unfortunately, this composition is for four voices.

A few years ago I had the good fortune to come across another setting, by John Baldwin of Windsor, in his manuscript commonplace book preserved in the Royal Music Library and now in the British Museum;[32] it is in three parts, is accompanied by the proper words, and is signed "John: baldwine" and clearly dated 1592. Without any question this is it, preserved in Baldwin's handsome script. It

Figure 3. From Baldwin's Setting for "In the Merry Month of May"

has not hitherto been either scored, printed, or identified with Breton and the Elvetham festivities. The three independent parts go together perfectly and merrily in the score that follows.

After dinner, for an hour and a half, Her Highness watched a tennis or handball match, five players to a side, before her window, played by my Lord Hertford's servants, all, Somersetshire men.

After supper there were tremendous displays of fireworks and a banquet of a thousand dishes of sugar-sweets, served by no less than two hundred gentlemen and lighted by a hundred torch-bearers. The incredible menu is, for the satisfaction of the "curious," set down in the first two quartos of *The Honorable Entertainment,* Hertford apparently having it excised from the third so as to avoid the appearance of ostentation. Even Elizabethan digestions must have been sorely strained.

Figure 4. "In the Merry Month of May"

Figure 4. *"In the Merry Month of May" (continued)*

Figure 4. "*In the Merry Month of May*" (*continued*)

Figure 4. "*In the Merry Month of May*" *(continued)*

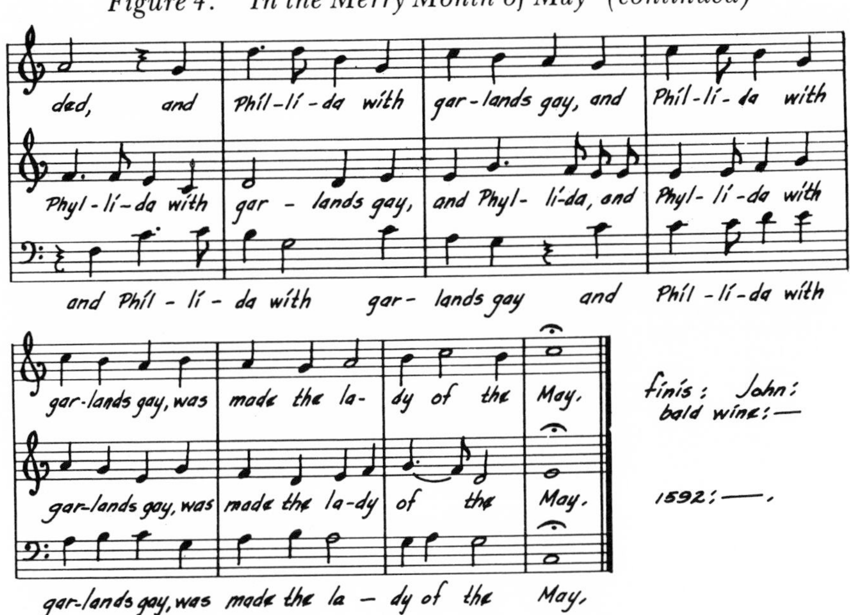

THE FOURTH DAY (THE DEPARTURE):
THURSDAY, SEPTEMBER 23, 1591

In the morning, Her Majesty again looked out of her gallery window over the garden, where three cornets (the same that had played the jigs in the pinnace the day before) performed "fantastic dances," while the Fairy Queen, followed by her maids, entered with a garland in the form of an imperial crown, which she fixed upon a silvered staff stuck into the ground, and made a formal blank-verse speech:

> I that abide in places under-ground,
> Aureola, the Quene of Fairy Land
>
> . . . . .
>
> . . . salute you with this chaplet,
> Giuen me by Auberon, the fairy King
>
> . . . . . .
>
> (For amorous starres fall nightly in my lap), Etc.

> After this speech, the Fairy Quene and her maides daunced about the garden, singing a song of sixe parts, with the musicke of an exquisite consort, wherein was the lute, bandora, base-violl, citterne, treble-violl, and flute. And this was the Fairies Song:
>
> *Elisa* is the fairest Queene
> That euer trod vpon this greene.

Elisaes eyes are blessed starres,
Inducing peace, subduing warres.
Elisaes hand is christall bright,
Her wordes are balme, her lookes are light.
Elisaes brest is that faire hill,
Wher vertue dwels, and sacred skill,
O blessed bee each day and houre,
Where sweete *Elisa* builds her bowre.

The words could have been contrived by Lyly, Watson, Breton, or anyone else involved in the festivities, or by Edward Johnson, who without any doubt composed the music. In the British Museum there is a set of part books,[33] dated only "temp. Elizabeth," containing a five-part setting of "Elisa is ye fayrest quene" and "Com agayne," both signed "E. Johnson."

The performers of the instrumental parts were obviously those

Figure 5. "Elisa Is the Fairest Queen"

who had provided the "broken consort" on the first evening of the Queen's visit. Putting together Johnson's parts, one may construct the score for treble voice and consort. Although it is in five parts only, the singer's part could be doubled by the recorder or treble viol. To add a sixth part would be easy for any musician who was present on the occasion.

"This spectacle so delighted her Maiestie that shee commanded to heare it sung and to be danced three times over, and called for divers Lords and Ladies to behold it: and then dismist the Actors with thankes, and a gracious larges, which of her exceeding goodness she bestowed upon them."

One hour later the royal procession departed, with all the performers paying their respects: Nereus and his company on one side, Sylvanus and his followers on the other, and before her the three Graces and the three Hours who had at first welcomed her,

Figure 5. "Elisa Is the Fairest Queen" (continued)

"all of them on euerie side wringing their hands, and shewing signe of sorrow for her departure." The Poet then made a short oration in twenty-two lines of blank verse, ending:

> O, either stay, or soone returne againe,
> For sommers parting is the countries paine.

It was raining hard; nevertheless, the Queen held up her coach and pulled off her mask in order to hear the following song of farewell, performed by a group of musicians hidden in a bower, with two singers "that were cunning" and with the broken consort with whose kind of music she was now familiar.

> Come againe faire Natures treasure,
> Whose lookes yeeld ioyes exceeding measure.
>
> O come againe heau'ns chiefe delight,
> Thine absence makes eternall night.
>
> O come againe worlds starbright eye,
> Whose presence doth adorne the skie.
>
> O come againe sweet beauties Sunne:
> When thou art gone, our ioyes are done.

Edward Johnson was again the composer.[34] The composition, for two singing voices and consort, may be scored as follows.

Figure 6. "Come Again, Fair Nature's Treasure"

To these strains, then, Queen Elizabeth departed in her coach in a driving rain. And she was so pleased that "shee openly protested to my Lord of Hertford, that the beginning, processe, and end of this entertainment was so honorable, as hereafter hee should finde the rewarde thereof in her especiall favour. . . ." The Earl of Hertford's company of actors were invited to perform at the Queen's Royal Court, for the first and last time, in January, 1592.

One must unhappily report that Hertford did not long continue to enjoy his sovereign's "especiall favour." His troubles continued until his death in 1621, and his two sons never attained the royal dignities that he had hoped for them.

One aftermath of this entertainment, however, is of special interest. William Shakespeare was twenty-seven years old when the event took place. His earliest plays were beginning to attract notice at James Burbage's Theatre in Shoreditch. Elvetham was only about thirty miles from London. The spectacular shows as reported in *The Honorable Entertainment* could not have failed to interest him. He may even have been present as an observer, for he was known to Watson, Breton, Morley, and others.

When he composed his *Midsummer Night's Dream* around 1595, he caused his Oberon, King of the Fairies, ("Auberon" in the *Entertainment*) to utter the following words to the sprite, Robin Goodfellow:[35]

Figure 6. "Come Again, Fair Nature's Treasure" (continued)

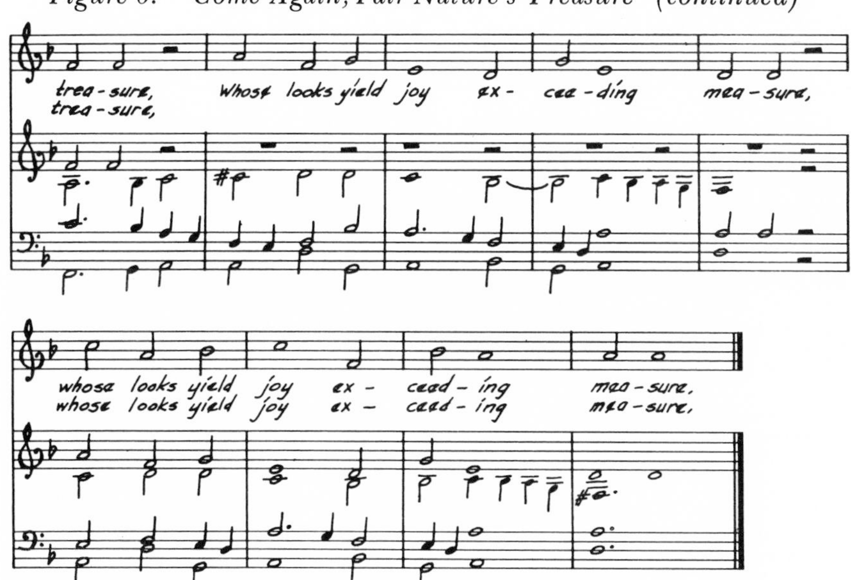

My gentle *Pucke* come hither: thou rembrest
Since once I sat vpon a promontory,
And heard a Meare-maide on a Dolphins backe,
Vttering such dulcet and harmonious breath,
That the rude sea grew ciuill at her song,
And certaine starres shot madly from their Spheares,
To heare the sea-maids musicke.

Puc. I remember.

Ob. That very time I saw (but thou couldst not)
Flying betweene the cold Moone and the earth,
Cupid all arm'd; a certaine aime he tooke
At a faire Vestall, throned by the West,

. . . . .

And the imperiall Votresse passed on,
In maiden meditation, fancy free.

This clearly is a recollection of a water show, with "sea-maids" singing sweetly and shooting stars (fireworks, as one may imagine); and the imperial votaress, the fair vestal throned in the West, can be none other than the Virgin Queen. A glance at the illustration in Nichols fortifies this supposition. Lyly's libretto, Hertford's pageantry, the lyrics and music of Watson, Breton, Baldwin, Johnson, and others, seem to have inspired at least one lovely passage in Shakespeare's *Dream*.

CAMPION'S ENTERTAINMENT AT BROUGHAM CASTLE, 1617

Ian Spink

KING James I spent the summer of 1617 in Scotland. Crossing the border on his return to London, he left Carlisle on August 6 and traveled south to Brougham Castle in Westmoreland, where he was to be the guest that night of Francis Clifford, Earl of Cumberland. Nichols says that the royal progress continued on to Appleby Castle the following day, but we shall see that the King must have stayed at least two nights at Brougham.[1]

The following year was published *The Ayres that were sung and played, at Brougham Castle in Westmerland, in the Kings Entertainment: Given by the Right Honourable the Earle of Cumberland, and his Right Noble Sonne the Lord Clifford. Composed by Mr. George Mason, and Mr. John Earsden. London: Printed by Thomas Snodham. Cum Privilegio. 1618.*[2]

No mention is made of the author of the entertainment, and (apart from these songs) neither a text nor a description ever seems to have been published. Vivian attributed it to Campion on the strength of a letter from the Earl to his son, which mentioned Campion in a likely connection; he also adduced some internal evidence in support of this theory—notably the similarity of image and occasion between the "Kings Good-night" (III) and one of Campion's Latin epigrams, "De regis reditu e Scotia," written about the same time.[3] The original of the letter seems to have disappeared, for the time being at any rate, but Vivian's source was no doubt Whitaker's *History of Craven*, where the letter is quoted rather more extensively.[4]

> Sonn, I have till now expected y'r l'res, according to your promis at y'r departure: so did Geo. Minson [Mason] y'r directions touching the musick, whereupon he mought the better have writt to doctor Campion. He is now gone to my L'd President's, and will be redy to do as he heares from yo'. For my own opinion, albeit I will not dislyke y'r device, I fynde plainly, upon better consideration, the charge for that entertaynment will grow very great, besyde the musick; and that, instead of less'ning, my charge in gen'all encreaseth, and newe paim'ts come on, w'ch, without better providence hereafter, cannot be p'formed.

The letter continues to preach economy without referring again to the entertainment. As it stands, it is hardly positive proof of Campion's authorship. If Mason did consult Campion (as he "mought"), was it merely for advice from a more experienced musician, or for directions from the author? In any case, the Earl seemed dissatisfied with the plan at this stage, and it cannot be assumed that the version alluded to here, or Campion's connection with it, was unaltered before performance. But whatever revision may have been made, Campion certainly seems to have remained associated in some capacity. Among the Clifford household accounts, the following entry dated July 18, 1617, is significant: "It^{m} given this day in Reward to Sr Wm Constable his coachman who came to knowe what day he could be readie wth his Coach to Carrie Doctor Campion from Londsbrough to Brawhum ij^{s} and to ye Stewards boy whoe brought a letter to Doctor Campion from M^{r} Jo: Tailor— vi^{d}."[5]

These records, few though they are, suggest that the entertainment may have been written in some such manner as follows. The Earl's letter indicates that he had trusted his son with preparing it, and the reference to "y'r device" suggests that the basic conception was Lord Clifford's also. But for the actual text a poet was required, and Campion was chosen. Apart from his obvious experience, there were other reasons for this choice. The Earl and his son had been the dedicatees of Campion's *Two Bookes of Ayres* (*ca.* 1613), the dedicatory poem of which indicates a relationship already established.

> What patron could I chuse, great *Lord,* but you?
> Grave words your years may challenge as their owne,
> And ev'ry note of Musicke is your due,
> Whose House the *Muses* pallace I have knowne.[6]

The first draft of the entertainment was possibly too extravagant, and perhaps it was subsequently pruned in deference to the Earl's protest. Campion did not himself set the songs but dispatched them to the Earl's musician, George Mason, who was joined by John Earsden in composing the music. Sometime after July 18, Campion traveled to Brougham Castle to supervise preparations and to be on hand if required.

Of John Earsden we know nothing at all—not even which of these songs are his. George Mason was a musician in the Earl's household at least as early as 1610, when his name occurs among the accounts for Christmas of that year (at a salary of £7.13.4 *p.a.*).[7] But Anthony Wood complicates matters by saying that he graduated Mus. B. from Cambridge in 1601, and J. E. West states that he was organist of Trinity College, Cambridge, from 1612 to 1629.[8] However, recent investigations have been unable to support these statements, so for the moment they must be discounted.[9] The only mention of Mason in the Clifford accounts that might relate to preparations for the entertainment occurs on the same day as the reference to Campion quoted above. "Item paid this day to a man of Hull wch was sent for to Londsbrough to play on the Lute at Brougham by Mr George Mason but was sent back, their being noe occasion to use him—vi^s^."[10] However, there would seem little point in trying to make much of this entry, though it deserves quoting.

THE ENTERTAINMENT

Brougham Castle is now a ruin. The Earl's niece and eventual heiress, Lady Anne Clifford, restored it and inscribed her work thus: "This Brougham Castle was repayred by the Ladie Anne Clifford, Countesse Dowager of Pembrooke, Dorsett, and Montgomery . . . in the yeares 1651 and 1652, after it had layen ruinous ever since about August 1617, when King James lay in it for a time in his Journie out of Skotland towards London, until this time."[11] However, it was sold for its stone early in the eighteenth century. The great hall and great chamber were both on the first floor and measured 41 by 21 feet, and 54 by 23 feet, respectively.[12] This was quite small by Whitehall standards, but not too small to prevent the Earl from putting on quite a spectacular show. The printed edition of the songs provides some hints as to the circumstances of their performance, and it is clear that there were in all three separate musical entertainments. The first consisted of "A Dialogue sung the first night, the King being at Supper" (I), "Another Dialogue, to be sung at the same time" (II), "The Lords Welcome, sung before the Kings Good-night" (X), and "The Kings Good-night" (III). As it appears, these items were sung at supper and before retiring on the night of the King's arrival, August 6. The reason "The Lords Welcome" was printed last in the collection, when it should obviously have been third, is not clear; but possibly it was because this was John Earsden's only contribution (an inferior one, it must be admitted) and was kept separate for that reason. The second entertainment comprised items IV to VIII, evidently belonging to a masque, and this must have been celebrated on the second night, since the last chorus ends:

> So humbly prostrate at thy sacred feet,
> Our nightly sports and prophesies wee end.

And finally, "The Farewell Song" (IX) was no doubt sung at some brief entertainment given just before the King's departure on August 8.

This timetable has been set out in detail because of Nichols' assertion that the King stayed one night at Brougham. The text of the songs and the accompanying rubrics do not support him in this, however, for if the King stayed one night, what is the significance of the phrase, "sung the first night"? And the final couplets of both "The Kings Good-night" and the last masque song imply an end to a separate night's entertainment. That the King did in fact stay on at Brougham until the eighth is proved by a royal warrant enabling the Privy Council of Scotland to bring to summary justice any "declairit outlaw or notorious malefactour . . . Gevin at Broome Castell, the aucht of August 1617."[13]

The first night's entertainment was merely complimentary table music, larded (no doubt) with a few speeches, the gist of which can easily be imagined. The general drift of the following night's masque is fairly clear from the text of the songs. In subject matter it seems to have been the usual sort of thing; an anti-masque combining exotic and rustic elements, culminating in the main masque with an apotheosis of the King as the embodiment of all virtue. A wandering band of gypsies arrives on the scene—a hallowed spot which they recognize as the dwelling place of Honour and Grace. They break into an "anticke dance" and then give place to a crowd of country lads and lassies. A ballad is sung, then follows a rustic dance. A gypsy steps forward and sings a song invoking "a chaine of prophecies." At this point, or hereabout, the scene may have been transformed, revealing the kingly attributes of Truth, Peace, Love, Honour, Long-life, and Illustrious Posterity in a tableau or procession, to the accompaniment of a final hymn of praise.

Despite the similarity of occasion between this and Campion's earlier *Cavendish House Entertainment* (1613), it is by no means a reworking of the same formula. It is true that both have rustic interludes (the rural setting of both dwellings was no doubt the reason for this), but the treatment seems Jonsonian rather, and generally dissimilar from Campion's four authentic masques. Indeed, consciously or unconciously, Jonson may have been influenced by reports of the Brougham Castle entertainment in his *Gipsies Metamorphosed,* performed almost exactly four years later, while the King was again in progress. Greg's outline of Jonson's masque shows the extent of the similarity.

> The masque itself opens with the appearence of the Gipsies, and after some introductory speeches the Jackman invites the spectators to have their fortunes told. The Captain tells the King's. . . . These concluded, enter eight country clowns and wenches, who supply what may be called an antimasque. . . . After this . . . is sung the ballad of Cock Lorel. . . . The rest of the company now reappear, "changed" from their Gipsy disguise to their own fashion of lords and gentlemen of the court. . . . The conclusion in praise of King and Prince consists of verses by the metamorphosed Gipsies alternating with songs by the Jackman.[14]

It can be seen that both masques have three stages in common. First, the arrival of the gypsies; second, the rural interlude or antimasque; and third ("unmasked now and cleare" as the Brougham Castle text expresses it) the gypsies' praise of the King in terms that are impressive enough, but all the more so because of the gypsies' supposed supernatural powers of divination. Jonson's masque is a work of considerable intricacy, more so than Campion's is likely to have been; but reduced to essentials, the relationship between the two seems quite pronounced and may indicate some sort of influence on Jonson by Campion.

TUNEFUL AND DECLAMATORY AYRES

Elsewhere I have suggested that the origins of the English declamatory ayre are to be found primarily in the songs written for the court masques performed between 1609 and 1613.[15] The idea that English composers began imitating Italian monodists and opera composers within a few years of 1600 seems hard to justify, in my opinion. For one thing, by the date of the earliest English declamatory songs (*ca.* 1609), only a handful of monodic collections had been published even in Italy, and although a few manuscripts may have penetrated England during the first decade of the century, so little indication of this now survives that it cannot have represented much of an influence at the time. Two songs by Caccini were printed in Robert Dowland's *Musicall Banquet* (1610), and a manuscript of his songs dating from before 1618 or so is extant at St. Michael's College, Tenbury. The emigrant Italian Angelo Notari, who arrived from Venice about 1610, was aware of the monodic style, as his *Prime Musiche Nuove* (London, 1613) shows; but apart from the queen's Italian musician, Giovanni Maria Lugaro, no other important Italian musician is known to have visited England during the early years of James I's reign. On the other hand, Italian music and musicians were certainly in fashion. John Cooper (alias Giovanni Coperario) affected an Italian version of his name, possibly after a visit to Italy about 1600; and Campion's patron, Sir Thomas Monson, is reported to have been "at infinite charge in breeding some [singers] in Italy."[16] John Dowland had been there in 1595, but without an immediately noticeable change in the style of his songs. Constantijn Huygens, while in London, refers to a visit to the house of the Ambassador of Savoy, Giovanni Francesco Biondi "ou il y a un collège de musiciens touts Italiens," but this was not until 1618.[17] It is true that the works of many Italian madrigalists were well known, but monodic publications do not seem to have been in demand at all. And had they exerted any influence, it might be expected that the general style of the English ayre would show some change before or about 1610, whereas in fact this tendency is only traceable in a dozen or so of the more than 550 lute songs published up to 1622. Significantly, most of the dozen can be classified as masque songs.

It seems more likely that the peculiar conditions of masque performance affected the style of song and singing, reinforced perhaps by a vague awareness of what was happening in Italy. The English ayre, as practiced by Dowland and his school, was either semicontrapuntal in conception—almost madrigalian—with the lute accompaniment simulating a polyphonic texture, or else purely melodic. In either case, it was essentially chamber music of a most intimate kind. It was too exquisite in style for the stage, especially for the bombast of the court masque in which the demands of audibility necessitated a more rhetorical and exaggerated type of declamation, with a simpler harmonic accompaniment in support. Such an inflated, heroic style was very different from the beguiling subtleties of the English lute song.

Declamatory traits can be observed increasingly in Alfonso Ferrabosco II's surviving masque songs for Jonson's *Masque of Blackness* (1605), *Lord Haddington's Masque* (1608), *Masque of Beauty* (1608), *Masque of Queens* (1609), *Oberon* (1611), and *Love freed from Ignorance and Folly* (1611);[18] in John Dowland's ceremonial "Far from the triumphing court" and the two songs "Welcome black night" and "Cease these false sports," probably written for a masque celebrating the wedding of his patron, Theophilus, Lord Howard de Walden, to Lady Elizabeth Home in March 1611/12;[19] and still more so in Nicholas Lanier's "Bring away this sacred tree" from Campion's *Squire's Masque* (1613).[20] If anything, the style is even more developed in some of Mason's songs for the Brougham Castle entertainment. It might have been supposed that his isolated position in the border country would have prevented his being acquainted with the latest musical trends at court. But in fact, such an important household as the Cliffords' could hardly be regarded as provincial. The estates may have been more than three hundred miles from London, but though the Earl was naturally retiring, his son was very much a man about town, and both were forced to play the courtier because of their position.

Some of the differences between the two styles of ayre have already been suggested. The declamatory style sought to make the rhythm and melody of the voice part dependent on the accents, quantities, and inflections of the verse, at the expense of purely musical considerations. Hand in hand with this went a continuo type of bass that was realized on a lute or theorbo in chordal style. Written-out tablature became rarer, and the bass part was not even figured, as a rule.

A clear contrast is provided between the melodic and declamatory styles in the following examples.[21]

At the beginning of the second verse of "The shadowes dark'ning our intents" (VII), the declamation clearly follows and exaggerates the rhetorical qualities of the verse (Figure 7). The extent to which the music depends on the words can be gauged by considering for a moment the music without them—it becomes meaningless. On the

Figure 7. "The Shadows Dark'ning Our Intents"

Moderate speed

The sha - dows dark-ning our in - tents, Must

fade, and truth now take her place: Who in our right E-gyp-tian race,

A chain of pro-phe-cies pre-sents; With which_ the star-ry sky con-sents,

And all the un - der e - le - ments. Thou that art all di - vine give ear,

other hand, the beginning of "Welcome, welcome king of guests" (III) shows no such dependence: rhythmically and melodically the music exists in its own right (Figure 8). It was at the dramatic climaxes of these sorts of entertainments that the declamatory style came into its own. Indeed, to a great extent it was the supernatural and triumphal aspects of the Jacobean masque that called the style into being. The gypsy's invocation, "The shadowes dark'ning our

Figure 7. "The Shadows Dark'ning Our Intents" (continued)

20

And grace our hum-ble songs, That speak what to thy state be-longs.

Un-mask-ed now, and clear, Which we in sev - 'ral strains di -

25

-vide, And heav'n - born Truth our notes shall guide, One by

30

one,— while we re-late That which shall tie both Time— and Fate.

intents," and the ensuing pageant of Truth, Peace, Love, Honour, etc., which concludes the masque, are more or less highly declamatory in style; so too is the second and more serious of the first night's dialogues, and also the final "Farewell Song." Apart from the bass "character-song" "Come follow me my wandring mates" (IV), the music of the anti-masque is essentially tuneful, as indeed one would expect from the titles of the songs—"A Ballad" (V) and "The Dance" (VI).

Figure 8. "Welcome, Welcome King of Guests"

Although the accounts for the entertainment have disappeared, the score gives some indication of the musical resources required. The structure of the ensemble numbers (VI and VIII) indicates the need for six singers; solo episodes being allotted to two basses, three tenors, and a treble—or more likely four tenors, one reading from a treble clef at the octave below.[22] The three solo songs are shared between a bass and two tenors, one song each. In addition, there were undoubtedly speaking parts and probably a troup of

Figure 8. "Welcome, Welcome King of Guests" (continued)

20
earth, Shall watch for— thy de light. Knees shall bend, From
-dorn The ro - ses— of the East, As the north Hath

25
friend to friend, While full cups do thee— right. And so great
now brought forth; The nor - thern morn is— best. And so best

Slower, getting softer

30 35
king, good night,good night, good night, good night,— good — night.
king, good rest, good rest, good rest, good rest,— good — rest.

good night, etc.
good rest, etc.

dancers as well as supers for the final tableau. So far as instruments are concerned, the printed tablature indicates a lute accompaniment (in two instances a bass lute), but other instruments of similar type were probably available, since a single instrument would hardly have been able to support the full chorus. The second dialogue (II) is the only song actually supplied with an instrumental bass part (that is, a bass part without words underlaid), but the omission elsewhere was perhaps an economy in the printing. Bass chorus parts almost certainly would have been doubled by the bass viol, especially since one seems to have been available. If the Carlisle waits were employed (or the musicians of some other town or nobleman), as they had been on previous occasions, the full chorus parts may have been doubled by instruments.[23] At Caversham, cornets, violins, and other "divers Instruments" had been available; and the instrumental resources used in Campion's court masques were, of course, extremely lavish.[24]

THE FIRST NIGHT'S MUSIC

The music for the first night consisted of four items; two dialogues sung at supper (I-II), "The Lords Welcome" (X) and "The Kings Good-night" (III). The dialogues are sharply contrasted in style. The first, in C major, is pleasantly tuneful and (like the words) rather banal—"Melodie now is needfull here, / It will helpe to mend our cheare." The second is much more impressive. C major turns to C minor, and the voices declaim:

> Now is the time, now is the hower
> When joy first blest this happy Bower.

Although in dialogue form, apparently the singers do not represent dramatic personages. Both dialogues end with a three-part chorus.

It has already been suggested that "The Lords Welcome" was Earsden's solitary contribution, a fact that caused it to be printed out of order at the back of the book. At any rate, Mason would seem to have been the senior partner (his name was printed on the title page in larger type), and the other songs show a certain consistency in style. For example, the striking similarity of cadence figure in numbers I, III, and VIII suggests a single composer, and in their turn these three songs are perfectly representative in style of the others, apart from "The Lords Welcome." This, with its uneasy changes in meter and general inexpertness, stands apart and may therefore be ascribed to the second composer, John Earsden.

"The Kings Good-night" is for tenor (treble clef) and bass, the last line of each verse being treated as a chorus in common time, echoing the phrase "Good-night" between voices rather charmingly. It is the imagery of the second verse of this song that Vivian found reflected in the epigram "De regis reditu e Scotia"—the King's return to England being a "northern dawn" outshining the usual "Roses of the East."[25]

THE SECOND NIGHT'S MUSIC: THE "ANTI-MASQUE"

The following night the main entertainment was presented. The first part or anti-masque, traditionally of a somewhat bizarre nature, featured gypsies and rustics. Reference to "our right Aegyptian race" is made explicit later on, but the popular conception of gypsies as a nomadic, clairvoyant, dusky, moon-worshiping race, is expressed in the first song (IV).

> Come follow me my wandring mates,
> Sonnes and daughters of the Fates:
> Friends of night, that oft have done
> Homage to the horned Moone.

Alone of the solo songs, this one is set for bass. As such it belongs to an interesting genre of early seventeenth-century "character songs" —usually play-songs expressing madness or the possession of supernatural powers, and sometimes of a humorous nature. The tone quality of the low voice and the dramatic style of declamation combine to conjure up the particular atmosphere required, in this case a mixture of the sinister and the exotic. Often, the voice merely "divides" the thorough-bass; that is, it fits syllables to the instrumental bass part with little attempt at melodic independence. Some idea of the general style, as well as particular details of expression, can be gained from Figure 9. The song suggests that an "anticke dance" followed.

Then comes the ballad of "Queen Dido" (V). Whether this is sung by one of the gypsies, or one of the rustics (who enter hereabout), or some other character, is not clear. Nor is the reason clear for the doubtful moral lesson of the last verse—it preaches rank infidelity without a hint of irony. And whatever the covert practices

Figure 9. "Come Follow Me My Wand'ring Mates"

Moderate speed

Come fol-low me my wand'r - ing mates, Sons and daugh-ters of the

fates: Friends of night, ——— that oft have done Ho-mage

to ——— the hor-ned moon. Fair-ly march, ——— and shun not light,

With such stars as these made bright. Yet bend you low ——— your cur-led

of the court might have been, it is unlikely that overt approval of such a doctrine could have been tolerated. Possibly the missing text makes clear that a contrast is intended between this heartlessness and the idyllic country lovers of the following dance. "Sib is all in all to me, / There is no Queene of Love but she."

Despite its title, it is doubtful that this song was really a traditional ballad, though it may be said to have become one later. There certainly was a "Dido Ballad" as early as 1565, known under various names such as "The Wanderynge Prince," "Queen Dido," "Troy Town" (after its first line, "When Troy Town for ten-years wars"), and the tune was very popular.[26] But the stanzas of "Troy Town" have six lines, each of eight syllables. Campion's ballad has ten lines to each verse and is rather more intricate metrically. They are obviously related in subject matter, but no version of "Dido was the Carthage Queen" earlier than Mason's *Ayres* is known at present. Stafford Smith, however, observed in a note on this item that "the last verse of the famous Ballad 'Dido Queen' was on this occasion, added to the more ancient song. The editor [Smith] has in his possession an older copy, without it."[27] If Smith was not mistaken, then of course Campion's authorship must be questioned and the traditional nature of the ballad asserted. But he may have confused the two ballads in his mind, intending to point out that the "moral" of the last verse is not to be found in the older and (as it happens) different version. Campion's "ballad" was printed again (without music, and with a few textual variants) in *Love's Court of Conscience* (1637), and again in D'Urfey's *Wit and Mirth; Or Pills to Purge Melancholy,* V (1714), also VI (1720), to a new tune.

It is more than likely that here we have an imitation of the ballad style on the part of both the poet and the composer. The tune is forthright in character and admirably suited to dancing. The "Dance" (VI) that follows continues in the same vein, employing similar melodic phrases and cadence figures. The first section is divided between six soloists, each of whom sings a couplet in praise of one of their number, though not necessarily of the opposite sex, since a bass sings:

> Tommy hath a looke as bright,
> As is the rosie morning light.

Each having sung his piece, they all sing together:

> Let us in a lovers round,
> Circle all this hallowed ground,

breaking into three time at "Softly, softly, trip and goe, trip and goe." A description of the dance follows:

> Forward then, and backe again;
> Here and there, and every where;

Winding to and winding fro;
Skipping hye and lowting low.
And like lovers hand in hand
March around, and make a stand.

The final couplet is marked *"Chorus,"* but (as in the case of the previous four lines, marked *"All"*) only a treble part and lute accompaniment is provided. Possibly, chorus parts were not printed, in this instance, but condensed into the accompaniment.

THE MAIN MASQUE

Country sports and all pretense are set aside, and the solemn moment has arrived when the gypsy ushers in "a chaine of prophecies" (VII):

And Heaven-borne Truth our Notes shall guide,
One by one, while wee relate
That which shall tye both Time, and Fate.

It is here that the dramatic capabilities of the declamatory ayre are seen at their best, for no other style could create the sense of awe and pregnant anticipation of this moment. The change to a bass lute accompaniment also adds to the effect. Verbal and musical ideas unfold together, reaching a pitch at the words "Unmasked now and cleare" (see Figure 7). At this moment of climax the scene was probably transformed from what was presumably a rural setting to some nobler prospect appropriate to a pageant of kingly virtues. Whether Truth, Peace, Love, Honour, and the rest actually sing, or whether they only form a procession or tableau, cannot be said for certain. Each "virtue" has a solo verse, the last phrase of which is echoed in a four-part chorus, like a kind of vocal ritornello between verses (Figure 10). But since the solo voices required are the same as in the previous ensemble number (VI), perhaps they merely constituted an off-stage chorus in both, the "rustics" in VI and the "virtues" in VIII being masquers. A final chorus concludes the night's entertainment:

Truth, Peace, Love, Honour and Long-life attend
Thee, and all those that from thy loynes descend.
With us the Angels in this *Chorus* meet:
So humbly prostrate at thy sacred feet,
Our nightly sports and prophesies wee end.

Figure 10. "Truth, Sprung from Heav'n"

THE FAREWELL

The circumstances of this final show are more difficult to establish. Presumably, it was given sometime on August 8 before the King's departure as part of a farewell entertainment such as Campion had provided at Caversham House four years previously. This had taken place in "an Arbour in the lower Garden" and the sentiments of "a mournefull parting song" are closely paralleled.[28] But despite the appalling, sycophantic hyperbole of the words, which must surely have sickened even in 1617, "The Farewell Song" (IX) achieves an effect of genuine pathos through its music. Again a declamatory style is employed, smoother and more sustained in movement than before but nevertheless looking forward to Henry Lawes rather than back to the Elizabethans. As with "The shadowes dark'ning our intents" (VII), the solemnity of the occasion is underlined by the use of a bass lute accompaniment. The music for both verses is substantially the same, but the second verse has been written out in full since certain declamatory features of the first verse would not have fitted the second. These necessary modifications are interesting, for they show the composer's concern over such details—incidentally, it reveals an incipient tendency to compose "from the bass up."

These *Ayres* have been understandably disregarded by musical historians up to now. Being in the new, anti-lyrical, early seventeenth-century declamatory style, for the most part, and displaying an inferior technique in the traditional sense, they failed to excite either the interest or the admiration of Fellowes and Warlock in the 1920's —Warlock said that they "contain no music of any particular interest except one very robust tune, 'Dido was the Carthage Queen.' "[29] At least he had looked at them, as had Parry (in Stafford Smith's edition). But they are not unimportant when considered as a representative and remarkably complete example of Jacobean masque songs. In them, more so perhaps than in any previous surviving masque music, we find an attempt at musical characterization and a sense of dramatic atmosphere conveyed by musical means. Some of the effects may be naive by later standards, but the music is not less interesting for that reason.

A full appreciation of these songs really depends on one's ability to view them within their dramatic context, and it has been one of the purposes of the present study to fill in this background. But it is a reciprocal process, and an enhanced knowledge and understanding of certain aspects of the drama—in this case the development of the Stuart masque—follows almost inevitably.

PATTERNS OF MUSIC AND ACTION IN FLETCHERIAN DRAMA

R. W. Ingram

JACOBEANS at all levels of society, at work and at play, delighted in music. All the music in Fletcherian drama is there to please, and, although some of it is there for no other reason, it is the intent here to suggest that Fletcher exploited the general delight in and knowledge of music for the benefit of his plays.

It is important, however, to remember that by "music" is meant songs, dances, and all instrumental music, from conventional flourishes and alarums to concerted masque music. Too often attention has been centered on songs alone and their value as poetry has been allowed to decide their worth as musical effect. No attention will be given here to the poetic merit of such songs as are mentioned. Their musical effect is what is being examined, and it is the sound of music in the dramatic context that is of first importance.

So long as the plays are hardly ever performed and are known only in reading, it will remain very difficult to appreciate the meaning and intention of the music in them. To the reader, a direction for music may simply be an interruption to the text, whereas in the theater, the music, vital though it may be to the scene, can steal upon the ear without asserting its presence to the detriment of the action. Musical entertainments more obvious than such "mood music" (such as songs or masques), while existing in their own right as entertainments, may well be integral parts of the play, parts that especially demand to be seen as well as heard. The plays must be read with such considerations in mind and with a sympathetic attempt to visualize them in theatrical performance. When this is done, their strength and appeal is made clearer. The extent to which this strength and appeal depends upon the skilful deployment of musical sounds is the topic of this paper.

The first indications of Fletcher's use of and fondness for music are seen in the musical imagery of the plays and in the ways in which a liking for or a dislike of music is used to mark certain characters and even to urge the plot forward. But Fletcher also made more directly dramatic uses of music: for example, he used it to sharpen the reversals of expectation and the clashes of emotion on which he so often relied for theatrical effect. The proliferation of songs and musical effects in certain plays raises a fundamental issue: how much music can a play contain and what is the relation between music, words, and action over the length of the whole play? Fletcher's solution to this problem, demonstrated in a representative tragicomedy, comedy, and tragedy, forms the concluding section of this study. First, however, some indication of the nature of Fletcherian drama and its special aptness for musical embellishment must be made, together with an explanation for calling it "Fletcherian" and using Fletcher's name as if he were sole author of the canon of Beaumont and Fletcher.

Humphrey Moseley in a prefatory letter to *Comedies and Tragedies written by Francis Beaumont and John Fletcher Gentlemen* (1647) remarked that he had considered publishing Fletcher's works separately "but since never parted while they lived, I conceived it not equitable to separate their ashes" (I, xiv).[1] Such sentiments have long ceased to hinder attempts at separation, and now at least a dozen hands have been authoritatively discovered in the canon. The dominance of Fletcher, however, has never been doubted. Twenty-six of the thirty-five commendatory poems in the 1647 folio were addressed to him alone: Cyrus Hoy finds his hand in fifty-one of the fifty-four plays he studied.[2] The corpus of plays have a unity of style and feeling and differ in degree rather than in kind. This kind may fairly be labeled "Fletcherian." In this paper it will therefore be both convenient and accurate to refer generally to Fletcher as the author. Most of the musical passages are found either in those plays by him alone or in scenes from collaborative plays generally allowed to be his. In fact, Fletcher may be said to be the musical intelligence behind the collection as a whole.

The appeal of Fletcherian drama lay in suspense. Reliance was placed on surprise. Unusual situations and startling actions followed hard upon each other's heels with dazzling rapidity. The action is set in an unreal world where consistency of motive and character must not be sought. The logic of the plays holds good only in the live theater, where audiences were cunningly persuaded into a willing suspension of disbelief. As Herrick said in his commendatory poem:

> Here's words with lines, and lines with Scenes consent,
> To raise an Act to full astonishment.
>
> (I, xli)

In this drama of "astonishment," music was a strong persuasive element. Its power and economy of suggestion were gratefully accepted and brilliantly developed by Fletcher, whose theater afforded sparse scenic effects and had cramping temporal limits. Music could set a mood or intensify one already existing; it could unobtrusively lower the pitch of emotion and ease tension without dissipating it entirely. Its versatility was unlimited, for there was no mood or situation it could not match. Rapid transitions between diverse moods and the contrast of emotions within a single scene especially benefited from musical aids. An excellent example of this occurs in the last act of *Valentinian* (V, ii). Valentinian has been poisoned and writhes on his deathbed. A lullaby is ordered to soothe him. The juxtaposition of the violence of the dying man and the gentleness of the song sharpens the emotions roused both aurally and visually. The bizarre union typically poises the audience between opposing moods of agony and gentleness in that ambiguity of feeling that Fletcherian drama so frequently sought.

Fletcher's use of music was facilitated by the common musical background that author and audience shared. Music played a significant and inescapable part in Jacobean daily life. An audience drawn from such a society would have been puzzled and disturbed if the stage world ignored music, and a puzzled and disturbed audience bodes ill for a playwright. Situations that called for music in everyday life also demanded it when they occurred in a play. This bred many of the stage's musical conventions; flourishes for royalty, music for banquets, trumpets and drums in alarums on the battlefield. The familiar sounds at once set the scene, firmly and succinctly evoked mood, and put the audience in the desired frame of mind. The very familiarity of these conventions could be turned to dramatic use when the expectations they aroused were deceived.

With so much music heard, it followed naturally that music should be much spoken about and that it should supply many images in conversation. Musical vocabulary is rich and Fletcher ransacked it for every kind of allusion, image, and joke. A host of technical terms—note, crotchet, quaver, division, change, noise, prick, fret, ravish, fiddle—supplied copious material for puns, quibbles, and double entendres. The great number of these commonplace figures emphasizes those that are more unusual. In *Thierry and Theodoret,* Thierry finely hits off the imperious nature of his wife when he says that she will "meet death like a measure" (IV, i). In the same play there is the grotesquely effective "if I should talk in my sleep, and they hear me, they would make a Recorder of my windpipe" (V, i). Overtones of Lear's last happy words to Cordelia before they go off to prison appear in *The Custom of the Country*: "your thoughts in cages / To sing to no ears then but mine" (I, i). People become instruments and consorts; thus, when everyone seems to fall in happily with his plans, Sir Perfidious Oldcraft remarks:

> Why this is musical now, and Tuesday next
> Shall tune your Instruments, that's the day set.
> (*Wit at Several Weapons,* III, i)

Aptly enough, the collapse of his plans is musically managed, for he is forced to pay exorbitantly for a band of musicians whose playing had covered the elopement of his daughter.

In a society where fondness for music is natural, anyone who dislikes it is marked at once as eccentric or even untrustworthy. Gondarino, *The Woman Hater,* is such a person, though his intense dislike of music is but a part of his general character of embittered misogynist. Such firm opponents of music, however, are rare. Greater use is made of humorously irritated reaction than of active dislike. Soldiers are prime examples of this and in two plays we can see how Fletcher uses them, showing soldiers struggling with sophisticated social musical diversions. Jacomo, *The Captain,* has little time for soft music. He considers it fit only for carpet knights, and the theme of the play is his conversion from this anti-romantic stand. The difficulties inherent in the task are amusingly set out when his lady, in a neat reversal of the usual procedure in love affairs, serenades the man. Jacomo falls asleep during the performance and wakes after it is over, hazily muttering about paying the fiddlers, thus implying that the music has been of the sort offered drinkers at taverns by strolling musicians. In *The Wild Goose Chase,* Pinac displays a characteristically soldierly yet understandable distaste for music, considering the musical obstacle race which he is made to undergo by the teasing Lillia-Bianca. Like Jacomo and like his own friend Belleur, he is irked at finding himself at a disadvantage when it comes to courting his lady, for he has only some bluff ballads to serve as love songs (*Captain,* II, ii; *Wild Goose Chase,* II, ii; II, i). (More variations on this theme of music and soldiers are skilfully played in *The Mad Lover* and *The Humorous Lieutenant.*)

In contrast, the plays contain many ardent music-lovers. Old Antonio in *The Chances* is typical of these. When he is ill he has musicians attend him, he has his ward taught music, and his own speech is so full of musical allusions as to give away his great love of the art. A non-performer himself, Antonio's counterpart among performers is perhaps Merrythought in *The Knight of the Burning Pestle.* Richer sources of comic material among music-lovers are the earnest and bungling amateurs. In *The Elder Brother* a group of young court gallants planning wedding celebrations turns casually and naturally to thoughts of a masque. Egremont falls in eagerly with a suggestion that they run up a masque: "'Tis not half an hour's work, a Cupid and a Fiddle, and the thing's done: but let's be handsome, shall's be Gods or Nymphs?" This bold idea is squashed by Eustace, who protests: "What, Nymphs with beards?" "That's true," replies Cowsy, "We'll be Knights then; some wandering Knights, that light here on a sudden" (II, ii). When these hastily laid plans are frustrated later, their petulant cries, "W'are ready, what a scurvy trick's this," are answered by the cold comfort of the suggestion that they "perform it at some hall, where Citizens' Wives may see't for Sixpence a piece, and a cold Supper" (III, v).

The keenest amateur musicians in Fletcher's plays are Wildbrain and his friends in *The Nightwalker.* They are zealous bellringers who are undone by their pride and ardor in their hobby. Lurcher, the nightwalker, dupes them into ringing in darkness as a test of their skill; while they pull at the bells, stripped of all unnecessary clothing, he makes off with the clothes. Lurcher is adept at turning other people's love of music to his own crafty ends. Before tricking the bellringers, he had distracted the household servants with an enticing display of ballads. After the thefts he committed are discovered, they can excuse themselves by saying:

> He gave us Books Sir, dainty Books to busie us,
> And we were reading, in that which was the Brew-house,
> A great way off, we were singing Ballads too;
> And could not hear. (III, v)

At the other pole from amateurs are the professional theater musicians and even these Fletcher tries to make members of the society of the plays. A casual reference to them in the play is often enough to suggest that they are something more than non-actors who have to come and go as unobtrusively as possible. It is better still when they have something to say for themselves, even if it is only a line, such as the reassurance given by one of them to Maria in the opening scene of *The Coxcomb.* At other times, a passing remark chivying them to a "quicker time fellows" is enough (*Wild Goose Chase,* II, ii). The witty fiddler who assists Thomas in his hilarious wooing of Mary in *Monsieur Thomas* is the best example of musician as character. Elsewhere, the most unnoticed of musicians (those who simply supply flourishes) are spoken to. Duke Ferrand brusquely focuses attention on his irritation by testily calling out as a flourish sounds on his entry:

> no note more, on
> Forfeit of your fingers; do you
> Envie me a minutes slumber?
> (*Double Marriage,* I, i)

Penius, in *Bonduca,* has betrayed his country and dishonored himself and his soldiers. His anguish is well caught when, shamed at hearing the drums sound the call to battle, he shouts: "Back; cease your bawling Drums there, / I'll beat the Tubs about your brains else. Back!" (II, i).

The angry words of these two men surprise by their suddenness and the way they clash with the mood suggested by the music. They are examples in miniature of Fletcherian reversals. The stronger the two emotions that clash and the more telescoped the succession between them, the greater the impact on the audience. By using music, Fletcher was able to effect some powerful *coups de théâtre.* In *The Queen of Corinth,* the pathos of Merione's soliloquy in the temple is broken by the abrupt entry of Theanor and half a dozen of his followers, who dance fantastically about the girl "to a horrid Musick, and sprinkling water on her face." The initial mood and setting are cues for solemn religious music: instead there follows a dance of tormentors that takes on the semblance of a perverted sacrificial dance. The scene, admittedly, is melodramatic but theatrically effective in a typically Fletcherian way (II, i). It must be stressed again that many of the devices and scenes in the plays read much cheaper on the page than they would appear clothed in the action of the stage. A larger example of the technique is found in successive scenes of *A Wife for a Month.* The second act ends with a court wedding celebrated with revels and a masque of Cupid. The third act opens in the lonely monastery where the true king still mourns his father:

> The night grows on, lead softly to the Tomb,
> And sing not till I bid ye: let the Musick
> Play gently as he passes. . . .
>
> . . . . .
>
> Now sing the Funeral Song, and let him kneel
> For then he is pleas'd.
>
> (III, i)

The impact of this solemn scene is magnified because it follows hard upon the masque, the symbol of the corrupt court (much as Claudius' harsh, brash court music symbolizes his falsity in contrast to Hamlet's quiet music of the recorder).[3] The riot and revelry of the false king is set against the devotional music of the true king; loud dance is set next to elegaic song; the savage mockery of a wedding that is to end after one month in death is balanced by the proper remembrance of death. The masque and the funeral music and elegaic song are contrasting parts of one musical effect; music, in this instance, is the dominant element in the pattern of action as it reveals aurally and visually the clash of people and parties.

Something of the variety of effect is exemplified in the handling of songs. That from *The Lover's Progress* is perhaps more expressive of a change of mood than a direct reversal, but the contrast is effectively made. The hymn from *Cupid's Revenge* has repercussions throughout the play, setting up a mood against which the events of the play continually react. Two songs and two singers are used for comedic versions of reversal in *The Chances.* The scope then widens as a brilliant comic scene centered on a lullaby/love song from *Women Pleas'd* is examined first for its own merits and then as part of a gaily organized series of musical effects deployed over the second half of that play. These examples not only demonstrate the playwright's skill in fusing enjoyable music with dramatic needs, but also the unity of conception which makes the canon. The example from *The Lover's Progress* is from a scene of Massinger's; *Cupid's Revenge* is by Beaumont; *The Chances* and *Women Pleas'd* are by Fletcher. It is symptomatic of Fletcher's musical dominance that *Women Pleas'd* demands special notice for its large amount of musical entertainment. It is at this point that focus changes from character and the individual scene to the whole play, and the general problem of uniting music, words, and action in a single pattern over the length of the play comes to the forefront. Fletcher's handling of this problem is displayed in *The Prophetess, The Little French Lawyer,* and *Valentinian.* These three plays are examined in detail as demonstrations of Fletcher's range and his dramaturgical skill.

Lidian's song in *The Lover's Progress* (III, i) is contrived skilfully to push the action forward. It urges the power of Heaven and love and persuades Clarange not to forsake the church: the happy conclusion of the play follows from this decision. In addition, it reaffirms the mood of calm after the exciting nocturnal activities of the previous scene. More interesting, however, is the manner in which the persuasive and penetrative power of the song is insisted upon, as if to justify its importance in the action. Clarange originally asks that the song relieve his melancholy: "The speediest cure" for it, as he has heard tell. Even a sceptical friar admits its force as poetry:

> I confess however,
> It stands not with my order to be taken
> With such poetical Raptures: I was mov'd
> And strangely with it.

After hearing it sung, Clarange says:

> It is a heavenly hymn, no ditty father,
> It passes through my ears unto my soul
> And works divinely upon it.

Such words not only underline the importance of the song but also indicate the compelling value attached to the power of music.

The same point is made in *Cupid's Revenge;* in Act I occurs a spectacular ceremony in worship of Cupid. A central feature of the scene is a song promising men a world of fulfilled love. To the eye, the quasi-religious setting and formal ceremonial make the song a hymn. To the ear, it is a strangely optimistic love song. In any event, the song is ironic in that it heralds a time of unrest and crossed love while sounding like an epilogue to such a time. Cupid's wrath falls on Hidaspes and leads to her death. As she lies dying an attendant prays for her, making what amounts to a point-by-point submission to the opening hymn to Cupid. It comes too late and, as another waiting lady adds, it is not powerful enough, for it ought to have been sung rather than recited—a revealing comment on the power of music. In a purely dramaturgical manner, the opening song is interesting because of its implications and the purpose it serves later in the action. This extension of the function of a song is excellently used in *The Chances.*

Constantia, the heroine, sings primarily to pass the time and to cheer herself up—a barely legitimate excuse for introducing a pleasant song into the play. Extra effect is won, however, as two servants overhear her singing and, unaware that she is in the house, decide it must be a spirit. They are encouraged in their belief by their masters, who want the girl's presence kept secret. She later vanishes, and a desperate search is made. After some time, the searchers hear a woman singing in a nearby house. They are sure it is Constantia, whereas in reality it is a courtesan. This explains the sentiments of the song, suitable to a courtesan but hardly to the known predicament of Constantia. Thus the searchers are perturbed as well as pleased to hear the song. One opinion is that it is "applied for certain to some strange melancholy she is laden with." The scene is musically a quiet one but the calmness of the music is overshadowed by the relief, anxiety, and bewilderment of the searchers, the whole evoking another of those ambivalent emotional atmospheres Fletcher so adroitly created. The scene is racily concluded by a sharp reversal: sounds of fighting come from the sweet singer's room as she is revealed for the harsh-mouthed virago she is (II, ii; IV, iii).

The final example concentrates the effect in one scene of splendid comedy. The miserly Lopez in *Women Pleas'd,* having announced that he will be away for the night, sneaks back hoping to catch his wife Isabella at her suspected tricks. Instead, he finds her sleeping peacefully. Overcome by her beauty, he is filled with remorse by his suspicions. In this mood he sings a love song, but so softly as not to awaken her. However, when he bends to kiss her, he sees tied to her finger the string which should have warned her of her lover's approach. Enraged, he rushes out to find a stick to beat her with while Isabella takes the chance to substitute her maid in the bed so that she may answer Lopez' accusations the next day without a bruise to show. The gentle song is a charming interlude in a scene of subdued but bustling intrigue. Everyone save Lopez knows about the string, so that his song, although quiet and romantic, creates tension until the string is discovered. The words of the song, in this case, add to the piquancy of the situation. The doting husband sings of "*Cupid's* most cunning nets made of that hair." A moment later he is crying out, "a damned string 'tis." Over the whole scene (III, iv) floats the irony that so tender a song should be sung to so dissembling a wife, and by a miserly old man!

This gay scene is only one of several musical entertainments in the play. *Women Pleas'd* is Fletcher's version of *The Wife of Bath's Tale,* with the comical subplot of Lopez and his troubles thrown in for good measure. The musicality of the play is due not only to the variety of music offered but also to its concentration in the latter half of the play, where each action has some musical illustration and tangles are unravelled in an opulent and mysterious concluding masque. An insult offered the Duke of Siena during a banquet in Florence is the catalyst: it is quite unexpected and is thrown into higher relief because of the bright accompanying banquet music.[4] This is the situation parodied in Lopez' song to Cupid. Such pairing of situations is a feature of the play. Silvio, the young man who must find out what women most desire, is encouraged at one stage in his quest by a magical song from mid-air, mockingly echoed in the next scene as chimney sweep's boys sing while hidden inside the chimney (IV, ii, iii).

Siena and Florence go to war and the impact of hostility on a country village gives Fletcher his slight but sufficient pretext for an amusing skirmish against puritan attitudes about morris dancing. The villager's merry-making is rudely halted by the entry of soldiers somewhat in the same manner that the banquets were disturbed by the Duke of Siena's wrath. After the soldiers and "volunteers" depart, the dance continues, or so it is hoped. Hope-on-High-Bomby, however, the village's incomparable hobby, interprets these events as evil omens in accord with his wife's strictures and so denounces the morris as a device of Satan:

> And now no more shall hop on high Bomby,
> Follow the painted pipes of high pleasures,
> And with the wicked, dance the devils measures;
> Away thou pamper'd jade of vanity.

Fortunately, he is recovered from these Marlovian denunciations by the amusing arguments of his old companions. Dramatically, the scene is somewhat outside the needs of the play. It is primarily a pleasant musical interlude that contrasts neatly with the play's other generally more exotic music (IV, i).

In the last act, the hero delivers the answer and casts himself on the mercy of the crone. His uneasiness is increased by more mysterious "Musick in divers places." He reacts in the approved soldierly vein and, not unfairly, asks: "More of these Devils dumps? / Must I be ever haunted with these witchcrafts?" Then there is the direction: "Enter a Masquerado of several shapes, and Dances, after which enter *Belvidere* and disperses them." She resolves all the mysteries and the oddly irritating masque suffers a seachange into the traditional and happy musical finale of comedy.

The banquet, the country gaiety of the morris dance, and the splendors of the finale are as satisfyingly different as the four songs that are heard. The more cheerful music is allotted to the subplot and the mysterious effects to the main plot, but the grouping of all is so ordered that it not only makes its own varied pattern but differentiates and, in the end, unifies the different plots.

Fletcher's most exciting achievements occur when the pattern of action over an entire play is echoed by the musical pattern. There are more difficulties in managing this union than have commonly been recognized. Perhaps the most baffling of them is the gauging of what and how much music is popular and likely to appeal to an audience. One frequently finds the music in seventeenth-century drama (particularly and inevitably non-Shakespearean drama) dismissed as extraneous, something pleasant but contributing little or nothing to the drama and found only because the public liked and demanded it. As has been stated earlier, score music does exist on those terms but it is dangerous to apply rigid rules to the fluid drama of this period. Then, as now, audiences could not be relied upon to like what they were supposed to like. *The Knight of the Burning Pestle* was lavishly supplied with both music and a splendid musical character in Merrythought, but "the privy mark of Irony" about the play so disturbed the audience that the charms of music did not soothe their savage breasts. *The Faithful Shepherdess* was another commercial failure that "on the guilty Stage / Was martir'd betweene Ignorance and Rage" (I, lii). As Fletcher himself wrote in a prefatory note to it, "the people . . . missing Whitsun ales, creame, wasiel, and morris dances began to be angry." The pastoral and sweetly magical decorations of the play did not please any more than those of *Alba,* a play presented to James I in the hall of Christ Church at Oxford University in 1605. If Fletcher had heard of the failure of this play, he did not heed it: "The comedy began about between nine and ten and ended at one . . . the name of it was *Alba,* whereof I never saw reason . . . many rusticall songs and dances which made it tedious."[5]

Clearly, music alone could not make a play a popular success. Though he frequently called for it, Fletcher never forgot that he was, in the first place, writing a play. Though the richness of the musical elements sometimes moved the plays toward what could be called musical drama, the musical elements were always secondary to the dramatic. Nonetheless, at times Fletcher seemed deliberately to see how far and in what directions he could fuse music and drama. He tended to explore the possibilities of a particular device in a single play. In one set of plays the problems of the masque occupied his mind—*The Maid's Tragedy, The Faithful Shepherdess, The False One, The Mad Lover, The Four Plays in One.* In another, he concentrated on the contribution singing can make—*Beggars' Bush, The Maid in the Mill,* and *Monsieur Thomas.* Elsewhere, music either of one general kind or colored by some particular atmosphere is dealt with: vagabonds' music in *Beggars' Bush,* grotesquerie in *The Pilgrim,* magic and mystery in *The Prophetess.* Concentration on one sort of music did not, of course, mean that other sorts were ignored in a play. The three plays to be dealt with now each exploit music in different ways but always to the end of strengthening the structure and attractiveness of the play.

The variety of musical effects in *The Prophetess* is so arranged that it culminates in an impressive, almost operatic, gathering of musical entertainment in the last act. The combination of pastoral gaiety and supernatural effects is a little reminiscent of *The Winter's Tale.* Although Fletcher calls his play "A Tragical History," it is a splendidly exuberant sample of his tragicomic style. Shortly before writing it, he had explored some of the possibilities of music and the grotesque in *The Pilgrim,* a complicated Spanish comedy full of disguises, misunderstanding, and wanderings in strange woods. It had included birdsong displays, a lengthy musical show by Bedlamites (real and fake), and had ended in a grandiose religious ceremony liberally decked with music. In *The Prophetess* Fletcher works this vein of mysterious and exotic music very thoroughly. The play is a seventeenth-century "spectacular" that relies upon music to make its most stupendous effects. Activity on and beneath earth and in the heavens, all comes garnished with music. Delphia is the Prophetess and it is her power that calls forth the most telling musical effects. When the triumphant ruler cries out

> Shine clear, my Stars,
> That usher'd me to taste this common air
> In my entrance to the world, and give applause
> To this great work,
>
> (II, iii)

it is at her bidding that heavenly music is heard and the admiring court is astonished into cries of "Miraculous." Diocles swiftly points out the propitious nature of the omen, which is at once reinforced by a song of praise from the skies. Fletcher takes opportunity here for one of his startling sound contrasts; after the strange music of strings from the skies there is heard the blaring of the "Loud Musick" of the Emperor's retinue ("Loud Musick" being shorthand for wind and brass instruments). Other of Delphia's demonstrations include a musically based dumb show of the defeat of the Persian armies (the defeat itself is due to her power) (IV, i) and the comical efforts made for Geta, the foolish servant who rises to the bench and, having Delphia before him, agrees to acquit her if she will conjure him a fine dancing she-devil. With more music, she does (III, ii) and so pleases him that at the end of the play he asks if he may have the same partner called up to join him in the revels being arranged.

In the last act Diocles has retired to a country estate where allurements include singing bird-pots, subterranean music, and a song by the spirit of the well (V, iii). The spectacular conclusion throws everything else into the shade, however. Basically, it is a country festival with magical decorations. The country folk, oblivious of a civil war that is brewing, decide to present Diocles with a festival:

> All our merry Gambols, our may-Ladies,
> Our evening dances on the Green, our Songs,
> Our Holiday good cheer, our Bag-pipes now Boyes
> Shall make the wanton Lasses skip again.
>
> (V, i)

Eschewing "courtly entertainments" and "rare musicks" (a fair enough description of the previous musical entertainment the play had offered), they propose a wholesome fare of "honest and cheerful toyes from cheerful meanings." This mood of excited jollity is sustained and the Well Spirit's song only increases the general feeling of elation. The pastoral begins with a dance by shepherds and shepherdesses led by Pan and Ceres. The arrival of Diocles' rival, Maximinian, momentarily interrupts the dance, but after a last staggering display of heavenly power he is conveniently made to realize his "base and foul intentions" and, amid protestations of amity, the play ends with the revel in full swing again.

The last scene is one of well-contrived contrasts. Against a background of rustic dancing and peaceful merriment are thrown forward, in turn, magic music and song, warlike music, and heavenly wonders. The use of music and dance is almost operatic: action superimposed on a chorus, sounds as well as action carrying the plot on. The different kinds of music symbolize Delphia's magical powers, the peace that is sought in the country, and the world of court and of politics. The rustic sounds begin the scene, are heard intermittently throughout, and, in the end, prevail. In such a play, which sets out to be a glittering show piece with Delphia's magic as the pretext for the spectacular, it is an uneasy criticism that carps at the seemingly extraneous. Theoretically, all the music and trappings could be taken from this play, but thus denuded, the play would have been a complete theatrical failure. Fletcher is, however, careful to make this play not merely a collection of favorite effects, musical or otherwise, but to attach all his effects firmly to a clearly defined plot.

The Prophetess is probably the nearest thing to grand opera libretto that Fletcher wrote, for its story and incidental effects are remarkably akin to the bold conglomerations of some nineteenth-century works. There is, of course, too much action and too much dialogue for *The Prophetess* to be anything other than a play. In opera, the pattern of action is primarily a musical one. This is beyond the scope of drama, and Fletcher, even though straining a little at the limits of pure drama in *The Prophetess,* always manages to remain within those limits. His pattern is determined by the spoken word and action. Music is used ingeniously to bolster that action, and, especially in the two plays we now turn to, to reflect in musical terms the broad outlines of the main emotional design of the play.

The leading situations in *The Little French Lawyer* revolve around anger, merriment, and a fear that is at once comical and horrid. At one time or another each of these emotions receives musical illustration. As the play opens, Dinant, an unsuccessful suitor to Lamira lately married to Champernel, is angrily discussing the state of affairs with his friend Cleremont. The festive wedding party enters and the two discontents are lost in the gay crowd, their rough words drowned as the epithalamium, "Come away, bring on the Bride," is sung. After the loud chorus, Dinant thrusts forward and soon embroils the whole group in argument. The pattern of the scene is bold; a combination of musical celebration and a pugnacious rejected suitor and his friend provide another of those moments of conflicting emotions such as was created in the last act of *Valentinian.*[6]

The next major conflict is comical and also hinges on music. Lamira allows Dinant to visit her, but Champernel is privy to the invitation and pretends to be asleep upstairs. Cleremont is sent to watch by his side in case he wakes. Lamira has thoughtfully provided music: "We must have mirth to our wine, Man," but Dinant has none of the regular lover's zeal for it at this time: "Plague o' the Musick . . . this will disturb all." Lamira quiets him, but the penetrative sounds of the recorders have reached Cleremont's astounded ears and from above he shouts in what he hopes is a whisper:

> What a Devil ail you?
> How cold I sweat! a hogs pox stop your pipes,
> The thing will 'wake; now, now, methinks I find
> His sword just gliding through my throat. What's that?
> A vengeance choak your pipes. Are you there, Lady?
> Stop, stop those Rascals; do you bring me hither
> To be cut into minced meat? why, *Dinant?*

Dinant indignantly disclaims responsibility: "I have spoken and spoke; I am betray'd and lost too." Cleremont thinks he has not been heard clearly: "Do you hear me? do you understand me? Plague dam your whistles." Before the situation gets too riotously out of hand, Lamira innocently halts the music. But almost immediately the musicians return to their instruments and the young men's folly is revealed. The scene is finely comical, with much of its humor rising from the vigorous twist given the old convention of the lover serenading his lady. Such reversal of roles has been noticed before in *The Captain,* but this is a full-scale working out of all its possibilities, and the romantic music (played just a shade too loudly?) is a foil for the desperate actions of the frustrated young would-be lover and his friend (III, i).

The riposte of the disconcerted young men occurs in the next act and continues the musical battle. While Champernel and friends are out strolling, they hear delightful music coming from a wood. A song lends additional enticement and soon the party is happily dancing. Vague uneasiness is dispelled only to return as the ladies are threatened with abduction. Pleas on their behalf are fruitless, until Dinant and Cleremont appear and rescue them. There follows a bewildering series of rescues and recaptures that eventually resolve when the whole incredible business is revealed as a contrivance of Dinant's. The musical point of the matter is taken up after the interruption of the dancing when the ladies, having been thrown into a dark cave, are frightened by "A Horrid noise of Musique within. . . . A strange Musick. Sackbut & Troop Musick" and peeping faces. This is followed by an unspecified "New sound within." Thus, there is a startling contrast between the pastoral dance in the sunlit woods—a setting largely evoked by the music and dancing—and the warlike and essentially masculine music that terrifies the girls in their dark place of imprisonment (V, i).

This scene may be compared with one from *The Double Marriage,* written probably a year later than *The Little French Lawyer,* to give an additional proof of Fletcher's virtuosity with musical effects. In the later play the same device is used, but the contrast is between fear and courage and the altered context gives a quite new identity to what is basically the same musical effect. The setting is a sea fight, given loud reality by blaring trumpet calls and confused shouting and scuffling. Virolet and Ascanio have been thrown into a dark hold and their talk is suddenly interrupted by "strange Musick within, Hoboys."

> *Asc:* Hark, what noise is this?
> What horrid noise is the Sea pleas'd to sing.
> A hideous Dirge to our deliverance?
>
> *Vir:* Stand fast now *(Within strange cries, horrid noise Trumpets)*
>
> *Asc:* I am fixt.
>
> *Vir:* We fear ye not
> Let death appear in all shapes, we smile on him.
> (II, i)

This strange music cuts across a high-sounding speech of Virolet on the insignificance of death and thus gains an added impact. Its momentary upsetting of the men only emphasizes their staunchness in gathering themselves to defy it. They had been trying to diminish death with words. In a film today such a scene might have shown them brought up short by a violent explosion dangerously close to and shaking the walls of the hold. Such realism was beyond the resources of Fletcher's theater, but to produce such an effect he husbanded as carefully and tellingly as he was able means that might seem rather feeble to us today. The sequence of the different kinds of music and sounds, of noise and quiet, thunder of battle and solemn discussion of death startlingly interrupted, was his solution to the problem in terms of what was available to his theater.

The impact in *The Little French Lawyer* is rather more grotesque than violent, for the temper of the comedy did not require the strongest manipulation of the effect. The three central actions are not so much illustrated with music as built around musical sounds, each one contrasting with the other two. The wedding-party music, that of the ill-fortuned wooing, and that for the woodland dance is all cheerful and attractive, yet each is set in a scene or situation whose prevailing atmosphere works in opposition to that of the music. The last device of the dark cave and eerie music is set sharply apart from the rest of the music in the play and serves to cast a melodramatic shadow over the penultimate action before a typically unexpected reversal brings the happy ending.

Valentinian is a strongly constructed tragedy, by turn sordid and violent: "It begins as the tragedy of Lucina, continues as the tragedy of Maximus, and concludes as the tragedy of Valentinian, as Fletcher throws his sympathy first one way and then another."[7] Each of the three actions has its own musical accompaniment and the three blocks of sound are used to emphasize the central events of the tragedy.

In his relentless pursuit of the chaste Lucina, Valentinian makes his palace like "a Paradise . . . Full of fair shews and Musicks" (II, i). He relies heavily on music for setting the voluptuous mood: as Lucina approaches music and two bluntly sexual songs are heard, "Now the lusty Spring is seen" and "Hear ye Ladies that Despise." Fletcher once again turns the serenade convention with its romantic music to uneasy ends; the coarse intentions of Valentinian and the sensual atmosphere are at odds with music's sounds (for although the songs are blunt in their purpose it does not at all follow that their musical setting should in any way be parodistic of the regularly serious love song). This is pointed up directly when Lucina expressly commends the music while disavowing the words:

> I like the air well,
> But for the words, they are lascivious,
> And over light for Ladies.
>
> (II, iv)

The palace servants are taken aback at Lucina's endurance and wonder that the music has not softened her heart. "What, heard ye any Musick yet?" asks Ardelia. Lucina tersely replies: "Too much." For the confrontation with the emperor, servants dart off to make sure "the soft Musick" is ready. This quietly plays as the two meet and Valentinian denies all Lucina's appeals. The whole of this passionate scene is disconcertingly accompanied by the gentle sounds of music (II, iv).

Valentinian's own tragedy having begun with music, it is ironic and apt that music should be powerless to help him avert its catastrophe. He dies in agony, and again soothing music provides the unexpected accompaniment to violence:

> The soft Musick;
> And let one sing to fasten sleep upon him:
> Oh friends, the Emperour.
>
> (V, i)

This time both words and music are "easie, sweet, And as a purling stream," but to no avail.

The next sounds heard are the rousing flourishes that announce Maximus is Emperor. As earlier, there were descriptions of musical preparations, so again there is talk of the celebrations for the crowning. These are in a lighthearted manner that does not, however, ring humorously enough to silence the fears aroused by the preceding death-laden actions. Paulus, the poet, takes an Osric-like part as he burbles about what sort of masque and what device shall be arranged. He hopes there will be some songs and Licippus answers him in words oddly reminiscent of Lucina's:

> By any means some songs: but very short ones,
> And honest language *Paulus,* without bursting,
> The air will fall the sweeter.
>
> (V, v)

The slight jibing at the emptiness of some masques heard in *The Elder Brother* is here extended, as all kinds of devices and figures are considered. Paulus fancies Orpheus rising from the flames with crossed arms and is left to ponder on the difficulties Licippus points out of the fire's burning the lute-strings and the athleticism needed to play a lute with crossed arms. When the entertainment is presented, it contrasts strongly with the quiet music that has gone before. Now all is noise: "A Synnet with Trumpets With a Banket prepared, with Hoboies, Musick, Song, wreath." A martial entertainment is presented and to Maximus, who has sacrificed his honor to win position, the song "Honour that is ever living" is sung. The irony is fully pointed when Maximus drinks the wine poisoned by Valentinian's widow as the drinking song "God Lyeus ever young, / Ever honour'd, ever sung" is given. The presenter then calls upon the military dancers to make their "high measure turn into a charge" as they foot it "to the fulness of your war-like noise." The performance goes forward but Maximus sits strangely still amid this loud festivity and only when he is called upon to make thanks is it discovered that he is dead. The martial celebrations have proved as ill-omened a background as the earlier quieter music, and the loud music is turned for the close of the play into the solemn music of the dead march (V, viii).

Thus, music that has been ostensibly romantic, peaceful, and martial has been fitted admirably into the movement of the plot and all of it has been colored by the brooding atmosphere and violence of the accompanying action. Its variety has been one pole, its ironic aptness to the situations the other. It is in such scenes as the closing one of *Valentinian* that Fletcher's art is displayed at its best. It provides a suitable climax to the whole play; its music contrasts with that heard earlier and aids the exposition of events so well that, although the primary appeal of the scene is dramatic, music and action are so blended that each needs the other.

This is Fletcher's solution to the problem of introducing a variety of music into his play without blurring the larger dramatic pattern of action. The diversity of sounds is made to serve the ends of his play, whether it be tragicomedy, comedy, or tragedy. His mastery of musical techniques is rooted in his appreciation of the theatrical and dramatic worth of music and his understanding of how well the kaleidoscopic dramatic art which he practiced was suited to musical embellishment. The suitability of Fletcherian drama for decoration by music still leaves the actual art of that decoration to be judged. Many things that seem easy to do demand much if they are to be done with taste. If Fletcher and his fellows were entertainers to the gentry, they were notably sophisticated and skilful entertainers. The fact that these plays are scarcely ever performed today has tended to obscure Fletcher's fine command of the skills of playwriting and particularly the contribution which music made to that skilful craftsmanship. A play can be read, but the direction for music on the printed page cannot properly be "read." It stands apart from the printed text in a way that it does not on the stage. Incidental music is best heard rather than listened to and it cannot be too firmly insisted upon that action does not cease while its sounds are heard. Fletcher's skill was not only to introduce music so that the action was not disturbed but, at times, to make music and action an indivisible theatrical event. Inevitably, some of his work falls below his highest standards; there are some cheap, albeit glittering, tricks, music that is incidental in the worst sense of the word. However, over the whole range of his work his standards as a fine craftsman are well maintained. Una Ellis-Fermor wrote of the atmosphere of the plays: "The air is full of reverberant rhetoric, melting cadences of word and music" heard as on "the moonlit stage of an exquisite opera set."[8] The link with opera is suggestive, but opera depends for its life on music; it is music with drama whereas Fletcherian drama is drama with music. The play is the thing. Fletcherian drama always stood in danger of degenerating into a ragged collection of startling events and spectacular scenes garnished with music ad libitum; of all the later Stuart playwrights Fletcher made the most ingenious, consistent, and successful attempts to avoid this charivari. William Cartwright gave a playwright's praise to this feature in one of his commendatory poems:

> No vast uncivill bulke swells any Scene,
> The strength's ingenious, and the vigour cleane;
> None can prevent the Fancy, and see through
> At the first opening; all stand wondring how
> The thing will be untill it is; which thence
> With fresh delight still cheats, still takes the sence;
> The whole designe, the shadowes, the lights such
> That none can say he shewes or hides too much.
>
> (I, xxxvii)

The essential dramatic shape of the story is always kept in mind and Fletcher's music was a homogeneous part of the dramatic context, not merely an ornament carelessly and hopefully offered to a supposedly uncaring audience.

MILTON ON LAWES: THE TRINITY MS REVISIONS

MacDonald Emslie

MILTON'S well-known sonnet on Henry Lawes exists in five forms. The Trinity College Cambridge MS contains three copies of it; the first is a rough draft in Milton's hand, the second a fair copy in his hand (both these are on fol. 43), and the third is a fair copy by an amanuensis (on fol. 45). The first printed version of the sonnet appeared in *Choice Psalms put into Musick for three voices* (1648). Lastly, there is the second printed version, that of the second edition of Milton's Poems (1673). The earlier versions are particularly interesting with reference to contemporary methods of song-making.

Milton calls Lawes' song "tuneful" *and* "well-measur'd," which suggests he is thinking of Lawes as particularly a composer of declamatory ayre—which is what he was at this time. An examination of the first hundred or so songs in Lawes' autograph manuscript collection suggests that they are the work of the 1630's: it contains, for instance, Lawes' settings of the *Comus* songs (1634). While a third of these songs are simple tuneful ayres of the post-1622 kind, almost two-thirds of them are declamatory ayres. This English song form had been developed in court masques by Nicholas Lanier by 1614. We must therefore correct Milton's remark (which remains the same in all versions of the sonnet) that Lawes "*First* taught our English Musick how to span / Words with just note and accent." But we do not expect the exact truth from people writing complimentary verses about their friends, and in any case the remark seems to have been a stock compliment; in 1657 Lawes praised John Wilson in similar terms, saying that he was the first to give "the right accents and proportion" in English song.[2]

Milton, whose father was a composer as well as a scrivener, knew a great deal about music, and in the course of writing his sonnet he revealed various shifts in his musical thought. The most significant evidence of this is found in the Trinity MS's first version, which is headed "To my freind Mr Hen. Laws Feb. 9. 1645." Milton's first version began:

> Harry, whose tunefull & well-measur'd song
> first taught our English Music how to span
> words with just notes, wch till then us'd to scan
> with Midas eares, committing short & long. . . .

He is stressing the point that in earlier forms of song the composer did not pay so much regard to the natural accentuation of the words. But the third line is turgid. Milton apparently made as his first alteration a revision of the second part of the line; he put a cross after "notes" and wrote over the line "when most were wont"; he then wrote out the result in full in the right-hand margin: "when most were wont to scan." He was not, however, satisfied with the verses as they now stood: "words with just notes, when most were wont to scan / with Midas eares. . . ." It seems that he wished to emphasize the declamatory qualities of Lawes' ayres and that he thought "just" and "scan" were not sufficient to do this. Milton therefore made what is apparently the second alteration to this particular line; over it, at the left-hand side, intruding into the margin, he wrote "words with just note & accent, not to scan"—which is the version we all know. He then wrote the line out again completely, in the left-hand margin. His phrase "just note & accent" is a recognition of the qualities of declamatory ayre—the kind of setting Lawes had given his *Comus* lyrics. Just accentuation, a voice-line that respects and is based on the speech movement of the words, is what distinguishes declamatory song.

The sonnet goes on: "not to scan / With Midas eares, committing short & long." Milton complains here of the failure of earlier song composers to observe just accentuation. All the later versions of the sonnet read "committing" and Johnson's dictionary used the passage to define one sense of the verb "to commit": "to place in a state of hostility or incongruity: a latinism."[3] The first version of the sonnet has the word crossed out and marked with a cross; in the right-hand margin an alternative is offered: "misjoyning." This makes us sure about Milton's meaning; the fault of the earlier song composers was that they put long notes to short syllables or vice versa—that is, they did not observe just accent. When the sonnet was first shaping, Milton was concerned that its opening lines should clearly distinguish the nature of the declamatory ayre. The later underlining of "committing" is equivalent to "stet."

There are alterations in the early versions of lines 5 and 6, but these are not concerned with song-making. Lines 7 and 8 read in the first manuscript version: "to after age thou shalt be writt a man / that didst reform thy art, the cheif among." This is probably nearer the truth than the line 2 remark that Lawes first taught English song to span words with just note and accent. Lawes probably was the best known of the Caroline composers of declamatory song—though there were other musicians of equal ability, in particular, John Wilson.[4] But in the second manuscript version of the sonnet, Milton altered lines 7 and 8 to read: "To after-age thou shalt be writt the man / That with smooth aires couldst humor best our tongue." He deserts his general praise of Lawes' song-making to return to the great characteristic of declamatory ayre—that while being tuneful ("smooth aires") it followed the accentuation of English (it "humor[ed] best our tongue"). In the second manuscript version, Milton amended "aires" to "aire"; this revision makes the line refer specifically to the melodic quality of Lawes' voice-lines; they were shapely, while still keeping to the speech inflection of the text.

The next line, line 9, begins, in all versions, "Thou honourst vers." The essential difference between declamatory and earlier forms of song is in the relative importance of the words and music. Declamatory song bases itself on certain characteristics of the words: the words are of greater importance; the music elaborates and sustains them, but the musical contribution to the total song is less than it is in the tuneful forms of ayre and, of course, in the elaborate contrapuntal structure of the madrigal. Declamatory song composers are not infrequently praised by poets of this period because their music does not overwhelm the lyric.

Milton next calls Lawes "the Preist of Phoebus quire / that tun'st thir [theire][5] happiest lines in hymn or story." "Hymn" may not refer to the contents of the *Choice Psalms* of 1648, in which the sonnet was first published. The Trinity MS versions have headings dated 1645 and referring to "Ayres." Lawes did set devotional texts and his first published collection contains a setting of Greek entitled "Anacreon's Hymn." The second term, "story," is of greater interest. We discover what Milton meant by it only when the sonnet reaches print, in 1648. In the *Choice Psalms* the word is asterisked and there is a marginal note: "The story of Ariadne set by him in Music." This is the first song in Lawes' first published songbook, the *Ayres and Dialogues* of 1653. It is a recitative song and the text, by William Cartwright, appears to have been specially written for Lawes to set. As Milton's sonnet—at least by 1648—refers to this Ariadne song, it must have been written by that date. It may well have been written by 1645, the date given the sonnet in the Trinity MS. Cartwright died in 1643. The song's position in Lawes' autograph manuscript suggests a date about 1640. It is a direct-speech lament by Ariadne after she has been deserted by Theseus on the isle of Naxos. Recitative began in Italy as dramatic music, sung drama, opera. In this particular English recitative song a character is singing: the song gives the performer a dramatic role. And direct speech exchanges could, we find, be referred to as "story" in the seventeenth century. The title page of the Commonwealth production of Davenant's *Siege of Rhodes* tells us that the play had been "Made a Representation by the Art of Prospective in Scenes, And the Story sung in *Recitative* Musick." "Story" means the dramatic exchanges of the piece, as distinct from the song lyrics. (Incidentally, Lawes set the first and fifth entries of the play.) Milton could have derived this use of "story" from the word *"istoria,"* as used in Italian discussions about suitable texts for the new recitative music: "Il semplice proferire di qualche cosa a mente, come un Orazione, un Istoria."[6] It is noteworthy that when, in 1653, the song first appeared in print, the publisher John Playford thought it necessary to preface it with a paragraph outlining the Theseus-Ariadne story in order to explain to the ordinary performer the nature of the dramatic situation in which Ariadne was supposed to be at the moment the song began.

There remain for consideration the last three lines of Milton's sonnet. The first manuscript version before its revision is not of particular musical interest, and it is its revision that produces the text we are familiar with:

> Dante shall give Fame leave to set thee higher
> Then his Casella, whom he woo'd to sing,
> Met in the milder shades of Purgatory.

This ending of the sonnet is worth bothering about because of the odd conclusion reached by Willa McClung Evans: "The comparison between Lawes and Casella implied, I believe, that in Milton's dreams of writing a monumental poem he thought of Lawes as chanting his own great epic to lute accompaniment."[7] These are Miss Evans' dreams, not Milton's. The point of the sonnet's conclusion merely seems to be that Casella probably had set Dante's words, as Lawes had set Milton's, but whereas Dante put Casella in Purgatory, Milton says, by way of compliment, that Lawes' reward after death will be better than that. In *Purgatorio,* Canto II, Dante is in the milder shades of Purgatory, having only recently left Hell. When we turn to the canto we see that Milton is complimenting Lawes on the power of his song. Its lines 106-20 have Dante addressing Casella: "If a new law does not take from you memory or skill in that song of love that used to calm all my desires, may it please you to comfort my soul with it for a while, which, travelling here with its mortal part, is so much distressed." Casella responds with a song, "Amor che nella mente mi ragiona": " 'Love that discourses to me in my mind,' he then began, so sweetly that the sweetness still sounds within me. My master [i.e., Virgil] and I, and those who were with him, seemed so glad, as if the mind of none of them paid attention to anything else. We were all fixed and intent upon his notes." They are then interrupted by Cato, who urges the souls on to the purgatorial mount. Cato's complaint that the song beguiles the spirits is especially relevant to Lawes and the new ways of setting music to words. For in evolving recitative, the Italian Camerata believed they were getting back to classical methods of song-making. They particularly wished to achieve the rhetorical power reported of ancient Greek song. Milton's reference to the *Purgatorio* should therefore be taken as praise for the power of Lawes' song to hold the attention of an audience. The nature of declamatory song—the importance it gave to the words, to the direct meaningfulness of the song as heard in performance—went along with the rhetorical intention.

Verses by John Cobb give a clear account of how Lawes' songs were musical heightenings of the spoken delivery of the words and how they dealt with the words in meaningful groups:

> No pointing *Comma, Colon,* halfe so well
> Renders the Breath of Sense; they cannot tell
> The just Proportion how each word should go
> To rise and fall, run swiftly or march slow;
> Thou shew'st 'tis *Musick* only must do this,
> Which as thou handlest it can never miss;
> All may be *Sung* or *Read,* which thou hast drest,
> Both are the same, save that the *Singing's* best.
> Thy muse can make this sad, raise that to Life,
> Inflaming one, smoothing down th' others Strife,
> Meer Words, when measur'd best, are Words alone,
> Till quickned by their nearest Friend a Tone:
> And then, when *Sense* and perfect *Concords* meet,
> Though th' Story bitter be, Tunes make it sweet:
> Thy *Ariadne's* Griefs so fitly shown
> As bring's us *Pleasure* from her saddest *Groan.*[8]

Setting words with just note and accent, giving a musical heightening of their spoken delivery, can produce song whose words are completely intelligible in performance and which can have considerable rhetorical impact. As Horatio Moore put it:

> With Words and Ayres our Ears are doubly fed,
> What e'er thou set'st is at once *Sung* and sed.[9]

Musical settings of this kind focus more attention on the lyrics—and hence there is a greater concern about choosing good ones. Wilson commends Lawes for this in 1653, and four years later Lawes returns the compliment. For Berkenhead, Lawes is the composer who "Worded Sense pursues." Waller, praising Lawes for his choice of lyrics, says: "But you alone may truly boast / That not a syllable is lost" and concludes, "Let words and sense be set by Thee."[10] Lawes himself says: "I never lov'd to *Set* or *sing* words which I do not understand; and where I cannot, I desir'd help of others who were able to interpret."[11]

Milton's remarks in his sonnet about Lawes' songs are not, then, idle praise, but pertinent musical comment. There is a further example that may enforce this point. The Lady in *Comus,* seeking her brothers, sings the song "Sweet Echo"; Milton first made her address end: "So mast thou be translated to the skies / And hold a counterpoint to all heavns harmonies." This means that Echo will sing a part that will join contrapuntally with all the various parts that are sung in Heaven. In the Trinity MS "And hold a counterpoint" is obliterated, but the Bridgewater MS makes the reading clear.[12] The Trinity MS of *Comus* in its first revised state was used as a source for the Bridgewater MS version; in its second revised state it was used as a source for the first printed edition, 1637. The first revisions, which are few, are supposed to have been undertaken by Lawes for the purposes of the Ludlow production.[13] Lawes did not alter "And hold a counterpoint" in this song. But it was altered by Milton in the second revision—which is reflected in the 1637 edition—to "And give resounding grace."[14] Miss Darbishire, repeating Aldis Wright, compares this revision to one in "Blest pair of sirens," where "harsh chromatic jarres" is altered to "harsh ill sounding jarres."[15] Her comment, "the technical musical phrase altered to one of a familiar and general character," also derive from Aldis Wright, who noted a further revision in "Blest pair of sirens"—"Mixe y^{r} choice chords" altered to "wed yor divine sounds."[16] But Milton's alteration of the last line of "Sweet Echo" seems to have had technical musical issues as its point. As we should expect, Lawes' setting of the song, which survives in his autograph manuscript, is not at all contrapuntal; it is a declamatory ayre. The music of such song is relatively simple as it appears in printed songbooks and certain manuscripts. But other manuscripts show that able performers elaborated the voice-line with a considerable number of vocal ornaments—"graces." There was thus an appreciable musical contribution added in certain performances. Lawes was an accomplished singer; it is almost certain that he would embellish his own performances in this way, and it is quite possible that the Lady could do so too; several manuscript songbooks showing florid ornamentation belonged to lady singers. In any case, it is more appropriate, when the setting is a declamatory ayre, to talk of giving resounding grace than it is to talk of holding a counterpoint. Gracing was used especially at cadences—certainly at the final cadence of a song. And we are discussing the song's last line. The revision, then, need not be any the less technical, but just more technically suitable. And that seems to be the way of describing Milton's revisions of his sonnet to Lawes, too.

CARTWRIGHT'S DEBT TO LAWES

Willa McClung Evans

THE debt Cartwright owed to Lawes was perhaps no greater than that Lawes owed to Cartwright. Their collaboration in providing dramatic-musical entertainment extended over a period of years, during which each became obligated to the other for a variety of favors.

At the beginning of their relationship, sometime before March 26, 1635, Cartwright was an Oxford student whose knowledge of the theater had been picked up largely through observing or participating in performances of university plays.[1] Lawes was a middle-aged, professional musician; he had composed songs for concerts, masques, and dramas.[2] In view of their respective backgrounds, Cartwright's debt to Lawes was for encouragement, criticism, and that distinction craved by ambitious young poets of having verses set to music and "sung before the Presence at Whitehall." And Lawes in his turn needed the well-wrought stanzas, which Cartwright learned to supply, for songs to be used in teaching and court performance. The years of active personal collaboration between the two ended with Cartwright's death in 1643.[3]

A complete account of the Lawes-Cartwright relationship might well fill a volume. But as I have pointed to several aspects of their collaboration elsewhere,[4] I propose to treat here but one facet of their work together: Cartwright's debt to Lawes for a lesson in dramaturgy received during the staging of *The Royal Slave.* The lesson I have in mind does not pertain to the lyrics included in the body of the play, but to a pagan analogue of a Christian liturgical musical service introduced into the denouement. Two versions of Act V, scene vii, one with and one without music, provided the focal point of this discussion.

The first version of *The Royal Slave* as represented in a manuscript text containing stage directions[5] reveals how Cartwright ended his play, without music and without Lawes' help. It also points to the problem confronting the young playwright: how to endow the denouement of his play with the uncontrived casual character of fashionable Cavalier drama,[6] and at the same time provide an appropriately strong conclusion. Cartwright was a scholar, a son of Ben, and a student of Aristotle; he must have known well the devices of discovery, reversal, and resolution. He also yearned for the approval of the court. In the first (manuscript) version of Act V, scene vii, prepared presumably for the entertainment of the King and Queen at Oxford, he chose to attempt to please the court.[7] He delegated to the Court Architect, Inigo Jones, the responsibility of introducing the devices of discovery, reversal, and resolution, in a spectacle—an Interlude, presented between scenes. Cartwright's verbal ending is consequently very flat.

To understand how flat, it is necessary to review the plot.[8] At the opening of the play, Cratander, an Ephesian held captive as prisoner of war by the Persians, sits behind the bars of his dungeon cell, reading a book of philosophy. From this prison he is eventually led forth, dressed in robes of state, and invested as the mock king of Persia for a rule of three days. During this brief span, he is subjected to several opportunities to stray from the path of virtue; he is tempted[9] to escape, to set free his fellow prisoners, to accept the Queen's favors. But Cratander, like the Christ of *Paradise Regained,* resisted temptation without apparent effort.[10] At the end of the three days, Cratander was to be sacrificed on the altar of the Persian sun god so that the laws of the Persians could be carried out. The Queen interceded for the victim, but the King was not to be diverted from his purpose to enforce the law. The final scene revealed how Cratander was rescued and a happy ending brought about.

Scene vii opens where the previous scene had left off, and without change in setting. The background represents the interior of a temple with an altar, and fire burning thereon. But as the court audience enjoyed surprise and diversion, Inigo Jones staged a spectacle between scenes vi and vii to prevent monotony and amuse the spectators. The spectacle provided an eclipse of the sun and a shower of rain that put out the fire on the altar. After this display, a priest entered and explained (as did the narrator of silent cinema) what had taken place. The sun god was not pleased with and did not require the sacrifice. He had thus sent an omen (in the eclipse and the shower) to declare that the ritual should not proceed. Cratander was to be liberated, and a happy ending was thus accomplished! The device which discovered the presence of the god, reversed Cratander's fate, and resolved the situation, had been expressed in the spectacle. Jones, not Cartwright, had brought about the denouement. This was indeed the weakest way in which to end a play; this was without doubt the unmotivated intervention of a god; this was the example par excellence of a deus ex machina.

Besides such structural weakness, there was another, more serious objection to this ending. The deeper meaning of the scene pointed to dangerous theological doctrine. The sun god's proclamation that there was no need to enact the sacrifice in a ceremonial of thanksgiving and reunion perilously paralleled Calvin's teaching that it was not necessary to stress the earthly suffering and crucifixion of Christ as part of the communion ritual celebrating the Last Supper.[11] G. Blakemore Evans believed that Cartwright had no intention of providing deeper meanings for his plays; that there was no message other than that which appeared on the "polite surface."[12] This may be true;[13] but Cartwright's metaphysically minded audience and his censors—behind whom loomed the powerful shadow of the University Chancellor, the Archbishop of Canterbury—were not unmindful of interpretations that might be twisted to advance unorthodox doctrine. If the play was ever actually staged as the manuscript versions represent the ending, it is surprising that Cartwright escaped with his ears. He soon changed the ending; and he printed the play with the new, altered denouement. Whether the changes were made before or after the Oxford performances is of little relevance to this study. Change it he did, both its superficial form and its deeper meaning.

To a casual reader, the obvious difference between the manuscript and the final printed text is the transposition of Inigo Jones' Interlude from between scenes vi and vii to a position within scene vii, and the addition of a processional and a song. The difference was of greater significance, however, than so simple an explanation indicates. It amounted to a startling conversion of Act V, scene vii, into an elaborate pagan ceremony, analogous to the Anglican ritual for the sacrament of the Eucharist. Harbage recognized the solemn character of *The Royal Slave* in his reference to its "elevation of tone and grandiloquence of style," as contributing "an almost religious atmosphere."[14] And Ruoff emphasized the popularity of the sacrificial motif, without observing the reason for its appeal to seventeenth-century Cavalier audiences, in his identification of scenes analogous to Act V, scene vii, in several other contemporary plays.[15]

As composer of the music for the song that was introduced, and by virtue of his early training and immediate professional activities, Lawes was instrumental in bringing about the changes introduced in Act V, scene vii. His early training had been that of a chorister at Salisbury Cathedral, where, if anywhere in England he would have become familiar with the origin and function of the parts of the liturgy. The Sarum ritual had been one of the oldest and purest forms of service in England; and its tradition was proudly pointed to if no longer practiced. A knowledge of the original forms and functions of the fixed parts of the Ordinary was essential in order to parallel on the stage (without too closely imitating) the musical service of the Eucharist. Lawes' position as Composer of the King's Musick had acquainted him with the court's tastes in drama, masques, and musical entertainments. As a Gentleman of the Chapel Royal, he had long known Laud, who had at one time been the King's Chaplain. Thus, Lawes was in a position to gauge how closely the liturgy of the church could be represented on the stage without offense to the Archbishop. And as Lawes had performed in court masques, he knew the professional actors and singers who could be counted on for the Hampton Court performance and what each could contribute to the entertainment. No other man in the kingdom had precisely the background and qualifications Lawes possessed, and which were required in the composer who was to make the changes that appeared in the new ending of *The Royal Slave*.[16] But Lawes was not a scholar. His feeling for dramatic appeals was based on his own experience and observation, not upon Aristotle's precepts.[17] When he set out to improve the ending of *The Royal Slave,* his aim was to provide a climactic conclusion which would please a Catholic Queen, an Anglican King, and the Archbishop of Canterbury.

His method was to employ secular songs that would suggest the origin and function of parts of a religious service. But in doing this, he avoided the use of musical themes reminiscent of those traditionally associated with the Sarum rite. Also, instead of resorting to the use of polyphony, the texture of contemporary motet and anthem, Lawes turned to secular monody—the form of the mid-seventeenth-century English ayre—with which his name has been principally associated. Except for one brief passage of polyphonic texture, the music for the last scene of *The Royal Slave* was monodic or harmonic.

The first obvious change in the ending of the play was the character of the stage sets used in scene vi. The manuscript had called for backdrops representing the interior of a temple. The new scene was to be that of a palace court. It provided a more appropriate environment for a festive reunion between soldiers returning from the wars and the loved ones left at home. There was dancing and gay carnival. Such pomp and feast and revelry relieved the necessity for diversion which Jones' Interlude previously had supplied. The Interlude was thus omitted between scenes vi and vii.

The backdrops for scene vii, however, still represented a temple, an altar, and "one busie putting fire thereon."[18] The contrast between the festive gaiety of scene vi and the preparations for Cratander's sacrifice of scene vii was, however, striking and impressive. Compatible with the temple interior and with the liturgical rites to follow, the scene opened with a processional. Processionals served functionally in ritualistic services;[19] they made a dramatic impact by intensifying expectancy. This processional suggested in the onward rhythmic movement of marching the ruthless inevitability of Cratander's approaching doom. A processional set the tone of awe for majesty, appropriate in a play presented before the King and the Queen. And a processional was itself a spectacle—the suitable beginning for a triumphal conclusion.

Heading the procession came the rogue, Molops, whose previous conduct made his mere presence increase pity and fear for Cratander. Molops carried a Sagar, the sword of state and emblem of Persian power. Held triumphantly at the head of the procession, it symbolized authority, sovereignty, earthly and heavenly justice; but it was more pointedly reminiscent of the Christian emblem carried at the head of religious processionals, the cross.[20]

After Molops came two pairs of slaves, two pairs of lords, two pairs of priests, and then, walking humbly and alone, Cratander. His singleness represented solitude in the midst of worldly pomp; his footing, the Way the saints and martyrs had trod and, prophetically, the path that Laud and Charles I were also to follow. By this I do not mean to imply that Cartwright or Lawes prognosticated the events of the 1640's, or that the Archbishop and the King were regarded in any way symbolic of Christian sacrifice. The fact that both were executed in the next decade, however, may explain the peculiarly strong audience response to the motif of sacrifice, noted by Ruoff.[21]

After Cratander, came the entrance of majesty: the King and Queen, attended by members of the court, and last of all, the masquers. They stepped solemnly around the stage and took their appointed places beside the altar, thus forming a tableau.[22] When they were in position, the service proceeded with the singing of a hymn, an invocation to the sun god, chanted by a priest. The first line of the lyric was a salute, a cry, an all hail; the second, was a plea for mercy. Its analogical base was the *Kyrie,* which in its origins had been a cry, an all hail, addressed to a god or an emperor, followed by a petition for deliverance from taxes and other burdens.[23] It had come in the fourth century to form the "core of the litanic response, Lord! have mercy upon us!" The pagan parallel used in *The Royal Slave* as the first priest's song first hailed the source of the sun god's power, then petitioned his mercy for the sacrificial victim:

> Thou o bright Sun who seest all,
> Look down upon our Captives fall.

Lawes' score[24] possessed the character of a secular but solemn ayre; it called for a tenor voice and emphasized, as did all of Lawes' monodies, the meaning of the words. The first four syllables—the salutation—are accompanied by notes which provide a rising melodic progression. The petition "Look down, Look down" is dramatized by a melodic drop of each verbal "down." The word "fall" is represented by a drop of five intervals. The modulation accompanying "Tis not a Man, but Vertue dyes" delays the chant and draws it out so that the ear becomes restless in anticipation of its accomplishment.

As preparation for climactic dramatic action, the processional followed by this simulation of a *Kyrie* stimulated anticipation, awe, and dread. It provided a prayerful attitude in which the audience could participate. And the choral response to the priest's solo further created the illusion of liturgical worship in its declaration that the

Figure 11. "Thou O Bright Sun"

Figure 12. "But Thou O Sun"

service was a ritual of thanksgiving. As the word "eucharist" means the giving of thanks, the deeper meaning intended could not escape an audience that was supersensitive to perceptions relevant to the liturgy. "While thus we pay our thanks" sets the tone of the choral response. It also echoes the character of praise and thanks expressed in the theme, "early in the morning, our praise shall rise to thee," of the *Sanctus*. The rest of the choral song in *The Royal Slave,* except perhaps for the syllables bearing the rhyme (be, Victory; thee, Trinity), bear little resemblance to a liturgical base; in fact, the rest of the song does not make sense. The words were offered apparently merely to provide the verbal line with which to extend a musical pattern. "And grant us either Peace or Victorye" was archaistic, for the Persians had won the victory and could dictate the peace.

At the end of this supplication, Molops stepped forward and delivered the Sagar to King Arsammes. His gesture paralleled the onward movement of the liturgical service marked by the carrying forth of the chalice.[25] This part of the stage ceremonial was designedly impressive; it occupied the eye, stimulated pity and fear for Cratander, kept the audience apprehensive because an awareness of the liturgical base warned of the approaching re-enactment of the sacrifice. After receiving the Sagar, the King, Arsammes, stood poised to deliver the death blow. Before his sword could descend, however, the action was again delayed. This time a second priest interceded in musical supplication:

> But thou o Sun mayst set, and then
> In brightnesse rise next morn again.
> He, when he shall once leave this light,
> Will make, and have eternall night.

Lawes' score calls for a bass voice. The depth of the tones foreshadowed Cratánder's descent into the tomb. The man of virtue—like the Lamb—was to be prepared for the sacrifice. In the solemnity of the music and the slow pace of the supplication, this hymn functioned as does the *Agnus Dei* of the liturgy, as an expression of the very nadir of woe and despair. Cratander's "night" was intensified in the musical score by the melodic drop of a fifth, to low G, held for four counts.

The prolongation of misery, before the introduction of the devices of discovery, reversal, and resolution, was a lesson Cartwright needed to learn. Without such intensification of impending doom which the deliberation of this supplication compelled, there would have been little suspense and, as a result, little cause for later rejoicing. Lawes was in no hurry to bring the action to a premature resolution. Music could, and did, sustain the emotional tension as long as the convention of entertainment warranted.

Then, the final chorus implemented with Jones' spectacle introduced the dramatic devices of discovery, reversal, and resolution. The stage directions explain that while the chorus was singing, the sun was eclipsed and a shower of rain dashed out the fire. The stage directions do not point out at what moment the sun was darkened, nor at what passage of the song the rain dashed out the fire. But the words of the song and the musical setting provide evidence with which to reconstruct the scene. The eclipse began, presumably, on the last words of the bass solo, "eternal night." And the darkness was continued during the first singing of the chorus:

> Good deedes may passe for Sacrifice, o than
> Accept the Vertues, and give back the Man. . . .

The score for the first singing of the chorus is a polyphonic arrangement intended to contribute confusion, bewilderment, and horror to the darkness. An alto begins the passage, singing "Good deedes may passe." As the alto sings "passe," the treble enters with "Good deedes," etc. When the treble reaches "may" the alto is vocalizing "sacrifice." The bass remained silent until the upper voices had completed their lines and then boomed forth, "o than." To a court that had grown accustomed to concordant monody, the discord and syncopation of the polyphonic music symbolized the "descent into hell," alluded to in the apostle's creed.[26] And the combined auditory appeals and darkness paralleled the unnatural horrors, portrayed in the Gospel According to St. Matthew 27:45-54, attendant upon the gloom, earthquake, and opening of graves just after the crucifixion. In this portion of the scene, the god made his will known, his presence felt. This discovery of the presence of the god began the operation of turning the plot. It represented a moment of sustained tension. Lawes drew it out during the singing of two lines and demonstrated to Cartwright how intense suspense may be prolonged. This too was a significant part of Cartwright's lesson in dramaturgy.

During the second singing of the same words, the "reversal" of

Figure 13. "Good Deedes May Passe," first singing

the plot occurred. The rain dashed out the fire, signifying that Cratander's fate was changed, reversed; the captive hero was to be liberated. The music accompanying this part of the song and spectacle was concordant. The harmony symbolized a return to law, order, and peace and contrasted strikingly with the previous discord and confusion. The "reversal" thus extended over the whole performance of the chorus, the first half symbolizing the anticipated doom, the last half, the change of affairs and release of the prisoner.

Figure 14. "Good Deedes May Passe," second singing

The first half expressed the nadir of despair, the second half, new hope.

The full promise of hope was expressed in the words "give backe the man." These final words are set to a progression of accidentals that lead from minor discords to major concords. The modulation exemplified Cratander's return from death, or, in the terms of a liturgical analogue the promise of resurrection, the *Gloria*. Lawes was particularly distinguished for the modulations with which he concluded his ayres; they often symbolized progression from fear and despair to hope and happiness as promised in the resurrection.[27]

The remainder of Act V, scene vii, was performed as originally represented in the manuscript texts. A priest explained that an eclipse had occurred and a shower of rain had dashed out the fire, hence the god had willed that Cratander should not be sacrificed. Obviously, the new musical version did not require such exposition. The discovery, reversal, and resolution had taken place naturally as part of a religious service. The miracle of the eclipse and the shower had been motivated: they were the god's response to Cratander's virtues and to the prayers invoked in the religious ceremonial. None of the philosophical speeches was omitted. Inigo Jones had no cause to be jealous or angry. Cavalier drama with its demands for casual, natural action had been implemented by the addition of a plot and a climax.

The most important change insofar as censors were concerned was the new twist in meaning that the parallel to the liturgical service offered. It was a shift of emphasis. When Jones' spectacle had been staged as an Interlude, between scenes, it had focused attention upon the omen's message: that a re-enactment of the sacrifice in ritual was not required and should not be permitted. In the altered form of Act V, scene vii, which included the musical service, the attention of the audience shifted from concentration upon the Calvinist complexion of the sun god's message to wonder at the power of virtue and prayer that provoked a miracle. Philosophical virtue as demonstrated in Cratander's character could transcend the evils of the flesh, the perils of the law, and liberate the soul from the physical bonds of earthly slavery. And corollary to this manifestation of the power of virtue and prayer, the implication that if a god were to intervene in men's affairs, if a miracle were to be performed, the time and the place for such a divine gesture would be in response to prayer, and it would occur during a celebration of the sacrament. Pursuing this line of thought a little further, the miracle thus performed becomes identified with the miracle the Catholic church associated with the celebration of the sacrament, transubstantiation. Such an interpretation pointed to, without defining, what was regarded as Laud's theological leaning and the Queen's belief. Surcharged with such timely tensions, *The Royal Slave* aroused interest in and excitement over its deeper meanings, which Cratander's danger and liberation alone could not have accomplished.

And Cartwright did not forget his lesson in dramaturgy. Into the text of his *Ariadne,*[28] which Lawes also set to music, the poet inserted delays that song could convert into suspense: a nadir of woe, which notes could embellish with despair; the discovery of a god, which music could charge with tension; and a reversal of the victim's fate, to be accompanied by a musical modulation pointing to a triumphal destiny.

THE MUSIC FOR THE LYRICS IN EARLY SEVENTEENTH-CENTURY ENGLISH DRAMA: A BIBLIOGRAPHY OF THE PRIMARY SOURCES

Vincent Duckles

It is dangerous to claim complete coverage for any bibliographical study, but an attempt to make a comprehensive survey of the musical settings for the Jacobean-Caroline drama must inevitably fall short of its objective. We are still in the process of recovering the work of those musicians who collaborated with Ben Jonson, with Beaumont and Fletcher, with Richard Brome, or with Sir William Davenant. Only within recent years has the music of the early English theater attracted the kind of attention that scholars have long devoted to the texts. The study of Shakespeare music is in a class by itself. Here, at least, there is a well-established tradition of scholarship, but it is safe to say that the problems related to Shakespeare's use of music will continue to stimulate research for a long time to come.

Incomplete as the present listing may be, I think its users will be impressed by the quantity of music that has survived in the manuscripts and early printed sources. Most of these settings have been observed in one connection or another as the byproducts of literary or musical investigations. A substantial number of them are available in modern editions of assorted qualities, but no attempt has yet been made to bring all the information together from the widely scattered sources. This compilation is offered as an attempt to treat the music of early English drama as a body of materials worthy of study in its own right. It is not intended to suggest that song can be disassociated from the larger context of the theater, but it may serve to correct an emphasis that has been weighted almost entirely in the direction of literature.

In one respect this bibliography is incomplete by design. It is concerned solely with the musical settings of texts and does not take into account the comparatively small number of dances, "symphonies," and other instrumental pieces that have been identified as belonging with certain masques or plays.

Song found its way into seventeenth-century English drama from two avenues: (1) it was lifted bodily from the repertory of traditional melody with which all playgoers of the time were familiar; or (2) it was composed for a specific dramatic occasion by one of the musicians associated with the playhouse. The pursuit of one or another of these paths has led scholars into rather widely separated territories. Men such as Edward F. Rimbault, William Chappell, or Frank Kidson explored the popular vein. Their work has culminated in the authoritative study by Claude M. Simpson, *The British Broadside Ballad and its Music* (1966), to which frequent reference will be made in the following pages. The deliberately composed song has attracted much attention in recent years in the work of John P. Cutts, MacDonald Emslie, and Ian Spink. Both categories of song are treated in this bibliography, the chief criterion for inclusion being that the setting is a product of the late sixteenth or early seventeenth centuries. The texts all derive from the plays, but it would be a mistake to claim that the settings they prompted were all utilized in the original productions, or even in revivals. Just as a preexisting song could be adapted for playhouse use, so a dramatic lyric could gain currency as a good singable text and be set by a musician who had no direct connection with the stage. The precise relationship between these settings and the plays from which they were derived could be the subject of extended and detailed study. The purpose of this bibliography is simply to direct the student to the primary sources and the modern editions of musical settings based on the Jacobean-Caroline drama, a period from about 1603 to 1642.

Specialists in the English theater will note that these dates correspond to the chronological limits adopted by William R. Bowden in his work on *The English Dramatic Lyric, 1603-1642* (1951). The

Appendix to Bowden's study, which lists most of the identifiable songs from the drama of the period, has, in fact, provided the basic framework for the present bibliography. Bowden, unfortunately, makes no mention of musical sources. His survey is further restricted by the fact that he excludes treatment of the English masque, and the use of song in Shakespearean drama. There are recent studies that make up for this deficiency, at least in part. Andrew J. Sabol has edited most of the surviving songs from the masques in his *Songs and Dances for the Stuart Masque* (1959); John H. Long has directed his attention to the use of music in Shakespeare's comedies, and F. W. Sternfeld has devoted himself to *Music in Shakespearean Tragedy* (1963). A vast amount of information on Shakespeare song has been assembled by Peter J. Seng in *The Vocal Songs in the Plays of Shakespeare: A Critical History* (1967). Two other indispensable tools should be mentioned: Alfred Harbage's *Annals of English Drama, 975-1700* (Philadelphia, 1940) has provided the authority for the dates of first performances of the masques and plays, and *English Song-Books, 1651-1702* (London, 1940) by Cyrus L. Day and Eleanore B. Murrie, is a sure guide to the dramatic songs that appear in the printed collections of the second half of the seventeenth century. Finally, no student of the music of English drama can fail to acknowledge a debt to John P. Cutts, who has made the contents of many of the major manuscript sources more readily accessible in a series of detailed descriptions and inventories published over the past fifteen years. Some indication of the scope of his work is given in connection with the list of sources that follows. Cutts' inventories, although some details could be called into question, furnish a standard numbering system by means of which the songs can be located in their respective manuscripts.

MANUSCRIPT SOURCES AND RELATED STUDIES

A useful listing of the "Sources of English Song, 1620-1660," with commentary, has been compiled by Ian Spink in *Miscellanea Musicologica, Adelaide Studies in Musicology,* I (1966), 117-138. In the list below only those studies are cited that treat the source under consideration comprehensively.

Birmingham, City Reference Library

MS 57,316. A fragment containing settings from Shakespeare's *The Tempest.*

Cambridge, Fitzwilliam Museum

MS 52.D (the "John Bull MS"). The last portion of this source contains a collection of songs before 1630.

Cambridge, King's College Library

MS KC.1. A parchment roll containing rounds and canons of the Elizabethan period. See Jill Vlasto, "An Elizabethan Anthology of Rounds," *Musical Quarterly,* XL (1954), 222-234.

Dublin, Trinity College Library

MS F.5.13. An early seventeenth-century source of songs and catches; treble part only. The companion bass part is in the Edinburgh University Library, see below.

Edinburgh, University Library

MS Dc.1.69. A late seventeenth-century source containing much earlier material, including music by John Wilson. Compiled by Edward Lowe. See John P. Cutts, "Seventeenth-Century Songs and Lyrics in Edinburgh University Library, Music MS Dc.1.69," *Musica Disciplina,* XIII (1959), 169-194.

MS LA.III.483. A bass part, the corresponding treble of which is found in the Trinity College Library, Dublin; see above.

Glasgow, University Library

MS R.d.58 ("John Playford's Commonplace Book").

London, British Museum

MS Egerton 2013. A rather inaccurate, poorly written source, before 1650, containing 73 solo songs, part songs, lute music, etc.

MS Egerton 2971. Early seventeenth-century English and Italian songs.

MS Add. 10,337 ("Elizabeth Rogers' Virginal Book"). Songs and keyboard music before 1650.

MS Add. 10,338. A collection compiled by George Jeffreys, *ca.* 1660.

MS Add. 11,608. Some 75 English solo songs, part songs, and dialogues, *ca.* 1655. The source is especially interesting for its embellished variants.

MS Add. 15,117. An early seventeenth-century source including some sixteenth-century music. Best known for "The Willow Song," "O Death, rock me asleep."

MSS Add. 17,786-791. A set of early seventeenth-century part books of songs for voice and viols.

MSS Add. 17,799-800. A transcription by Matthew Locke of the music for Shirley's masque, *Cupid and Death, ca.* 1660. See Edward J. Dent's edition of the masque in *Musica Britannica,* II (1951).

MS Add. 24,665. Compiled by Giles Earle, *ca.* 1615-1626. See Peter Warlock, *Giles Earle, His Booke* (London, 1932), an edition of the texts with commentary on the music.

MS Add. 29,396. Compiled by Edward Lowe, Oxford musician and organist of the Chapel Royal, *ca.* 1660.

MS Add. 29,481. Twenty-four songs of the early seventeenth century.

MS Add. 31,432. William Lawes' autograph manuscript, compiled before 1646. See John P. Cutts, "British Museum Add. MS 31432:

William Lawes's Writing for the Theatre and the Court," *The Library,* 5th Ser., VII (1952), 225-234.

MS Loan 35. Henry Lawes' autograph manuscript, containing some 384 songs, *ca.* 1634-1650.

London, Lambeth Palace

MS 1041. A mid-seventeenth-century source of English and French songs, compiled for "The Lady Ann Blount."

New York, Public Library

MS Drexel 4041. An important collection of 150 solo and part songs before 1660; a rich source of theater music of the time. See John P. Cutts, "Drexel Manuscript 4041 . . . Earl Ferrers' MS, A Treasure-House of Early 17th-Century Song and Dramatic Lyric," *Musica Disciplina,* XVIII (1964), 151-202.

MS Drexel 4175 ("Ann Twice, her booke"), a fragment containing 18 solo songs, formerly in the collection of J. Stafford Smith. See John P. Cutts, "Songs unto the Violl and Lute, Drexel MS 4175," *Musica Disciplina,* XVI (1962), 73-92.

MS Drexel 4257 ("John Gamble's Commonplace Book"). An important collection of 325 songs, compiled before 1659. See Vincent Duckles, "John Gamble's Commonplace Book: A Critical Edition of NYPL MS Drexel 4257" (unpublished Ph.D. dissertation, University of California, Berkeley, 1953).

Oxford, Bodleian Library

MS Mus.b.1. Songs and lute music by John Wilson, compiled by the composer before 1656. See John P. Cutts, "Seventeenth-Century Lyrics: Oxford, Bodleian, MS Mus.b.1," *Musica Disciplina,* X (1956), 142-209.

MS Mus.Sch.b.2. Vocal and instrumental music by William Lawes in the hand of the composer, before 1645.

MS Don.c.57. A collection of solo songs, *ca.* 1625-1650, formerly in the library of Colonel Probert. See John P. Cutts, "A Bodleian Song-Book: Don.c.57," *Music & Letters,* XXXIV (1953), 192-211.

Oxford, Christ Church College

MS 87 ("Elizabeth Davenant's MS"). 24 songs, before 1624. See John P. Cutts, "Mrs. Elizabeth Davenant 1624: Christ Church MS Mus. 87," *Review of English Studies,* X (1959), 26-37.

MS 439. 74 songs, *ca.* 1620-1630.

MSS 736-38. 3-voice settings by Thomas Ford and John Jenkins, *ca.* 1630. See Vincent Duckles, "John Jenkins's Settings of Lyrics by George Herbert," *Musical Quarterly,* XLVIII (1962), 461-475.

Paris, Conservatoire

MS Res.2489.

Tenbury

MSS 1018 & 1019. Two early seventeenth-century sources of English songs and Italian monodies, before 1620.

Washington, Folger Library

MS v.a.159. A collection of lute music.

MODERN MUSICAL EDITIONS, WITH ABBREVIATIONS

Chappell Chappell, William. *Popular Music of the Olden Time,* 1 vol. in 2 (paged continuously), London, 1855-1859. Reissued by Dover Publications, Inc., New York, 1965.

Chappell-Wooldridge Chappell, William. *Old English Popular Music.* 2 vols. New ed., revised by H. E. Wooldridge. London, 1893. Reissued by Brussel, New York, 1961. 2 vols. in 1.

Cutts *Musique* Cutts, John P. *Musique de la troupe de Shakespeare.* Paris, 1959.

Fellowes *EMS* Fellowes, Edmund H. *The English Madrigal School.* 36 vols. London, 1913-1924. (New ed. by Thurston Dart in progress.)

Fellowes *LSW 1* Fellowes, Edmund H. *The English School of Lutenist Song Writers.* 1st Ser. 15 vols. London, 1920-1932.

Fellowes *LSW 2* Fellowes, Edmund H. *The English School of Lutenist Song Writers.* 2nd Ser. 17 vols. London, 1920-1932. (New editions of both series are in progress.)

Fellowes *Songs and Lyrics* Fellowes, Edmund H. *Songs and Lyrics from the Plays of Beaumont and Fletcher.* London, 1928.

Gibbon *Melody* Gibbon, John Murray. *Melody and the Lyric.* London, 1930.

Jackson *English Melodies* Jackson, Vincent. *English Melodies from the Thirteenth to the Eighteenth Century.* London, 1910.

Long *Shakespeare* Long, John H. *Shakespeare's Use of Music.* 2 vols. Gainesville, Florida, 1955-1961.

Mus. Brit. 2 Cupid and Death, by Matthew Locke and Christopher Gibbons. Edward J. Dent (ed.). (*Musica Britannica,* II.) London, 1951.

Sabol *Songs and Dances* Sabol, Andrew. *Songs and Dances for the Stuart Masque.* Providence, R.I., 1959.

Simpson *Broadside Ballad* Simpson, Claude M. *The British Broadside Ballad and its Music.* Rutgers, N.J., 1966.

Smith *Musica Antiqua* Smith, John Stafford. *Musica Antiqua.* 2 vols. London, 1812.

Spink *Johnson* Spink, Ian (ed.) *Robert Johnson: Ayres, Songs and Dialogues.* London, 1961. (English Lute-Songs. 2nd Ser., XVII.)

Sternfeld *Music* Sternfeld, Frederick W. *Music in Shakespearean Tragedy.* London, 1963.

Sternfeld *Songs* Sternfeld, Frederick W. *Songs from Shakespeare's Tragedies.* London, 1964.

Ward *Simpson* Ward, John M. "Simpson: The British Broadside Ballad and Its Music, a Review and an Article," *Journal of the American Musicological Society,* XX (1967), 28-86.

Warlock *Pam* Warlock, Peter (ed.). *Thomas Ravenscroft: Pammelia and Other Rounds and Catches.* London, 1928.

Warlock and Wilson *English Ayres* Warlock, Peter, and Philip Wilson. *English Ayres, Elizabethan and Jacobean.* 6 vols. London, 1927-1931.

BIBLIOGRAPHY

NOTE: No attempt has been made to cite all of the sources for the popular airs sung in the early English drama. Abundant details regarding these tunes, particularly in their instrumental versions, can be found in *Chappell, Chappell-Wooldridge,* and above all in Claude Simpson's *The British Broadside Ballad* and the supplementary article prepared by John Ward, given in the preceding list.

ANONYMOUS WORKS

Every Woman in Her Humour (1603-1608)

1. "Fortune my foe"

   One of the most popular melodies of the late sixteenth and early seventeenth centuries. There is a keyboard arrangement by Byrd in the *Fitzwilliam Virginal Book* and several anonymous versions are in lute and keyboard sources of the time. The song is introduced in *The Maid's Metamorphoses* and *The Two Merry Milkmaids* and is alluded to in a number of dramatic works.

   See *Chappell,* p. 162; *Chappell-Wooldridge,* I, 76; Gibbon *Melody,* p. 49; Jackson *English Melodies,* p. 21; Simpson *Broadside Ballad,* No. 144, p. 225.

2. "Here's none but only I"

   London, British Museum, MS Egerton 2971, fol. 15. Oxford, Christ Church, MS 439, fol. 20.

3. "My love can sing no other song"

   Printed in Robert Jones' *First Book of Ayres* (1600), No. 19, where the first line begins: "My mistress sings no other song."

   See Fellowes *LSW 2,* V.

4. "Sister, awake, close not your eyes"

   Printed in Thomas Bateson's *First Set of Madrigals* (1604), No. 21.

   See Fellowes *EMS,* XXI.

5. "Sleep, wayward thoughts"

   London, British Museum, Add. MS 24,665, fol. 28v; Add. MS 29,481, fol. 2. Oxford, Christ Church, MS 439, p. 46.

   Printed in Fellowes *LSW 1,* II, and in numerous other modern editions.

Flowers, Masque of (1614)

The original print of 1614 contains six leaves of music for four voices comprising a choral dialogue between the companies of Silenas and of Kawasha: "Ahey for and a ho" / "Kawasha comes in majesty" / "Ahey for and a ho." The composer, although not named, is assumed to be John Wilson.

"Kawasha comes in majesty"

Edinburgh, University Library, MS Dc.1.69, No. 94.

Printed in John Wilson's *Cheerful Ayres* (1660), pp. 18-21.

The vocal and instrumental music for the *Masque of Flowers* is edited in Sabol *Songs and Dances,* pp. 58-60.

The Ghost, or the Woman Wears the Breeches (1640)

"Come, Chloris, hie we to the bower"

New York, Public Library, MS Drexel 4041, No. 87. London, British Museum, Add. MS 11,608, fol. 8b; MS Loan 35 (Henry Lawes' autograph MS), No. 156. Edinburgh, University Library, MS Dc.1.69, No. 122 (a 3-voice setting attributed to William Lawes).

First printed in Henry Lawes' *Ayres and Dialogues* (1653), Pt. II, p. 16. The song is found in some fifteen printed collections of the seventeenth century, an indication of its contemporary popularity. The lyric in the song books is attributed to Henry Reynolds.

Hatton (Lady) Masque (1636)

"Bacchus, Iacchus, fill our brains"

New York, Public Library, MS Drexel 4257, No. 69, with text beginning: "Let soldiers fight for pay or praise." London, British Museum, MS Loan 35 (Henry Lawes' autograph MS), No. 79. Here described as "A baccanall song, in a Mask before their Majestys, 1636."

Printed in Henry Lawes' *Ayres and Dialogues* (1653), Pt. II, p. 9; *The Musical Companion* (1673), p. 72. The lyric is by Townshend.

Edited in Jackson *English Melodies,* p. 102.

The Knave in Grain (1639)

"Three merry men, and three merry men be we"

The refrain from the catch "Hold thy peace," found in Ravenscroft's *Deuteromelia* (1609). Another tune to the same catch is found in Cambridge, King's College, MS KC 1, No. 32 (*ca.* 1580). *Chappell,* p. 216, associates the "Three merry men" catch with music found in "John Playford's Commonplace Book" in the Glasgow University Library MS R.d.58-61. The same information is given in *Chappell-Wooldridge,* I, 197.

This catch, or snatches from it, appears in many early plays, including Shakespeare's *Twelfth Night,* Barry's *Ram-Alley,* Fletcher's *The Bloody Brother,* and Dekker's *Westward Ho.*

The tune, after *Chappell,* is printed in Gibbon *Melody,* p. 79.

The Maid's Metamorphoses (1599-1600)

1. "By the moon we sport and play"

Printed in Ravenscroft's *A Briefe Discourse* (1614) as "The Urchin's Dance." Transcribed in Gibbon *Melody,* p. 132.

2. "Fortune, my foe"
   See comments under *Every Woman in Her Humour,* p. 123.
3. "Round about a faire ring a"
   In Ravenscroft's *A Briefe Discourse* (1614) as "The Elves Dance" by John Bennet.

Mountebanks, The Mask of Gray's Inn (1618)
"What is't you lack"
New York Public Library, MS Drexel 4175, No. 29 (incomplete). London, British Museum, Add. MS 29,481, fols. 17v-19.
See Sabol *Songs and Dances,* pp. 63-67.

Philotus (1603)
"What if a day, or a month, or a year"
London, British Museum, Add. MS 24,665, fol. 25v. Oxford, Christ Church, MS 439, p. 115. Dublin, Trinity College, MS F.5.13, p. 37.
Printed in Richard Alison's *An Howres Recreation* (1606), Nos. 17-18; Forbes' *Cantus, Songs and Fancies* (1662) and later editions. Thomas Campion is credited with music and lyric.
See *Chappell,* p. 310; *Chappell-Wooldridge,* I, 100; Simpson *Broadside Ballad,* p. 752; Fellowes EMS, XXXIII; Jackson *English Melodies,* p. 70; Warlock and Wilson *English Ayres,* VI, 28.

The Thracian Wonder (1590-1600)
"Art thou gone in haste"
New York, Public Library, MS Drexel 4257, No. 34. London, British Museum, MS Loan 35, No. 384.
The play's attribution to Webster and Rowley has been rejected by most authorities. The mid-seventeenth-century setting by Henry Lawes could have had no connection with the original production.

The Two Merry Milkmaids (1619-1620)
"Fortune, my foe"
See comments under *Every Woman in Her Humour,* p. 123.

Vices, Masque of (*ca.* 1630)
"Say daunce how shall we go"
London, British Museum, Add. MS 10,338, fol. 28v.
A 3-voice song from an unknown masque. The MS is in the hand of George Jeffreys, who may be the composer.

LODOWICK BARRY

Ram-Alley (1607-1608)
"And three merry men, and three merry men"
See comments under *The Knave in Grain,* p. 124.

FRANCIS BEAUMONT AND JOHN FLETCHER

The Beggar's Bush (*ca.* 1615-1622)

1. "Bring out your coney-skins, maids, to me"
   There is a late seventeenth-century setting by Ackroyde in *Vinculum Societatis* (1687), pp. 6-7. Quoted in Gibbon *Melody*, p. 122.
2. "Cast your caps and cares away"
   Oxford, Bodleian, MS Mus.b.1 (John Wilson's MS), No. 56; MS Don.c.57, No. 136. New York Public Library, MS Drexel 4041, No. 106. Edinburgh, University Library, MS Dc.1.69, No. 95.
   Printed in Wilson's *Cheerful Ayres* (1660), pp. 22-23; *The Musical Companion* (1673), p. 70.
   Modern editions include Cutts *Musique*, p. 93; Fellowes *Songs and Lyrics*, p. 49 (after MS Don.c.57); Gibbon *Melody*, p. 124.
3. "Have you any work for the sow gelder?"
   Edinburgh, University Library, MS Dc.1.69, No. 48.
   Printed in Wilson's *Cheerful Ayres* (1660), pp. 12-13.
   Edited in Cutts *Musique*, p. 95.
4. "He ran at me first in the shape of a ram"
   New York, Public Library, MS Drexel 4257, No. 67, where the text begins: "I met with the Devil in the shape of a ram."
   There is another late seventeenth-century setting by Thomas Wroth printed in Durfey's *Wit and Mirth: or Pills to Purge Melancholy* (1706), under the title "The gelding of the Devil."
   Edited, after the Drexel MS, in Cutts *Musique*, p. 94.

The Bloody Brother (*ca.* 1624/25)

1. "Bring out the cold chine"
   New York, Public Library, MS Drexel 4041, No. 128 (text only). Edinburgh, University Library, MS Ec.1.69, No. 6.
   Printed in *Select Ayres and Dialogues* (1659) and *The Treasury of Musick* (1669), pp. 86-87; *Catch that Catch Can* (1667), pp. 100-101; *The Musical Companion* (1673), pp. 68-69.
   The specific connection of this song with the play is a conjecture by Cutts made in his inventory of MS Drexel 4041 printed in *Musica Disciplina*, XVIII (1964), 196. The evidence is not entirely conclusive.
2. "Drink today and drown all sorrow"
   London, British Museum, Add. MS 29,396, fol. 18v.
   This 3-voice setting, attributed to Chilmead, has been edited by Fellowes in *Songs and Lyrics*, p. 56; E. S. Lindsey in "The Music of the Songs in Fletcher's Plays," *Studies in Philology*, XXI (1924), 325-355; Cutts *Musique*, pp. 83-84.
3. "Three merry boys, and three merry boys"
   See comments under *The Knave in Grain*, p. 124.
4. "Take, O take those lips away"

This famous song, also introduced in Shakespeare's *Measure for Measure* (1604), occurs in five contemporary MSS and four seventeenth-century prints. It has been treated frequently by modern editors. The composer is John Wilson.

Oxford, Bodleian, MS Mus.b.1, No. 13; Christ Church MS 434, fol. 1. New York Public Library, MS Drexel 4041, No. 44; MS Drexel 4257, No. 16. London, British Museum, Add. MS 11,608, fol. 56.

Printed in *Select Musicall Ayres* (1652), p. 2; *Select Musicall Ayres* (1653), p. 24; *Select Ayres* (1659) and *The Treasury of Musick* (1669), p. 1.

For modern editions see Cutts *Musique,* pp. 1-85; Long *Shakespeare,* II, 22; Sternfeld *Music,* pp. 94-96; Sternfeld *Songs,* No. 10; Gibbon *Melody,* p. 123; Jackson *English Melodies,* p. 94.

The Captain (1609-1612)

1. "Away, delights, go seek some other dwelling"

New York, Public Library, MS Drexel 4257, No. 109 (attributed to Robert Johnson).

See Cutts *Musique,* p. 28; Spink *Johnson,* pp. 28-29.

2. "Come hither, you that love, and hear me sing"

New York, Public Library, MS Drexel 4257, No. 108 (Robert Johnson). Edinburgh, University Library, MS Dc.1.69, No. 47.

Printed in Wilson's *Cheerful Ayres* (1660), pp. 14-15.

See Cutts *Musique,* pp. 29-30; Spink *Johnson,* pp. 30-31.

3. "Tell me, dearest, what is love"

New York, Public Library, MS Drexel 4257, No. 35; MS Drexel 4041, No. 124; MS Drexel 4175, No. 17.

Cutts has edited the versions from the two latter sources in Cutts *Musique,* pp. 27-28. It was also transcribed, after MS Drexel 4175, in Smith *Musica Antiqua,* I, 55, and is edited in Spink *Johnson,* p. 69. The song, a miniature dialogue, is also introduced in *The Knight of the Burning Pestle.*

The Chances (1613-1625)

"Come away, thou lady gay"

Oxford, Bodleian, MS Don.c.57, No. 119 (Robert Johnson).

Edited in Cutts *Musique,* p. 52; Spink *Johnson,* pp. 37-39.

The Coxcomb (1608-1610)

"Then set your foot to my foot, and up tails all"

Snatch from an old popular song, the tune of which is found in the *Fitzwilliam Virginal Book* and in Playford's *Dancing Master* (1650). See *Chappell,* p. 196; *Chappell-Wooldridge,* I, 149; Simpson *Broadside Ballad,* p. 727.

Cupid's Revenge (1607-1612)

"Lovers, rejoyce, your pains shall be rewarded"

London, British Museum, Add. MS 31,432, fol. 36 (William Lawes).

The Faithful Shepherdess (1608-1609)

1. "Come, shepherds, come, come away"
   New York, Public Library, MS Drexel 4041, No. 19 (William Lawes).
2. "Do not fear to put thy feet"
   Edinburgh, University Library, MS Dc.1.69, No. 96.
   Printed in Wilson's *Cheerful Ayres* (1660), pp. 24-25; *Select Ayres and Dialogues* (1659) and *The Treasury of Musick* (1669), p. 98. The setting is by John Wilson.
3. "Sing his praises that doth keep"
   Edinburgh, University Library, MS Dc.1.69, No. 15 (William Lawes).

The False One (1619-1622)

"Look out, bright eyes, and clear the air"
Oxford, Bodleian, MS Mus.b.1, No. 47 (John Wilson).
Edited in Cutts *Musique,* p. 88.

The Humourous Lieutenant (1619)

"I obey, I obey, and am come to view the day"
New York, Public Library, MS Drexel 4041, No. 38 (attributed to J. H. [John Hilton?]; Cutts reads T. H. [Thomas Holmes?]).
Edited in Cutts *Musique,* pp. 80-81.

The Knight of the Burning Pestle (1607-1610)

The music in this play consists chiefly of snatches of popular song sung by Merrythought. Most of these have been identified by Alexander Dyce, who edited the play in 1843-1846, or by E. S. Lindsey in "The Original Music for Beaumont's Play, *The Knight of the Burning Pestle,*" *Studies in Philology,* XXVI (1929), 435-443.

1. "Nose, nose, jolly red nose"
   A phrase taken from the *Freeman's Song,* "Of all the birds that ever I see," in Ravenscroft's *Deuteromelia* (1609).
   See *Chappell,* p. 75; *Chappell-Wooldridge,* I, 141.
2. "But yet, or ere you part"
   The refrain from Dowland's song "Wilt thou unkind thus reave me," from his *First Book of Ayres* (1597), No. 15.
   See Fellowes *LSW 1,* II.
3. "I am three merry men"
   See comments under *The Knave in Grain,* p. 124 above.
4. "Troll the black bowl to me"
   From a 4-voice catch in Ravenscroft's *Pammelia* (1609). Also found in Dublin, Trinity College, MS F.5.13.
   Edited in Warlock *Pam,* No. 62.
5. "As you come from Walsingham"

The tune "Walsingham" dates from the sixteenth century. Instrumental compositions based on it are found in great number in collections such as the *Fitzwilliam Virginal Book, Lady Neville's Book,* Barley's *New Book of Tabliture* (1596), Holborne's *Cittharn Schoole* (1597), etc.

See *Chappell,* p. 121; *Chappell-Wooldridge,* I, 69; Simpson *Broadside Ballad,* p. 741; Ward *Simpson,* p. 79-83.

6. "Why, an if she be"

A phrase taken from the song "Farewell, dear love," in Robert Jones' *First Book of Ayres* (1600), No. 12.

Edited in Fellowes *LSW 2,* V.

7. "Go from my window" / "Begone, begone, my juggy, my puggy"

Two stanzas from a popular song dating from the sixteenth century. The melody is found in instrumental settings in the *Fitzwilliam Virginal Book,* the Cambridge lute MSS, "Jane Pickering's Lute Book" (British Museum MS Egerton 2046), and in such early prints as Barley's *New Book of Tabliture* (1596), Morley's *First Book of Consort Lessons* (1599), and Robinson's *Schoole of Musick* (1603). The song is employed by many dramatists: Beaumont and Fletcher in *Monsieur Thomas* and *The Woman's Prize,* Brewer in *The Love-sick King,* Middleton in *Blurt, Master Constable,* etc.

Tune and commentary can be found in *Chappell,* p. 140; *Chappell-Wooldridge,* I, 146-147; Simpson *Broadside Ballad,* p. 257.

8. "Who can sing a merrier note"

A phrase from the catch "Sing we now merrily, our purses be empty," from Ravenscroft's *Pammelia* (1609).

Edited in Warlock *Pam,* p. 26.

9. "Hey, ho, nobody at home"

Catch from Ravenscroft's *Pammelia* (1609).

Edited in Warlock *Pam,* p. 22.

10. "Sing wee and chant it"

From Morley's *First Book of Balletts* (1595), No. 4.

Edited in Fellowes *EMS,* IV.

11. "Fortune, my foe"

See comments under *Every Woman in Her Humour,* p. 123 above.

12. "Tell me, dearest, what is love"

See comments under Beaumont and Fletcher's *The Captain,* p. 127 above.

The Lover's Progress (1623)

1. "Adieu, fond love, farewell you wanton powers"

London, British Museum, MS Egerton 2013, fol. 47v.

Edited in Cutts *Musique,* pp. 97-99; Spink *Johnson,* pp. 56-57. Both Cutts and Spink accept this anonymous setting as a work by Robert Johnson. Spink's edition corrects the original, which is defective and misleading.

2. "Tis late and cold, stir up the fire"

London, British Museum, Add. MS 11,608, fol. 20 (Robert Johnson); Add. MS 29,396, fol. 39v-40; Add. MS 29,481, fol. 25v (a different setting, incomplete).

The settings from all three sources edited in Cutts *Musique,* pp. 100-103. See also Spink *Johnson,* p. 42. Anthony Lewis has edited the Add. MS 11,608 version in his *William Shakespeare: Two Songs from The Tempest . . .* (Paris, 1936).

Love's Cure (1625)

"Turn thy beauteous face away"

Oxford, Bodleian, MS Mus.b.1, No. 28 (John Wilson). Edinburgh, University Library, MS Dc.1.69, No. 34.

Printed in Wilson's *Cheerful Ayres* (1660), pp. 140-141.

Edited in Cutts *Musique,* p. 110, after the Bodleian MS.

The Loyal Subject (1618)

"Will you buy any honesty"

Edinburgh, University Library, MS Dc.1.69, No. 43 (John Wilson).

Printed in Wilson's *Cheerful Ayres* (1660), pp. 4-5.

Edited in Cutts *Musique,* p. 77.

The Mad Lover (1615-1619)

1. "All these lie howling on the Stygian shore
O love no more, O love no more"

New York, Public Library, MS Drexel 4041, No. 111 (William Lawes).

Cutts has identified these two lines of verse as the last couplet of a song beginning "This lion was a man of war that died." No further music is given in the source, and Cutts' attempt to adapt the preceding nine lines of text to the music of an adjacent song by William Lawes is unconvincing.

See Cutts *Musique,* pp. 65-66.

2. "Arm, arm, the scouts are all come in"

New York, Public Library, MS Drexel 4041, No. 34 (R.J.).

Edited in Cutts *Musique,* pp. 67-69; Spink *Johnson,* p. 19.

3. "Caron, O Caron, thou wafter of the souls to bliss"

London, British Museum, Add. MS 10,337, fol. 37 (Richard Balls).

Edited in Cutts *Musique,* pp. 62-64.

4. "Go, happy heart, for thou shalt lie"

Cambridge, Fitzwilliam Museum, MS 52.D, fols. 98v-99 (John Wilson). Oxford, Bodleian, MS Mus.b.1, No. 27 (John Wilson); MS Don.c.57, No. 113; Christ Church, MS 87, fols. 7-8.

Edited in Fellowes *Songs and Lyrics,* pp. 51-53 (after MS Don.c.57); Cutts *Musique,* pp. 70-72 (after MS Mus.b.1 and the Fitzwilliam Museum MS).

5. "Orpheus I am, come from the deeps below"

Cambridge, Fitzwilliam Museum, MS 52.D, fol. 99v. Dublin, Trinity College, MS F.5.13, fol. 30 (treble only). Edinburgh, University Library, MS La.III.483, fols. 200-201 (bass).

The Dublin and Edinburgh MSS are separated partbooks of the same original set. The song is also listed in the Index to New York, Public Library, MS Drexel 4175, but is missing from the MS itself. Cutts and Spink both credit the setting to Robert Johnson.

Edited in Cutts *Musique,* pp. 58-61; Spink *Johnson,* p. 66.

The Maid in the Mill (1623)

1. "Come follow me, you country lasses"

New York, Public Library, MS Drexel 4041, No. 22 (J.J.).

Edited in Cutts *Musique,* p. 104. Cutts makes no conjecture as to the identity of the composer, J.J. [John Jenkins?].

2. "You shall have crowns of roses"

New York, Public Library, MS Drexel 4041, No. 23.

This is the second strophe of the preceding lyric; the music is not the same as that for the first strophe.

Edited in Cutts *Musique,* p. 105.

3. "How long shall I pine for love"

A late seventeenth-century setting of this lyric is found in Durfey's *Wit and Mirth: or Pills to Purge Melancholy* (1706), p. 171.

Monsieur Thomas (1610-1616)

"Come up to my window, love"

An adaptation of the song "Go from my window." The song is one of a group of snatches from nine popular ballads introduced in Act III, scene iii of this play. See comments under *The Knight of the Burning Pestle,* p. 128 above.

The Nice Valor (1615-1625)

"Hence all you vain delights"

London, British Museum, MS Egerton 2013, fol. 3v (John Hilton). Oxford, Bodleian, MS F.575, fol. 7v (another setting, anonymous, with lute accompaniment).

Edited in Cutts *Musique,* pp. 106-109 (after the Oxford and British Museum MSS). See also Fellowes *Songs and Lyrics,* p. 63; Lindsey's study, "The Music of the Songs in Fletcher's Plays," *Studies in Philology,* XXI (1924), 353.

The Pilgrim (1621)

"Down, down, be still you seas"

New York, Public Library, MS Drexel 4041, No. 17. Edinburgh, University Library, MS Dc.1.69, No. 71.

Printed in Wilson's *Cheerful Ayres* (1660), pp. 112-113.

Cutts conjectures that the Wilson setting, above, may have been introduced in the play in the place now occupied by the lyric "Down, ye angry waters all" (Act III, scene vii). Similarities in imagery make the suggestion a plausible one. See Cutts *Musique,* p. 89.

The Queen of Corinth (1616-1618)

1. "Weep no more, nor sigh, nor groan"

   Oxford, Bodleian, MS Mus.b.1, No. 43 (John Wilson); MS Don.c.57 (another setting, distinct from Wilson's, entered twice: on fol. 29 and fol. 81. The second entry bears an attribution to Stephen Mace).

   Edited in Cutts *Musique,* p. 75 (after MS Mus.b.1); Fellowes *Songs and Lyrics,* pp. 61-63 (after MS Don.c.57).

2. "Court ladies laugh and wonder"

   Oxford, Bodleian, MS Mus.b.1, No. 44 (John Wilson).
   Edited in Cutts *Musique,* p. 76.

The Spanish Curate (1622)

1. "Dearest, do not now delay me"

   New York, Public Library, MS Drexel 4257, No. 17. London, British Museum, MS Loan 35, No. 123 (Henry Lawes).

   Printed in Henry Lawes' *Ayres and Dialogues* (1653), Pt. I, p. 20, and in *Select Ayres and Dialogues* (1653), p. 10. In the 1653 publication the lyric is attributed to Henry Harrington.

   Edited in Cutts *Musique,* p. 96.

2. "Let the bells now ring, and let the boys sing"

   A late seventeenth-century setting by Rogers is printed in *The Musical Companion* (1673), pp. 170-171.

Valentinian (1610-1614)

1. "Now the lusty spring is seen"

   Edinburgh, University Library, MS Dc.1.69, No. 76.
   Printed in Wilson's *Cheerful Ayres* (1660), pp. 136-137.
   Edited in Cutts *Musique,* p. 34.

2. "Care-charming sleep, thou easer of all woes"

   Oxford, Bodleian, MS Don.c.57, No. 20; Christ Church, MS 87, No. 7 (another setting). Cambridge, Fitzwilliam Museum, MS 52D, No. 12 (Robert Johnson). London, British Museum, Add. MS 11,608, fol. 18v.

   Edited in Fellowes *Songs and Lyrics,* pp. 54-56 (after MS Don.c. 57; Cutts *Musique,* pp. 35-38 (after Don.c.57, Fitzwilliam and Christ Church MSS); Anthony Lewis' *William Shakespeare: Two Songs from The Tempest . . .* (Paris, 1936), pp. 7-12 (after Add. MS 11,608).

3. "God Lyaeus, ever young"

   Edinburgh, University Library, MS Dc.1.69, No. 148.

Printed in Wilson's *Cheerful Ayres* (1660), pp. 130-131.
Edited in Cutts *Musique,* p. 39.

4. "Hear, ye ladies that despise"
No setting survives for this lyric. We know that music existed because of an entry in the table of contents for New York, Public Library, MS Drexel 4175. The pages that contained the song are missing.

The Wild Goose Chase (1619-1622)
"From the honored dead I bring"
Oxford, Bodleian, MS Mus.b.1, No. 52 (John Wilson).
Edited in Cutts *Musique,* p. 90.

Wit Without Money (1614-1620)
"The fit's upon me now"
There is a dance tune with this title quoted in the 7th edition of Playford's *Dancing Master* (1686), p. 205.
See *Chappell,* p. 176; *Chappell-Wooldridge,* II, 29; Simpson *Broadside Ballad,* p. 218.

The Woman's Prize (1604-1617)
"Begone, my juggy, my puggy"
A paraphrase of the popular song "Go from my window."
See comments under Beaumont and Fletcher's *The Knight of the Burning Pestle,* p. 128 above.

Woman Pleased (1619-1622)
"O fair sweet face, O eyes celestial"
Oxford, Bodleian, MS Mus.b.1, No. 45 (John Wilson). Edinburgh, University Library, MS Dc.1.69, Nos. 44-45. London, British Museum, MS Egerton 2013, fol. 12v.
Edited in Cutts *Musique,* pp. 86-87.

DAUBRIDGECOURT BELCHIER

Hans Beer-Pot (1618)
"As you come from Walsingham"
A verse from the famous ballad "Walsingham." See comments under Beaumont and Fletcher's *The Knight of the Burning Pestle,* p. 128 above.

WILLIAM BERKELEY

The Lost Lady (1637)
"Where did you borrow that last sigh"
New York, Public Library, MS Drexel 4041, No. 5. London, British Museum, Add. MS 31,432, fol. 17 (William Lawes).

ANTHONY BREWER

The Love-Sick King (1607-1610)

"Begone, begone, my juggy, my puggy"

Another paraphrase of "Go from my window." See comments under Beaumont and Fletcher's *The Knight of the Burning Pestle,* p. 128 above.

RICHARD BROME

The Jovial Crew (1641)

1. "From hunger and cold who lives more free"

   Printed in *Select Ayres and Dialogues* (1659) and *The Treasury of Musick* (1669), p. 36; *The Musical Companion* (1673), p. 96. The music is attributed to J. G. (possibly John Goodgroome or John Gamble).

   See Simpson *Broadside Ballad,* p. 244.
2. "There was an old man at Walton Cross"

   Printed in *Catch that Catch Can* (1652) and later editions. Music by John Hilton.
3. "Round boys, a round, let mirth fly aloft"

   Printed in *Catch that Catch Can* (1667), p. 78 (William Lawes); *The Musical Companion* (1673), p. 56.

The Northern Lass (1629)

1. "Some say my love is but a man"

   New York, Public Library, MS Drexel 4041, No. 11 (John Wilson).
2. "Nor love, nor fate dare I accuse"

   New York, Public Library, MS Drexel 4041, No. 12; MS Drexel 4257, No. 99 (John Wilson).

   There is also a late seventeenth-century setting of the lyric by R. Simson in *Quadratum Musicum* (1687), p. 6.
3. "A bonny, bonny bird I had"

   New York, Public Library, MS Drexel 4041, No. 15; MS Drexel 4257, No. 45 (John Wilson).
4. "Peace, wayward bairn, O cease thy moan"

   New York, Public Library, MS Drexel 4257, No. 46. London, British Museum, Add. MS 10,337, fol. 57.

   This is a lyric contrived to fit a preexisting tune usually associated with the song "Ballow, my babe," possibly of Scottish provenance.

   The melody is printed, after Drexel 4257, in *Music of Scotland, 1500-1700* (1957), p. 186 (*Musica Britannica,* XV), adapted to a translation of the chorale "Vom Himmel hoch." For further discussion of the melody and the texts associated with it, see *The Percy Folio Manuscript,* ed. J. W. Hales and F. J. Furnivall (London, 1867-1868), and Simpson *Broadside Ballad,* p. 31.

5. "As I was gathering April flowers"
   New York, Public Library, MS Drexel 4257, No. 47 (John Wilson); MS Drexel 4041, No. 21.

The Queen and Concubine (1630-1640)
"What if a day, or a month, or a year"
   See comments under the anonymous play, *Philotus* (1603), p. 125 above.

WILLIAM BROWNE

Ulysses and Circe, Inner Temple Masque (1615)
"Steer hither, steer your wingéd prize"
   Tenbury, St. Michael's College, MS 1019, fol. 6.
   Edited in Sabol *Songs and Dances,* pp. 61-62.

THOMAS CAMPION

Entertainment at Brougham Castle (1617-1618)
   The music for the nine songs in this production was composed by George Mason and John Earsden and published in 1618 under the title *The Ayres that were Sung and Played at Brougham Castle in Westmerland in the King's Entertainment* (1618). The writer of the text is not identified, but it has generally been accepted as the work of Thomas Campion.
1. "Tune thy cheerful voice to mine"
2. "Now is the time, now is the hour"
3. "Welcome, welcome, king of guests"
4. "Come follow me, my wandring mates"
5. "Dido was the Carthage Queen"
6. "Robin is a lovely lad"
7. "The shadowes darkning our intents"
8. "O stay! sweet is the least delay"
9. "Welcome is the word"

   All of the settings were printed in J. Stafford Smith's *Musica Antiqua,* II, 150-165. [See Spink's essay, pp. 57-74 above. *Ed.*]

Lord Hayes Masque (1607)
   The text of this masque, with the music to five songs, was printed in 1607 under the title *The Description of a Maske . . . in Honor of the Lord Hayes* (London: John Windet for John Brown). The songs are as follows:
1. "Now hath Flora" (music by Campion)
2. "Move now with measur'd sound" (music by Campion)
3. "Shows and nightly revels" (music by Thomas Lupo)
4. "Triumph now" (music by Thomas Giles)
5. "Time that leads" (music by Thomas Lupo)

The five songs have been edited by G. E. P. Arkwright in *The Old English Edition,* I (London, 1889) and by Sabol *Songs and Dances,* pp. 26-33.

The Squire's Masque (1613)

Printed, with the music for four songs, as *The Description of a Mask: presented . . . at the Mariage of the Right Honourable the Earle of Somerset* (London: Printed by E. A. for Laurence Lisle).

1. "Bring away this sacred tree (music by Nicholas Lanier)

   This song is preserved in the MS sources, below, with a different text beginning "Weep no more, my wearied eyes."

   Dublin, Trinity College, MS F.5.13, p. 107. Cambridge, Fitzwilliam Museum, MS 52.D, fol. 99. New York, Public Library, MS Drexel 4257, No. 168.

   Edited in Smith's *Musica Antiqua,* I, 60; Sabol *Songs and Dances,* pp. 52-53.
2. "Go, happy man, like th'evening star" (music by Coperario)

   Edited in Sabol *Songs and Dances,* p. 54.
3. "While dancing rests, fit place to music granting" (music by Coperario)

   Edited in Sabol *Songs and Dances,* p. 55.
4. "Come ashore, come merry mates" (music by Coperario)

   Edited in Smith's *Musica Antiqua,* I, 61; Sabol *Songs and Dances,* pp. 56-57.

WILLIAM CARTWRIGHT

The Lady-Errant (1635-1638)

"Wake, my Adonis, do not die"

Printed in Playford's *Select Musicall Ayres and Dialogues* (1652), Pt. I, pp. 28-29 (music by Charles Coleman); *Select Musicall Ayres and Dialogues* (1653), Pt. I, pp. 26-27; *Select Ayres and Dialogues* (1659) and *The Treasury of Musick* (1669), pp. 4-5.

The Ordinary (1634-1635)

"Come, O come, I brook no stay"

New York, Public Library, MS Drexel 4257, No. 236. London, British Museum, MS Loan 35, No. 103 (Henry Lawes).

Printed in *Select Ayres* (1659) and *The Treasury of Musick* (1669), p. 61; *Musick's Delight on the Cithren* (1666), No. 91.

The Royal Slave (1636)

1. "A pox on the jailor and on his fat jowls"

   Printed in *Catch that Catch Can* (1652), p. 29 (John Hilton). Hilton's music is also found in the editions of 1658 and 1663. A setting by William Lawes appears in the edition of 1667, p. 74, and in *The Musical Companion* (1673), p. 53.

2. "Come, my sweet, whil'st every strain"
London, British Museum, MS Loan 35, No. 74 (Henry Lawes).
Printed in Henry Lawes' *Ayres and Dialogues* (1653), Pt. I, p. 32; *Select Ayres* (1659) and *The Treasury of Musick* (1669), p. 26.
3. "Come from the dungeon to the throne" (tenor solo)
"So beasts for sacrifice we feed" (chorus)
"Wash with thy blood what wars hath done" (soprano solo)
"Thou, O bright sun, who see'st all" (tenor solo)
"Whilst thus we pay our tributes" (chorus)
"But thou, O sun, may'st set" (bass solo)
"Good deeds may pass for sacrifice" (chorus)
The above series of settings by Henry Lawes are grouped as a unit in New York, Public Library, MS Drexel 4041, Nos. 112ff. The song "Come from the dungeon to the throne" is also found in British Museum, MS Loan 35, No. 75; Add. MS 29,396, fol. 15; Paris, Conservatoire, MS Rés. 2489.
Printed in *Select Ayres* (1659) and *The Treasury of Musick* (1669), p. 26; *Catch that Catch Can* (1667), pp. 166-167; *The Musical Companion* (1673).
4. "Now the sun is fled"
New York, Public Library, MS Drexel 4041, No. 114. Paris, Conservatoire, MS Rés. 2489, fols. 36-37, where attributed to William Lawes.

WILLIAM CAVENDISH

The Variety (1638-1639)

1. "I swear by Muscadel"
New York, Public Library, MS Drexel 4041, No. 52. Edinburgh, University Library, MS Dc.1.69, No. 26. Oxford, Bodleian, MS Don.c.57, fol. 143 (John Wilson).
Printed in Wilson's *Cheerful Ayres* (1660), pp. 108-109.
2. "Thine eyes to me like suns appear"
New York, Public Library, MS Drexel 4041, No. 50 (John Wilson). Edinburgh, University Library, MS Dc.1.69, No. 62.
Printed in Wilson's *Cheerful Ayres* (1660), p. 53.
3. "I'd have thee merry, laugh and smile"
New York, Public Library, MS Drexel 4041, No. 51 (John Wilson). Edinburgh, University Library, MS Dc.1.69, No. 63.
Printed in Wilson's *Cheerful Ayres* (1660), p. 57.
4. "The hart he loves the high wood"
A late seventeenth-century printing is in *Catch that Catch Can* (1685), No. 58, and in *The Second Book of the Pleasant Musical Companion* (1686), Pt. 1, No. 52.
5. "Have you felt the wool of beaver"
Taken from the famous lyric "See the chariot at hand," by Ben

Jonson. See commentary under Jonson's *The Devil is an Ass*, p. 144 below.

ABRAHAM COWLEY

Love's Riddle (1632-1633)

"It is a punishment to love"

New York, Public Library, MS Drexel 4257, No. 164. Oxford, Bodleian, MS Don.c.57, No. 69.

Printed in *New Ayres and Dialogues* (1678), p. 65 (William Webb).

SAMUEL DANIEL

Hymen's Triumph (1614)

"From the temple to the board"

Tenbury, St. Michael's College, MS 1018, fol. 12.

WILLIAM DAVENANT

Britannia Triumphans (1638)

Music by William Lawes for this court masque is preserved in the composer's autograph in Oxford, Bodleian, MS Mus.Sch.B.2:

1. "Britanocles, the great and good, appears" (chorus)
2. "Why move these princes" (solo with chorus)
3. "So well Britanocles o're seas doth reign" (solo with chorus)
4. "Wise Nature, that the dew of sleep prepares" (solo with chorus)
5. "To bed, to bed" (chorus)

The source also includes some instrumental music from the masque. See Murray Lefkowitz, *William Lawes* (London, 1960), pp. 224 ff.

The Just Italian (1629)

"This lady, ripe and calm and fresh"

New York, Public Library, MS Drexel 4041, No. 77 (John Atkins).

Love and Honor (1634)

1. "O draw your curtains and appear"

   New York, Public Library, MS Drexel 4041, No. 10 (William Lawes). London, British Museum, Add. MS 31,432, fol. 39 (William Lawes).

   Printed in *New Ayres and Dialogues* (1678), pp. 44-45.
2. "No morning red and blushing fair"

   No setting for this song survives, but a place was provided for it in New York, Public Library, MS Drexel 4257, No. 123, where the text incipit is found without music.

The Triumphs of the Prince d'Amour (1636)

Solos, dialogues, and choruses, as well as instrumental "symphonies," by William Lawes are found in the composer's autograph in the Bodleian Library, MS Mus.Sch.B.2. See Murray Lefkowitz, *William Lawes* (London, 1960), pp. 221 ff.

1. "Behold how this conjunction thrives" (duet for tenor and bass with chorus)
2. "The angry steed, the fife and drum" (tenor with chorus)
3. "The balm's rich sweat, the myrrh's sweet tears" (soprano and bass with chorus)
4. "And may your language be of force" (soprano, tenor, and bass with chorus)
5. "May our three gods so long conjoin" (4-part chorus)

   All of the above settings are edited in Sabol *Songs and Dances,* pp. 102-115. There is an incomplete version of No. 1, "Behold how this conjunction thrives," in Edinburgh, University Library, MS Dc.1.69, No. 128.
6. "Whither so gladly and so fast"

   London, British Museum, MS Loan 35, No. 78 (Henry Lawes).

   Printed in Henry Lawes' *Select Ayres and Dialogues* (1669), Bk. II, p. 39. This setting is also edited in Sabol *Songs and Dances,* pp. 100-101.

The Unfortunate Lovers (1638)

1. "Run to Love's lottery, maids, and rejoice"

   A setting by Alphonso Marsh printed in Playford's *Choice Songs and Ayres* (1673), pp. 5-7; Playford's *Choice Ayres, Songs and Dialogues* (1675 and 1676), pp. 5-6.
2. "Ye fiends and furies, come along"

   London, British Museum, Add. MS 31,432, fol. 41v (William Lawes).

   Printed in *New Ayres and Dialogues* (1678), pp. 60-64.

THOMAS DEKKER

If It Be Not Good (1610-1612)

"The fit's upon me now"

A snatch sung to the dance tune of the same title in Playford's *Dancing Master,* 7th ed. (1686), p. 205. Also introduced in Beaumont and Fletcher's *Wit Without Money.*

See *Chappell,* p. 176; *Chappell-Wooldridge,* II, 29; Simpson *Broadside Ballad,* p. 218.

Patient Grissill (1600)

"Golden slumber kiss your eyes"

Chappell adapted this text to the dance tune "Mayfair," found in the 1657 edition of Playford's *Dancing Master.* The union is a felicitous one, but there is no evidence that the dance tune was employed in the original production. It was an extremely popular melody and survived well into the eighteenth century in ballad operas. See *Chappell,* p. 587; *Chappell-Wooldridge,* II, 113; Jackson *English Melodies,* p. 149.

The Weakest Goeth to the Wall (1599-1600)

1. "King Richard's gone to Walsingham"

   Probably sung to the ballad tune "Walsingham." See comments under *The Knight of the Burning Pestle,* pp. 128-129 above.

2. "John Dory bought him an ambling nag"

   Taken from "A freemens song" printed in Ravenscroft's *Deuteromelia* (1609). Here the text begins "As it fell on a holy day."

   Edited in Warlock *Pam,* p. 27.

   See also *Chappell,* p. 67; *Chappell-Wooldridge,* I, 93; Simpson *Broadside Ballad,* p. 398.

The Welsh Ambassador (1602-1623)

"Three merry men, and three merry men"

See comments under *The Knave in Grain,* p. 124 above.

Westward Ho (1604)

"Three merry men, and three merry men"

See comments under *The Knave in Grain,* p. 124 above.

JOHN DENHAM

The Sophy (1641)

"Somnus, the humble God that dwells"

New York, Public Library, MS Drexel 4041, No. 27 (William Lawes).

JOHN FORD

The Fancies Chaste and Noble (1630-1636)

1. "Whoop, do me no harm, good woman"

   A snatch probably sung to the tune "Whoops, do me no harm, good man," printed in William Corkine's *First Book of Ayres* (1610).

   See *Chappell,* p. 208; *Chappell-Wooldridge,* I, 96; Simpson *Broadside Ballad,* p. 777.

2. "The fit's upon me now"

   See comments under Beaumont and Fletcher's *Wit Without Money,* p. 133 above.

The Lady's Trial (1638)

1. "Pleasure, beauty, youth attend thee"

   New York, Public Library, MS Drexel 4257, No. 178; MS Drexel

4041, No. 68. London, British Museum, Add. MS 31,432, fol. 19 (William Lawes).

Printed in Henry Lawes' *Select Ayres and Dialogues* (1669), Bk. II, p. 23. Both of the Lawes brothers have been credited with the song in the contemporary sources. The weight of the evidence inclines toward William, however, since the song occurs in his autograph MS along with another setting from the same play; see below.

2. "What ho! we come to be merry"

London, British Museum, Add. MS 31,432, fol. 18v (William Lawes).

The Lover's Melancholy (1628)

"Fly hence, shadows that do keep"

Oxford, Bodleian, MS Mus.b.1, fol. 99 (John Wilson). Edinburgh, University Library, MS Dc.1.69, No. 76.

Printed in Wilson's *Cheerful Ayres* (1660), pp. 88-89.

HENRY GLAPTHORNE

Argalus and Parthenia (1637-1639)

"Love's a child, and ought to be"

London, British Museum, Add. MS 31,432, fol. 25v (William Lawes).

Printed in *New Ayres and Dialogues* (1678), pp. 58-59.

THOMAS GOFFE

The Courageous Turk (1618)

"Drop, golden showers, gentle sleep"

Oxford, Christ Church, MS 87, fols. 3v-4.

WILLIAM HABINGTON

The Queen of Aragon (1640)

"Fine young folly though you wear"

Printed in *Select Musicall Ayres and Dialogues* (1653), Pt. III, p. 33 (music by William Tompkins); *Select Ayres and Dialogues* (1659) and *The Treasury of Musick* (1669), p. 103. In *Catch that Catch Can* (1667), p. 182, there is another setting by William Howes.

RICHARD HATTON

In British Museum Add. MS 10,338, fols. 33-39v, are four settings described as "Songs made for some Comedyes a 4 voc. (1631), Sir R. Hatton." The songs are listed as follows:

1. "You that have been this evening's light"
2. "Fond maids, take warning while you may"
3. "Cupid blushes to behold"
4. "Hymen hath together tied"

The play or plays from which these songs are taken have not been identified. The MS is in the hand of George Jeffreys, who may be the composer of the settings.

PETER HAUSTED

The Rival Friends (1631)

1. "Drowsy Phoebus, come away"
   London, British Museum, Add. MS 10,338, fols. 43-51.
2. "Have pity, grief, I cannot pay"
   London, British Museum, Add. MS 10,338, fol. 45v; MS Loan 35, No. 81 (Henry Lawes).
3. "Newly from a poatch't toad"
   London, British Museum, Add. MS 10,338, fol. 18 (Thomas Holmes).
4. "Cruel, but once again one poor kiss"
   London, British Museum, Add. MS 10,338, fol. 46; MS Loan 35, No. 82 (Henry Lawes).
   This song, not printed with the text of the play, carries a marginal annotation in Add. MS 10,338 in the hand of George Jeffreys: "This song was made for the Comodie but I think not sung."

THOMAS HEYWOOD

The Rape of Lucrece (1603-1608)

1. "Now what is love, I will thee tell"
   Printed in Robert Jones' *Second Book of Songs and Ayres* (1601), No. 9. The lyric has been attributed to Sir Walter Raleigh. Edited in Fellowes *ELS 2,* VI.
2. "Arise, my juggy, my puggy"
   An adaptation of the popular song "Go from my window." See comments under Beaumont and Fletcher's *The Knight of the Burning Pestle,* p. 129 above.

BARTON HOLIDAY

Technogamia, or The Marriage of the Arts (1619)

"Tobacco's a musician"

A setting is printed by Edward F. Rimbault in *A Little Book of Songs and Ballads* (London, 1851), from "a manuscript set of partbooks in the handwriting of Thomas Weelkes, 1609."

BEN JONSON

Augers, Masque of (1622)

1. "Do not expect to hear"

London, British Museum, Add. MS 11,608, fol. 17v (Nicholas Lanier).

Edited in Sabol *Songs and Dances,* pp. 74-75.

2. "Though it may seem rude"

A late seventeenth-century setting is found in Durfey's *Wit and Mirth, or Pills to Purge Melancholy,* Pt. II (1700), pp. 38-39, and later editions. The song is also introduced in Thomas Randolph's *The Drinking Academy* (1629).

Bartholomew Fair (1614)

"My masters and friends, and good people draw near"

The song makes a late appearance in Durfey's *Wit and Mirth, or Pills to Purge Melancholy,* Pt. II (1700), pp. 1-2, and later editions. The tune is an old one, being an adaptation of "Packington's Pound," found in the *Fitzwilliam Virginal Book,* the Cambridge lute MSS, Barley's *New Book of Tabliture* (1596), etc.

The melody is given in Gibbon *Melody,* p. 150. See also *Chappell,* p. 123; *Chappell-Wooldridge,* I, 259; Simpson *Broadside Ballad,* p. 568.

Beauty, Masque of (1608)

1. "So Beauty on the waters stood"

Printed in Alfonso Ferrabosco's *Ayres* (1609), No. 21.

Edited in Fellowes *ELS 2,* XV; Sabol *Songs and Dances,* p. 34.

2. "If all these Cupids now were blind"
3. "It was no policy of court"
4. "Yes, were the loves or false or straying"

The three preceding lyrics are given as one composite setting in Ferrabosco's *Ayres* (1609), Nos. 28-30; they are also found in Oxford, Christ Church, MS 439, Nos. 71, 72, 74.

Edited in Fellowes *ELS 2,* XV; Sabol *Songs and Dances,* pp. 35-38.

5. "Had those that dwell in error foul"

Printed in Ferrabosco's *Ayres* (1609), No. 22.

Edited in Fellowes *ELS 2,* XV; Sabol *Songs and Dances,* p. 39.

Blackness, Masque of (1605)

"Come away, come away, we grow jealous of your stay"

Oxford, Christ Church, MS 439, No. 27.

Printed in Ferrabosco's *Ayres* (1609), No. 3.

Edited in Fellowes *ELS 2,* XV; Sabol *Songs and Dances,* p. 25.

Cynthia's Revels (1601)

1. "Slow, fresh fount, keep time with my salt tears"

Printed in Henry Youll's *Canzonets to Three Voyces* (1608), No. 8.

Edited in Fellowes *EMS,* XXVIII.

2. "O that joy so soon should waste"
Oxford, Christ Church, MS 439, No. 33. London, British Museum, MS Loan 35, No. 5 (another setting by Henry Lawes).

The Devil is an Ass (1616)
"Do but look on her eyes, they do light"
London, British Museum, Add. MS 29,481, fol. 21; Add. MS 15,117, fol. 17b. Oxford, Christ Church, MS 87, fols, 4v-5. Dublin, Trinity College, MS F.5.13, No. 51 (melody only, the bass part is found in Edinburgh, University Library, MS La.III.483, fol. 201). New York, Public Library, MS Drexel 4257, No. 2; MS Drexel 4175, No. 19.

The text in the play is the second stanza of a lyric that appears in Jonson's *Underwoods* (1641), beginning "See the chariot at hand." Most of the sources begin with a third stanza, "Have you seen the white lily grow." The song is also introduced in Cavendish's *The Variety* and Suckling's *The Sad One.* Some authorities (e.g., Warlock) credit the song to Alfonso Ferrabosco; others (e.g., Cutts and Spink) consider Robert Johnson the composer.

There are numerous modern editions of the setting: Dolmetsch's *Select English Songs and Dialogues* (London, 1898); Potter's *Reliquary of English Song* (New York, 1915) I, 28 (with a facsimile of the setting in Add. MS 15,117); Cutts *Musique,* pp. 54-56; Spink *Johnson,* pp. 64-65.

Entertainment of the King and Queen . . . at Highgate (1604)
"See, O see, who comes here a-maying"
Printed in Martin Peerson's *Private Musicke* (London, 1620), No. 24.

Entertainment at Welbeck (1633)
"What softer sounds are these"
London, British Museum, Add. MS 31,432, fol. 20v (William Lawes).

Epicoene, or The Silent Woman (1609)
"Still to be neat, still to be dressed"
New York, Public Library, MS Drexel 4257, No. 179 (William Lawes); MS Drexel 4041, No. 64.

Printed in Playford's *Select Ayres and Dialogues,* II (1669), 51.

Edited by Rimbault in his *Musical Illustrations of Bishop Percy's Reliques* (London, 1850), p. 67; Lefkowitz in his biographical study of *William Lawes* (London, 1960), pp. 197-198.

The Fortunate Isles (1625)
"Come, noble nymphs, and do not hide"
Oxford, Bodleian, MS Don.c.57, No. 97.

Printed in *Select Ayres and Dialogues* (1659) and *The Treasury of Musick* (1669), p. 14 (music by William Webb).

Edited in Sabol *Songs and Dances,* pp. 76-77.

The song is also used in Jonson's *Neptune's Triumph* (1624).

The Gypsies Metamorphos'd (1621)

1. "Cook Lorrel would needs have the Devil his guest"

   New York, Public Library, MS Drexel 4257, No. 92 (text only).

   The tune which served as vehicle for a great many popular songs is found in Durfey's *Wit and Mirth, or Pills to Purge Melancholy,* Pt. II (1700), 101-103.

   Tune and commentary found in *Chappell,* p. 160; *Chappell-Wooldridge,* II, 40; Simpson *Broadside Ballad,* p. 129.

2. "From the famous peak of Derby"

   Printed in *The Musical Companion* (1673), pp. 88-89 (music by Robert Johnson).

   Edited in Sabol *Songs and Dances,* pp. 68-69; Spink *Johnson,* p. 40.

3. "To the old, long life and treasure"

   New York, Public Library, MS Drexel 4257, No. 177.

   The tune, somewhat modified, is also found in Playford's *Dancing Master* (1651), under the title "A Health."

   Edited in Sabol *Songs and Dances*, p. 70.

4. "Why this is a sport"

   London, British Museum, Add. MS 29,396, fols, 71v-72v (Edmund Chilmead).

   Edited in Sabol *Songs and Dances,* pp. 70-73.

Haddington Masque (1608)

1. "Why stays the bridegroom to invade"

   Oxford, Christ Church, MS 439, No. 49.

   Printed in Ferrabosco's *Ayres* (1609), No. 11.

   Edited in Fellowes *ELS 2,* XVI; Sabol *Songs and Dances,* pp. 40-41.

2. "Beauties, have you seen a toy"

   New York, Public Library, MS Drexel 4257, No. 37. London, British Museum, Add. MS 11,608, fol. 81; MS Loan 35, No. 67 (Henry Lawes).

   Printed in Henry Lawes' *The Second Book of Ayres and Dialogues* (1655), p. 41; Lawes' *Select Ayres and Dialogues,* II (1669), 75.

Love Freed from Ignorance and Folly (1611)

"O what a fault, nay what a sin"

Tenbury, St. Michael's College, MS 1018, fols. 36a-37b (Alfonso Ferrabosco).

Edited in Sabol *Songs and Dances,* pp. 47-50.

Neptune's Triumph (1624)

"Come, noble nymphs, and do not hide"

See comments under Jonson's *The Fortunate Isles,* pp. 144-145.

Oberon, The Masque of (1611)

1. "Buzz, quoth the blue fly"

   Printed in *Catch that Catch Can* (1667), p. 75 (music by Edmund Nelham).

2. "Gentle knights, know some measure"

   Tenbury, St. Michael's College, MS 1018, fols. 37v-38 (Ferrabosco).

   Edited in Sabol *Songs and Dances,* pp. 44-46; Cutts, "La musique dans les masques de Ben Jonson," in *Les Fêtes de la Renaissance* (Paris, 1956), pp. 298-299.

3. "Nay, nay, you must not stay"

   Tenbury, St. Michael's College, MS 1018, fol. 36 (Ferrabosco).

   Edited in Sabol *Songs and Dances,* pp. 43-44; Cutts, "La musique dans les masques de Ben Jonson," in *Les Fêtes de la Renaissance* (Paris, 1956), p. 300.

Poetaster (1601)

"If I freely may discover"

London, British Museum, Add. MS 24,665, fol. 59v; MS Loan 35, No. 9 (another setting by Henry Lawes). New York, Public Library, MS Drexel 4257, No. 9 (Lawes' setting).

The anonymous setting in "Giles Earle's Book" (Add. MS 24,665) is the earliest and may be the music used in the original production. The second strophe begins "She should be allowed her passions" and is sung to the same music.

Queens, Masque of (1609)

"If all the ages of the earth"

Oxford, Christ Church, MS 439, No. 73.

Printed in Ferrabosco's *Ayres* (1609), No. 23.

Edited in Fellowes *LSW 2,* XV; Sabol *Songs and Dances,* p. 42.

The Sad Shepherd (1612-1637)

"Though I am young and cannot tell"

Oxford, Bodleian, MS Mus.b.1, No. 164 (John Wilson).

Printed in *Select Musicall Ayres and Dialogues,* II (1652), 24; *Select Musicall Ayres and Dialogues,* III (1653), 24; *Select Ayres* (1659) and *The Treasury of Musick* (1669), p. 92; *Catch that Catch Can* (1667), pp. 216-217; *An Introduction to the Skill of Musick* (1672), p. 68; *The Musical Companion* (1673), pp. 202-203. The printed setting, by Nicholas Lanier, is quite distinct from Wilson's setting in Bodleian MS Mus.b.1.

The Vision of Delight (1617)

"I was not wearier where I lay"

London, British Museum, MS Egerton 2013, fol. 45v. New York, Public Library, MS Drexel 4175 (listed in the table of contents but missing from the source).

The Egerton MS version is transcribed and discussed by Mac-

Donald Emslie in "Nicholas Lanier's Innovations in English Song," *Music and Letters,* XLI (1960), 23 ff. Emslie attributes the setting to Lanier.

Volpone (1606)

"Come, my Celia, let us prove"

London, British Museum, Add. MS 15,117, fol. 20v.

Printed in Ferrabosco's *Ayres* (1609), No. 6.

Edited in Fellowes *LSW 2,* XV; Warlock and Wilson *English Ayres,* II, 25; Gibbon *Melody,* p. 142; Cutts *Musique,* pp. 3-5.

THOMAS KILLIGREW

The Princess (1635-1636)

"To Bacchus, we to Bacchus sing"

New York, Public Library, MS Drexel 4041, No. 115 (Charles Coleman).

Printed in *Select Musicall Ayres and Dialogues,* I (1652), 42-43; *Select Ayres and Dialogues* (1659) and *The Treasury of Musick* (1669), pp. 84-85.

The Prisoners (1635-1636)

"Ha, Posanos, by my loss of peace 'tis she"

London, British Museum, MS Loan 35, No. 272 (Henry Lawes).

The association of this song with Killigrew's play is merely a suggestion based on the fact that the play has a singing character named Pausanes.

WILLIAM KILLIGREW

Selindra (1662)

"Come, thou glorious object of my sight"

New York, Public Library, MS Drexel 4041, No. 85 (Henry Lawes). London, British Museum, MS Loan 35, No. 267 (Henry Lawes); MS Egerton 2013, fol. 20v (Nicholas Lanier).

Printed in Henry Lawes' *Ayres and Dialogues,* I (1653), 80-81; his *Select Ayres and Dialogues* (1669), Bk. II, pp. 22-23.

JOHN MARSTON

The Dutch Courtezan (1603-1604)

1. "The dark is my delight"

   London, British Museum, MS Egerton 2971, fol. 8v; Add. MS 24,665, fol. 58v.

2. "Mine mettre sing non oder song"

   A dialect version of a song in Robert Jones' *First Book of Ayres* (1600), No. 19.

Edited in Fellowes *LSW 2,* V. The song is also used in the anonymous play *Every Woman in Her Humour,* see p. 123 above.

Eastward Ho (1605) (with Chapman and Jonson)

1. "But a little higher"

   A snatch from the refrain of Campion's song "Mistress, since you so much desire," found in Rossiter's *Book of Ayres,* I (1601), No. 16. The song is entered in the index of New York, Public Library, MS Drexel 4175 but missing from the contents.

   Edited in Fellowes *LSW 1,* IV.

2. "Now, O now I must depart"

   A snatch from a song in Dowland's *First Book of Ayres* (1597), No. 6. Well known as an instrumental piece, "The Frog Galliard." See commentary by *Chappell,* p. 127; *Chappell-Wooldridge,* I, 274; Simpson *Broadside Ballad,* p. 242.

   Edited in Fellowes *LSW 1,* I.

PHILIP MASSINGER

The Fatal Dowry (1618-1619)

"Poor citizen, if thou wilt be"

Oxford, Bodleian, MS Don.c.57, No. 156.

The Picture (1629)

"The blushing rose, the purple flower"

New York, Public Library, MS Drexel 4257, No. 78.

THOMAS MAY

The Old Couple (1636)

"Dear, do not your fair beauty wrong"

London, British Museum, Add. MS 29,396, fols. 21v-22 (Robert Johnson). New York, Public Library, MS Drexel 4175, Nos. 41 and 51 (Robert Johnson). The song is entered twice in this source, once with lute accompaniment and once with unfigured bass.

Both versions are edited in Cutts *Musique,* pp. 49-51; Spink *Johnson,* pp. 6-8. First printed in J. Stafford Smith's *Musica Antiqua,* I, 53. As Spink points out, the lyric is *read* in the play, not sung.

JASPER MAYNE

The City Match (1637)

"We show no monstrous crocodile"

New York, Public Library, MS Drexel 4041, No. 7 (William Lawes).

THOMAS MIDDLETON

Blurt, Master-Constable (1601)

1. "What meat eats the Spaniard"

   London, British Museum, Add. MSS 17,786-91, No. 28. An anonymous setting for two voices and viols.

   Edited, with discussion, by Andrew Sabol: "Two Songs with Accompaniment for an Elizabethan Choirboy Play," *Studies in the Renaissance,* V (1958), 155-157.

2. "Go from my window"

   See comments under Beaumont and Fletcher's *The Knight of the Burning Pestle,* p. 129 above.

3. "Love for such a cherry lip"

   Printed in Ravenscroft's *A Brief Discourse* (1614), No. 15 (music by Edward Pearce).

   Edited by Andrew Sabol in "Two Songs with Accompaniment for an Elizabethan Choirboy Play," *Studies in the Renaissance,* V (1958), 158-159; Gibbon *Melody,* p. 132.

A Chaste Maid in Cheapside (1611-1613)

"Cupid is Venus' only joy"

New York, Public Library, MS Drexel 4175, Nos. 24 and 56. London, British Museum, Add. MS 29,481, fol. 6v (soprano only).

The song is entered twice in the Drexel MS, once with a lute accompaniment and once with unfigured bass. Both versions are edited in Cutts *Musique,* pp. 46-48.

More Dissemblers besides Women (1615-1623)

"Cupid is Venus' only joy"

The song is utilized in both this and the above play by Middleton.

The Spanish Gypsy (1623)

1. "Trip it, gypsies, trip it fine"

   Chappell suggests an adaptation of this text to the dance tune "The Gypsies Round," set by Byrd in the *Fitzwilliam Virginal Book,* No. 216. See *Chappell,* p. 171; *Chappell-Wooldridge,* I, 255-256; Gibbon *Melody,* p. 128.

2. "Come follow your leader, follow"

   Associated with the dance melody "The Spanish Gipsies," found in Playford's *Dancing Master* (1650) and later editions, and in *Musick's Delight on the Cithren* (1666).

   See *Chappell,* p. 272; *Chappell-Wooldridge,* I, 186-187; Gibbon *Melody,* p. 128; Simpson *Broadside Ballad,* p. 675.

The Widow (1607-1616)

"I keep my horse, I keep my whore"

London, British Museum, Add. MS 29,396, fol. 77v (William Lawes).

A late seventeenth-century setting is printed in Playford's *A Pleasant Musical Companion* (1686), II, No. 26.

Edited in Cutts *Musique,* p. 57 (after Add. MS 29,396).

The Witch (1613-1616)

1. "In a maiden-time professed"

   Oxford, Bodleian, MS Mus.b.1, fol. 21 (John Wilson). New York, Public Library, MS Drexel 4257, No. 32.

   Edited in Cutts *Musique,* p. 7. Cutts' attribution of the music to Robert Johnson is pure speculation.

2. "Come away, come away Hecket"

   Cambridge, Fitzwilliam Museum, MS 52.D. fols. 107-108. New York, Public Library, MS Drexel 4175, No. 54.

   Edited, after the Drexel MS, by J. Stafford Smith in *Musica Antiqua,* I, 48. Cutts *Musique,* pp. 8-13, gives the versions from both sources. Cutts' attribution to Robert Johnson is questionable.

JOHN MILTON

Comus, Masque of (1634)

Henry Lawes' settings of the five songs from this masque are found in the composer's autograph MS in the British Museum, MS Loan 35, fols. 68-72.

1. "From the heavens now I fly"
2. "Sweet Echo"
3. "Sabrina fair"
4. "Back, shepherds, back"
5. "Now my task is smoothly done"

The music has frequently been edited and commented upon. See Sabol *Songs and Dances,* pp. 91-99; *The Mask of Comus, Originally Called 'A Mask Presented at Ludlow Castle, 1634,'* ed. E. H. Visiak and Hubert J. Foss (London, 1937). See also the discussion in Willa M. Evans' *Henry Lawes* (London, 1941), pp. 79-109.

THOMAS NABBES

Hannibal and Scipio (1635)

"On, bravely on, the foe is met"

New York, Public Library, MS Drexel 4041, No. 120.

See the discussion by Cutts in *English Miscellany,* XIV (1963), 75-81.

THOMAS RANDOLPH

Aristippus (1626-1630)

1. "Those are slaves that heap up mountains"

Printed in *Catch that Catch Can* (1667), pp. 112-113 (music by William Gregory).

2. "Come, my lads that love Canary"
   London, British Museum, Add. MS 11,608, fol. 53.

The Drinking Academy (1629)

"Though it may seem rude for me to intrude"

Printed in Durfey's *Wit and Mirth, or Pills to Purge Melancholy,* Pt. II (1700), pp. 38-39. The song is also introduced in Jonson's *Masque of Augers* (1622).

SAMUEL ROWLEY

The Noble Soldier (1634)

"O sorrow say, where dost thou dwell"

Printed in Playford's *Choice Ayres, Songs and Dialogues* (1675), p. 77, and in the edition of 1676, p. 87 (music by Robert Smith).

WILLIAM ROWLEY

A Match at Midnight (1621-1637)

"Her loved her once, her loved her no more"

A parody of a popular tune found in Playford's *Dancing Master* (1652) and usually associated with a text by Robert Aytoun: "I loved thee once, I'll love no more." The song is found in New York, Public Library, MS 4257, No. 149. A more sophisticated setting of the Aytoun lyric by Henry Lawes is found in the composer's autograph MS, British Museum, MS Loan 35, No. 21, and in Lawes' *Select Ayres and Dialogues* (1669), Bk. II, p. 30.

See Simpson *Broadside Ballad,* p. 343.

JOSEPH RUTTER

The Cid, Second Part (1638-1640)

"Twas not his person nor his parts"

New York, Public Library, MS Drexel 4041, No. 26. Edinburgh, University Library, MS Dc.1.69, No. 97.

In British Museum, Add. MS 28,396, fol. 48v, there is a lyric, without music, "I will no more enamoured be," described as "An Answer to 'Twas not his person.'"

WILLIAM SHAKESPEARE

Music mentioned by Shakespeare, or utilized in the original productions of his plays, has been the subject of investigation and discussion since the seventeenth century. There have been numerous attempts to adapt Shakespearean lyrics to existing dance tunes or songs current during his time. Some of these attempts have been convincing enough, but for the purposes of the present bibliography, only those songs are cited that can be identified positively with Shakespeare texts in the sixteenth and seventeenth centuries. They may or may not have been used in the early productions of the plays; they do, at least, represent the core of the authentic Shakespearean music that has survived.

The bibliography of this field is extensive. I have not attempted to cite all of the commentary on Shakespearean song, since this information has been well covered in the work of three recent specialists: John H. Long, Frederick W. Sternfeld, and Peter J. Seng. Their major contributions are as follows:

Long, John H. *Shakespeare's Use of Music.* 2 vols. Gainesville, Florida, 1955-1961.

Sternfeld, Frederick W. *Music in Shakespearean Tragedy.* London, 1963.

Seng, Peter J. *The Vocal Songs in the Plays of Shakespeare, a Critical History.* Cambridge, Mass., 1967. (Seng's general bibliography, pp. 275-299, is particularly useful.)

As You Like It (1599-1600)

1. "What shall he have that killed the deer"

A catch by John Hilton printed in *Catch that Catch Can* (1652), p. 30, and in the editions of 1658 and 1663, p. 26.

See Ernest Brennecke's reconstruction of this catch and discussion of its possible performance in " 'What shall he have that killed the deer,' a Note on Shakespeare's Lyric and its Music," in *The Musical Times,* XCIII (1952), 347-351. Transcriptions of the catch also appear in Gibbon *Melody,* p. 111, and in Long *Shakespeare,* I (1955), 151.

2. "It was a lover and his lass"

Printed in Morley's *First Book of Ayres* (1600) and available in numerous modern editions.

See Fellowes *LSW 2,* XVII. A facsimile of the original printed music in the Folger Shakespeare Library is given in Long *Shakespeare,* I (1955), 154.

Cymbeline (1611)

"Hark, hark, the lark at heav'ns gate sings"

Oxford, Bodleian, MS Don.c.57, No. 70.

Edited in Cutts *Musique,* p. 6, where the name of Robert Johnson is advanced as the possible composer; Sternfeld *Songs,* p. 29. Other studies of this setting have been made by George A. Thewlis, "Some Notes on a Bodleian Manuscript: With an Unpublished Contemporary Setting of Shakespeare," in *Music and Letters,* XXII (1941), 32-35, and by Willa M. Evans in *PMLA,* LX (1945), 98-103.

Hamlet (1602)

The songs sung by Ophelia in *Hamlet,* IV, v, have been rather tenuously identified with certain dance tunes and popular melodies of the late sixteenth and early seventeenth centuries. The subject has been thoroughly treated by Sternfeld in his *Music,* chap. 3.

1. "How should I your true love know"

   Possibly sung to a variant of the Walsingham tune. See comments under Beaumont and Fletcher's *The Knight of the Burning Pestle,* pp. 128-129 above, and Sternfeld *Music,* pp. 59-62. See also Sternfeld *Songs,* pp. 8-10.

2. "Tomorrow is Saint Valentine's day"

   There is no authentic Elizabethan source, but the text has traditionally been adapted to a tune very similar to "A Soldier's Life," found in Playford's *Dancing Master* (1651), No. 65.

3. "They bore him barefaced on the bier"

   This has traditionally been associated with the Walsingham tune, or with a melody utilized for the snatch "And will he not come again." See No. 5, below.

4. "For bonny sweet robin is all my joy"

   Sternfeld has traced some thirty contemporary sources for this melody, six of which were printed between 1597 and 1621. These include Ravenscroft's *Pammelia* (1609), Robinson's *Schoole of Musicke* (1603), and Holborne's *Cittharn Schoole* (1597). An early instrumental version is found in the *Ballet Lute Book* (Dublin, Trinity College, MS D.1.21). See Sternfeld *Music,* pp. 76-77, and Sternfeld *Songs,* pp. 11-13.

5. "And will he not come again"

   This text is traditionally adapted to a variant of the dance tune "The Merry Milkmaids," printed in Playford's *Dancing Master* (1651), No. 31. Occasionally this melody is used for "They bore him barefaced on the bier," No. 3, above.

6. "In youth when I did love"

   This song of the grave digger in Act V, scene i, is a paraphrase of Thomas Lord Vaux's lyric "I loathe that I did love," first printed in Tottel's *Miscellany* (1557). Two contemporary melodies survive, one an early nineteenth-century copy from a source since lost, and one in British Museum, Add. MS 4900. See Sternfeld *Music,* pp. 151-155, where the melodies are edited and a facsimile of the British Museum source is given. See also Sternfeld *Songs,* pp. 14-16.

King Lear (1606)

1. "Then they for sudden joy did weep"

   The music for this song was discovered by Peter Seng written on a British Museum copy of Ravenscroft's *Pammelia* (1609). See *Shakespeare Quarterly,* IX (1958), 583-585, where a facsimile is given. Sternfeld *Music* gives the melody with suggested text underlay, p. 176. He also suggests the tune "Flying Fame" from Durfey's

Wit and Mirth, or Pills to Purge Melancholy (1707) as a possible vehicle. Both settings are edited in Sternfeld *Songs,* pp. 20-22.

2. "Come o'er the burn, Bessy, to me"

The earliest setting of this text is a sixteenth-century part song for three voices in the British Museum, Add. MS 5665, fols. 143v-144. The Shakespearean text, however, can best be adapted to a melody found in a Cambridge University Library lute MS (MS Dd.2.11, fol. 80v), or the *Weld Lute Book* in the possession of Lord Forester. See Sternfeld *Music,* pp. 183-188, and Sternfeld *Songs,* p. 26-28.

King Henry VIII (1613, possibly in collaboration with Fletcher)

"Orpheus with his lute made trees"

A 3-voice setting by Matthew Locke is found in *Catch that Catch Can* (1667), p. 174.

Measure for Measure (1604)

"Take, O take those lips away"

See comments under Beaumont and Fletcher's *The Bloody Brother,* pp. 126-127 above.

Much Ado About Nothing (1598-1600)

"Sigh no more, ladies"

Oxford, Christ Church, MSS 736-8 (3-voice setting by Thomas Ford).

Ford's setting is incomplete, lacking instrumental parts. It is transcribed in Gibbon *Melody,* p. 117, and in Long *Shakespeare,* I (1955), 132-133, after the Christ Church MSS. Peter Warlock has reconstructed the 3-voice setting as a solo song in *Four English Songs of the Early 17th-Century* (Oxford, 1925).

Othello (1604)

"The poor soul sat sighing"

London, British Museum, Add. MS 15,117, fol. 18. Washington, Folger Library, MS v.a.159, fol. 19 ("Lodge Book"). Dublin, Trinity College, MS d.3.30, p. 26 ("Dallis Book").

The "Lodge" and "Dallis" books are lute transcriptions without text. The song has been edited, after the British Museum MS, by Warlock and Wilson in *English Ayres,* I, 19; by E. H. Fellowes in R. Noble's *Shakespeare's Use of Song* (London, 1923); by J. P. Cutts in "A Reconsideration of the 'Willow Song,'" in *Journal of the American Musicological Society,* X (1957), 14-24; Cutts *Musique,* pp. 1-2; Sternfeld *Music,* pp. 39-49; Sternfeld *Songs,* pp. 2-7.

The Tempest (1611)

1. "Full fathom five thy father lies"

Birmingham, City Reference Library, MS 57,316 (Robert Johnson). New York, Public Library, MS Drexel 4041, No. 90 (words only).

Printed in Wilson's *Cheerful Ayres* (1660), pp. 6-7 (Robert Johnson). There is a late seventeenth-century setting by John Bannister in British Museum, Add. MS 29,396, fol. 110 (melody only). Bannister's setting is printed in *The Ariels Songs in the Play call'd The Tempest* (1675), p. 5.

Edited in Cutts *Musique,* p. 24; by Anthony Lewis in *William Shakespeare: Two Songs from The Tempest . . .* (Paris, 1936); Long *Shakespeare,* II (1961), 117, with a facsimile of the setting in *Cheerful Ayres.*

2. "Where the bee sucks there suck I"

Birmingham, City Reference Library, MS 57,316 (Robert Johnson). Oxford, Bodleian, MS Don.c.57, No. 135. London, British Museum, Add. MS 29,396, fol. 110 (Pelham Humfrey).

Printed in *Select Ayres and Dialogues* (1659) and *The Treasury of Musick* (1669), p. 96; Wilson's *Cheerful Ayres* (1660), pp. 8-9; *Catch that Catch Can* (1667), pp. 126-127; *The Musical Companion* (1673), pp. 174-175. Pelham Humfrey's setting is printed in *The Ariels Songs in the Play call'd The Tempest* (1675), p. 5.

Edited in Cutts *Musique,* p. 25; Anthony Lewis' *William Shakespeare: Two Songs from The Tempest* (Paris, 1936), pp. 4-6; Long *Shakespeare,* II (1961), 127. Long also gives a facsimile of the setting in the Bodleian MS (MS Don.c.57).

3. "Come unto these yellow sands"

A late seventeenth-century setting by John Bannister is printed in *The Ariels Songs in the Play call'd The Tempest* (1675), p. 2.

Twelfth Night (1602)

1. "Three merry men, and three merry men"

The popular drinking song also quoted in Barry's *Ram-Alley,* Beaumont and Fletcher's *The Bloody Brother,* and the anonymous play *The Knave in Grain.* See comments under the latter play, p. 124 above.

2. "Farewell, dear love"

Dublin, Trinity College, MS F.5.13, pp. 108-109.

Printed in Robert Jones' *First Book of Ayres* (1600), No. 12.

Edited in Fellowes *LSW 2,* V. The setting is also printed in J. Stafford Smith's *Musica Antiqua,* II, 204-205.

3. "O Mistris mine, where are you roming"

The melody to which this lyric is assumed to have been sung is found in a set of keyboard variations by Byrd in the *Fitzwilliam Virginal Book,* I, No. 66, and in Morley's *First Book of Consort Lessons* (1599), No. 19. This melody is also employed with a text by Campion in New York, Public Library, MS Drexel 4257, No. 118, "Long have mine eyes gazed with delight."

The song has appeared in numerous modern collections. One of the most authoritative versions is given by Sydney Beck in "The Case of 'O Mistresse Mine,' " in *Renaissance News,* VI (1953), 19-23.

The Winter's Tale (1611)

1. "Get you hence for I must go"

   New York, Public Library, MS Drexel 4175, No. 59; MS Drexel 4041, No. 141 (incomplete).

   Both versions are edited in Cutts *Musique,* pp. 17-19. Cutts' attribution to Robert Johnson is conjecture. Also edited and discussed in Long *Shakespeare,* II (1961), 81-85, with a facsimile from MS Drexel 4175; Spink *Johnson,* p. 62.

2. "Lawn as white as driven snow"

   Printed in Wilson's *Cheerful Ayres* (1660), pp. 64-65.

   Edited in Cutts *Musique,* pp. 20-21; Long *Shakespeare,* II (1961), 80, with a facsimile of the original print.

3. "Jog on, jog on the footpath way"

   Printed in *Catch that Catch Can* (1667), p. 85 (John Hilton); Playford's *Dancing Master* (1650); the *Fitzwilliam Virginal Book,* where the tune appears under the name "Hanskin."

   There are several modern editions: E. Naylor's *Shakespeare and Music* (London, 1931), p. 185; Long *Shakespeare,* II (1961), 74, with a facsimile of the original print of Hilton's setting. See also *Chappell,* p. 211; *Chappell-Wooldridge,* I, 159-160; Simpson *Broadside Ballad,* p. 392.

HENRY SHIRLEY

The Martyred Soldier (1620-1627)

"Victory, victory, Hell is beaten down"

Oxford, Bodleian, MS Don.c.57, No. 29.

JAMES SHIRLEY

Bird in a Cage (1633)

"There was an invisible fox by chance"

Printed in *Catch that Catch Can* (1667), p. 66 (John Hilton).

The Cardinal (1641)

"Come, my Daphne, come away"

London, British Museum, Add. MS 11,608, fol. 1 (William Lawes); Add. MS 31,432, fol. 43v (William Lawes).

Printed in *Select Musicall Ayres and Dialogues* (1652), II, 6-7; *Select Musicall Ayres and Dialogues* (1653), II, 4-5; *Select Ayres and Dialogues* (1659) and *The Treasury of Musick* (1669), pp. 74-75.

The Constant Maid (1637-1639)

"An old man is a bed full of bones"

A ballad sung to the tune of "Cook Laurel." See comments under Jonson's *The Gypsies Metamorphos'd,* p. 145 above. The tune designated as "An old man is a bed full of bones" appears in all editions of the *Dancing Master*. See Simpson *Broadside Ballad,* p. 129.

Contention of Ajax and Ulysses (1658-1659)

"The glories of our birth and state"

London, Lambeth Palace, MS 1041, No. 32 (Edward Coleman).

Printed in *Catch that Catch Can* (1667), pp. 146-147; Henry Lawes' *Select Ayres and Dialogues* (1669), Bk. II, pp. 74-75; *The Musical Companion* (1673), pp. 156-157, etc.

See Simpson *Broadside Ballad,* p. 255.

Court Secret (1642)

"What help of tongue need they require"

There is a late seventeenth-century setting by Robert King in *A Second Booke of Songs* (1695), pp. 41-42.

Cupid and Death (1653)

The music for this masque by Matthew Locke and Christopher Gibbons is found in Locke's autograph MS in the British Museum, Add. MS 17,799. It includes instrumental dances and entries, recitatives, choruses, and five songs:

1. "Though little be the God of Love"
2. "Victorious men of earth" (Gibbons)
   Also printed in Playford's *Choice Ayres and Songs,* Bk. III (1681), p. 39.
3. "Stay, Cupid, whither art thou flying"
4. "What will it, Death, advance thy name"
5. "Change, O change your fatal bows" (Gibbons)
   Also printed in Playford's *Choice Ayres and Songs,* Bk. III (1681), p. 38.

Complete music and text for the masque have been edited by Edward J. Dent in *Musica Britannica,* II (1951).

The Duke's Mistress (1636)

"What should my mistress do with hair"

New York, Public Library, MS Drexel 4041, No. 110 (William Lawes); MS Drexel 4257, No. 24.

The music for this song is given in Cutts *Musique,* pp. 65-66, where it is adapted rather arbitrarily to a text from Fletcher's *The Mad Lover.*

Love Tricks (1625)

1. "God of war, to Cupid yield"
   New York, Public Library, MS Drexel 4257, No. 218.
2. "Turn, Amaryllis, to thy swain"
   One of the most popular songs of its day, this lyric was set by John Hilton and by Thomas Brewer. Hilton's setting is preserved in *A Musicall Banquet* (1651), Pt. III, p. 8; *Catch that Catch Can*

(1652), p. 2, and in the 1658 and 1663 editions of the same collection. Brewer's setting appears in *Select Ayres and Dialogues* (1659) and *The Treasury of Musick* (1669), pp. 112-113, as well as in the 1660 and 1662 editions of Playford's *Brief Introduction to the Skill of Musick.*

The Triumph of Beauty (1646)

1. "Cease, warring thoughts"

   Oxford, Bodleian, MS Mus.Sch.b.2 (William Lawes).

   Another setting is printed in John Gamble's *Ayres and Dialogues* (1659), p. 9. The Lawes setting is edited, in part, in Murray Lefkowitz's *William Lawes* (London, 1960), pp. 231-233.

2. "Come, ye graces, come away"

   Printed in John Gamble's *Ayres and Dialogues* (1659), pp. 56-57.

3. "Jove sent thee, Paris, what is mine"

   Printed in John Gamble's *Ayres and Dialogues* (1659), pp. 81-84.

The Triumph of Peace (1634)

The instrumental "symphonies" and four songs from this masque are found in William Lawes' autograph MS in the Bodleian MS Mus.Sch.b.2.

1. "Hence, ye profane" (tenor solo with chorus)
2. "Wherefore do my sisters stay" (tenor with chorus)
3. "Think not I could absent myself"
4. "Come away, away, away" (incomplete chorus fragment)
5. "In envy of the night"

   London, British Museum, Add. MS 31,432, fol. 26 (William Lawes). New York, Public Library, MS Drexel 4041, No. 20.

   Most of William Lawes' music for the masque has been printed by Edward J. Dent in his *Foundations of English Opera* (Cambridge, 1928), pp. 30-37, with a few additions by Lefkowitz in his *William Lawes* (London, 1960), pp. 217-218.

WILLIAM STRODE

The Floating Island (1636)

1. "Come, heavy souls, oppressed with the weight"

   London, British Museum, MS Loan 35, No. 76 (Henry Lawes).

   Printed in Henry Lawes' *Ayres and Dialogues* (1653), Pt. I, p. 28.

2. "Hail, thou great Queen"

   London, British Museum, Add. MS 29,396, fol. 15v (Henry Lawes).

3. "My limbs I will fling" (Hilario's song)

   London, British Museum, Add. MS 29,396, fol. 27 (Henry Lawes).

4. "Once Venus's cheeks that shamed the morn"

   London, British Museum, MS Loan 35, No. 118 (Henry Lawes).

Printed in Henry Lawes' *Ayres and Dialogues,* III (1658 and 1669), 38-39.

5. "Sweet Morphe, lend a feeling ear"
   London, British Museum, MS Loan 35, No. 117 (Henry Lawes).

JOHN SUCKLING

Aglaura (1637)

1. "No, no, fair heretic, it needs must be"
   London, British Museum, MS Loan 35, Nos. 99-100 (Henry Lawes). New York, Public Library, MS Drexel 4041, No. 9 (Henry Lawes); MS Drexel 4257, No. 89.
   Printed in *Select Musicall Ayres and Dialogues* (1652), Pt. I, p. 38 (Henry Lawes); *Select Musicall Ayres and Dialogues* (1653), Pt. I, p. 12; *Select Ayres and Dialogues* (1659) and *The Treasury of Musick* (1669), p. 46.
2. "Why so pale and wan, fond lover"
   New York, Public Library, MS Drexel 4041, No. 7 (William Lawes).
   Edwin F. Rimbault printed this song in his *Musical Illustrations of Bishop Percy's Reliques of Ancient English Poetry . . .* (London, 1850), after the Drexel MS, and the melody was in turn copied by Gibbon *Melody,* p. 186.

The Goblins (1637-1640)

1. "A health, a health to the nut-brown lass"
   London, British Museum, Add. MS 31,432, fol. 21v (William Lawes). New York, Public Library, MS Drexel 4041, No. 108 (William Lawes).
2. "Some drink, boy"
   Printed in *Catch that Catch Can* (1667), p. 66.

The Sad One (1637-1640)

"Come away to the tavern I say"
Printed in *A Musicall Banquet* (1651), Pt. III, p. 10; *Catch that Catch Can* (1652, 1658, and 1663). Music by John Hilton.

The Tragedy of Brennoralt (1639)

"A hall, a hall to welcome our friend"
London, British Museum, Add. MS 31,432, fol. 7v (William Lawes).

JOHN WEBSTER

The Duchess of Malfi (1612-1614)

"O let us howl some heavy note"
London, British Museum, Add. MS 29,481, fol. 5v. New York, Public Library, MS Drexel 4041, No. 126 (Robert Johnson); MS

Drexel 4175, No. 42 (another setting is mentioned as No. 4 in the index of this MS but is missing from the contents).

The settings for all three versions are edited in Cutts *Musique*, pp. 40-45.

ROBERT WILD

The Benefice (1633)

1. "God prosper long our noble King"

   This text is traditionally sung to the old ballad tune "Chevy Chase." It is printed in the various editions of Durfey's *Wit and Mirth, or Pills to Purge Melancholy.*

   See Simpson *Broadside Ballad,* p. 96.

2. "I am confirmed a scholar can"

   A parody on Suckling's famous lyric "I am confirmed a woman can." The setting by Henry Lawes was widely known.

   New York, Public Library, MS Drexel 4041, No. 16; MS Drexel 4257, No. 115. British Museum, MS Loan 35, No. 89.

   Printed in *Select Musicall Ayres and Dialogues* (1652 and 1653); *Select Ayres and Dialogues* (1659) and *The Treasury of Musick* (1669), p. 38, etc.

   Edited in Dolmetsch's *Select English Songs and Dialogues,* Bk. I (London, 1898), pp. 20-23; Gibbon *Melody,* p. 185.

NOTES

MUSIC IN THE ENGLISH MYSTERY PLAYS

[1] A pioneer article on this subject is that by Fletcher Collins, "Music in the Craft Cycles," *PMLA,* XLVII (1932), 613-21.

For a discussion of music and musical dialogue in the best known of all the plays, see Nan C. Carpenter, "Music in the *Secunda Pastorum," Speculum,* XXVI (1951), 696-700.

R. W. Ingram, "The Use of Music in English Miracle Plays," *Anglia,* LXXV (1957), 55-76, briefly surveys music in the cycle plays and in some individual pageants. Of special value is a critical bibliography appended to the article.

John Stevens, "Music in the Medieval Drama," *Proceedings of the Royal Musical Association,* LXXXIV (1958), 81-95, gives an excellent brief account of the subject.

For a detailed investigation of music in the Chester cycle, see Nan C. Carpenter, "Music in the Chester Plays," *Papers on English Language and Literature,* I (1965), 195-216.

Two articles by Edmund A. Bowles contain much information about musical instruments in the Middle Ages (although both articles are only peripheral to the subject of music in British drama, drawing primarily upon Continental—especially French—sources): "Haut and Bas: The Grouping of Musical Instruments in the Middle Ages," *Musica Disciplina,* XX (1954), 115-40, and "The Role of Musical Instruments in Medieval Sacred Drama," *Musical Quarterly,* LXV (1959), 67-84.

[2] Standard works on the medieval drama are Edmund K. Chambers, *The Medieval Stage* (2 vols.; Oxford, 1903), and Karl Young, *The Drama of the Medieval Church* (2 vols.; Oxford, 1933). For the beginnings of liturgical drama, see Young, *Drama,* I, 178ff. and 201ff. See also, Hardin Craig, *English Religious Drama of the Middle Ages* (Oxford, 1955), pp. 19ff. (hereinafter

cited as *ERD*). Grace Frank, *The Medieval French Drama* (Oxford, 1954), gives a clear and simple explanation of this phenomenon, pp. 18ff.

[3] See Young, *Drama,* II, 307ff.; Craig, *ERD,* pp. 81ff.

[4] See Young, *Drama,* II, 311ff. for text of the St. Nicholas plays. See especially p. 327, n. 4.

[5] For a discussion of primitive notation, see Willi Apel, *The Notation of Polyphonic Music* (4th rev. ed.; Cambridge, 1949), pp. 204ff.

[6] See Young, *Drama,* II, 172ff. A facsimile of a page from this play is reproduced here and shows the chironomic notation.

[7] *Ibid.,* II, 219ff. See especially Plate XIX showing a page of this play with musical notation. Young's two volumes contain all known dramatic compositions performed by the medieval church as part of the liturgy, of public worship. Young tells us (I, xiv, n.), "A large proportion of the extant texts lack music in the MSS; but, fortunately, most of the longer and more significant plays have it." For the melodies to many of these, see E. de Coussemaker, *Drames liturgiques du Moyen Age* (Rennes, 1860).

[8] Young, *Drama,* II, 296.

[9] See *ibid.,* II, 290ff. for a description and text of the play. *Daniel* was first revived in 1958. Play and recording (Decca DL 9402) are by the New York Pro Musica, under the direction of Noah Greenberg. For the musical score, see *The Play of Daniel,* ed. Noah Greenberg (New York, 1959). And see Bowles, "The Role of Musical Instruments in Medieval Sacred Drama," pp. 83-84, for the use of instruments in *Daniel.*

[10] See Craig, *ERD,* pp. 96ff., for the story of the transition from church to town.

[11] See *ibid.,* pp. 127ff., for a discussion of the origin and development of the Corpus Christi festival.

[12] *Ibid.,* p. 133.

[13] But note that Martial Rose, in his introduction to *The Wakefield Mystery Plays* (London, 1961), argues quite cogently against a number of ideas long traditional in connection with the presentation of the craft plays. For example, he presents data to show that some of them, at least, were probably performed by one set of actors who played the main characters throughout (as against a new cast of characters for each scene), by religious guilds supported by trade guilds, in a fixed location (as against the traditional idea of the pageant wagon's movement from place to place). See especially pp. 26ff. See also F. M. Salter, *Medieval Drama in Chester* (Toronto, 1955), pp. 77ff. for data about professionals.

[14] The five MSS in which these plays are preserved, however, are very late —from 1591 to 1607. See Craig, *ERD,* pp. 166-98, for a thorough discussion of the Chester plays, without, however, any reference to music. See also Salter, *Drama in Chester,* for many interesting details about performance of the plays (including some payments to musicians, pp. 76-77).

[15] See Lucy Toulmin Smith (ed.), *The York Plays* (Oxford, 1885), xlv. For a full discussion of the plays, see Miss Smith's magnificent introduction. See also Craig, *ERD,* pp. 199ff.

[16] See Craig, *ERD,* pp. 214ff., for details of the relationship between the two cycles.

[17] See *ibid.,* pp. 239ff., for a full discussion of the *Ludus Coventriae* or Hegge plays.

[18] See *The Chester Plays,* ed. Thomas Wright (2 vols.; London, 1843 and

1847), I, 5. *The Chester Plays,* Pt. I, ed. Hermann Deimling (London, 1892), p. 12, has the direction "Tunc cantabunt" at this point. Other MSS specify "a songe" or "a songe Dignus es Domine" (see the concordance, *ibid.*)—probably the antiphon for Palm Sunday *(Dignus es domine deus noster accipere gloriam et honorem):* see the *Graduale Sarisburiense,* ed. W. H. Frere (London, 1894), p. 82.

[19] Deimling, *Chester Plays,* p. 13: "Tunc cantabunt et recedet Deus."

[20] Smith, *York Plays,* p. 2: *"Tunc cantant angeli Te deum."*

[21] *Ibid.,* p. 3.

[22] See James Orchard Halliwell (ed.), *Ludus Coventriae* (London, 1841), p. 20.

[23] *Ibid.: "Hic cantent angeli in cœlo.* 'Tibi omnes angeli, tibi cœli et universæ potestates, Tibi cherubyn et seraphyn incessabili voce proclamant, —Sanctus! Sanctus! Sanctus! Dominus Deus Sabaoth!' "

[24] Deimling, *Chester Plays,* p. 104.

[25] Smith, *York Plays,* pp. 98 and 101.

[26] For the musical portion of this scene, see Halliwell, *Ludus Coventriae,* pp. 112-16.

[27] Deimling, *Chester Plays,* p. 197. The rubric reads: "tunc ibunt, et Angelus cantabit 'Ecce dominus super nubem levem, et ingredietur Egiptum, et movebuntur simulacra Egipti a facie Domini Exercituum,' et si fieri poterit, cadet aliqua statua sive imago."

[28] See *ibid.,* p. 205, for this episode.

[29] *The Towneley Plays,* ed. George England and Alfred W. Pollard (London, 1897), p. 161.

[30] *Ibid.,* p. 185. The Canticle of Simeon, the *Nunc dimittis,* is definitely specified in the other three cycles in the scene in which Simeon receives Jesus in the Temple.

[31] *The Chester Plays,* ed. C. W. Matthews (London, 1916) (this is the continuation of the plays edited for the EETS left unfinished by Dr. Deimling), p. 329: " 'Te Deum laudamus, te Dominum confitemur.' Et sic Ibunt glorificantes Deum, cantantes 'Te Deum.' " Other MSS specify that Michael lead the singing as the procession begins. See Wright, *Chester Plays,* II, 79: *"Tunc eunt omnes, et incipiat Michell, Te Deum laudamus."* Wright's edition of the plays is based upon the so-called Devonshire MS and varies sometimes from the Deimling-Matthews edition based upon MS Harl. 2124. The concordance in the latter, however, generally notes the variations.

[32] Matthews, *Chester Plays,* p. 427: "Tunc Michael Archangelus adducet Henochum et Heliam ad Coelum et Cantabit: 'Gaudete Iusti in Domino etc.' "

[33] Smith, *York Plays,* p. 177: *"Tunc cantabant duo angeli Veni creator spiritus."*

[34] See Frank Ll. Harrison, *Music in Medieval Britain* (New York, 1958), p. 65. For the use of polyphonic settings of various parts of the liturgy in the church, see pp. 104-55.

[35] Smith, *York Plays,* p. 181: *"tunc cantant angeli, veni creator."*

[36] Halliwell, *Ludus Coventriae,* p. 211: *"Hic venient angeli cantantes et ministrantes ei:—'Gloria tibi, Domine!' "*

[37] For a full discussion of this antiphon, see Harrison, *Music in Medieval Britain,* pp. 91, 95, 99, etc.

[38] Matthews, *Chester Plays,* p. 337: "Tunc Cantabunt duo Angeli, 'Christus resurgens a mortuis, &c.,' et *Christus* tunc resurget ac Cantu finito dicat vt

sequitur": at which *Iesus resurgens* sings in many verses how he has redeemed man's soul.

[39] Smith, *York Plays,* 406, 416-17.

[40] England and Pollard, *Towneley Plays,* p. 313: *"Tunc cantabunt angeli 'Christus resurgens.'"*

[41] Matthews, *Chester Plays,* p. 367: "Tunc Iesus Ascendet et in ascendendo cantabit Ihesus vt sequitur: Ascendo ad Patrem meum et Patrem vestrum, Deum meum et Deum vestrum. Alleluia! Alleluya! (Et Cantico finito, stabit Ihesus in medio quasi supra Nubes.)" See the concordance, *ibid.,* for the many musical variations among the five MSS with their differing stage directions. And see Wright, *Chester Plays,* II, 117, for a lengthy dialogue sung by Jesus, two angels, and a chorus of angels. In one version of the play, "God singeth alonne."

[42] Matthews, *Chester Plays,* p. 369: "Tunc Ascendet et in ascendendo cantant Angeli Canticum subsequentem:

> Exaltare, domine, in virtute tua, cantabimus,
> et psallemus virtutes tuas. Alleluya."

[43] *Ibid.*: "Tunc descendent Angeli et cantabunt, 'Viri Galilei quid aspicitis in Cœlum?'"

[44] Smith, *York Plays,* p. 461.

[45] England and Pollard, *Towneley Plays,* p. 361: "& sic ascendit, cantantibus angelis 'Ascendo ad patrem meum.'"

[46] Halliwell, *Ludus Coventriae,* p. 378: *"Hic ascendit ab oculis eorum, et in cœlo cantent, etc."*

[47] Matthews, *Chester Plays,* p. 376: "Tunc omnes Apostoli, genu flectentes, cantent: 'veni Creator spiritus, mentes tuorum visita; Imple superna gratia, que tu creasti, pectora.'"

[48] *Ibid.,* p. 381: "Tunc Deus emittit Spiritum sanctum in spetie ignis et in mittendo cantent Duo Angeli 'Accipite spiritum sanctum, quorum remiseritis peccata, remittantur eius,' etc. et cantendo procitient ignem super apostolos."

[49] Smith, *York Plays,* p. 468: "Angelus tunc cantare. Veni creator spiritus." And see p. 469 for the reference to two angels singing the hymn.

[50] *Ibid.,* p. 479. The rubric follows: *"Et cantant antiphona scilicet Aue regina celorum."*

[51] See *ibid.,* pp. 483-90, for the musical references. And see pp. 524-27 for a discussion of these chants by the editor, who explains their composition from several antiphons used in services celebrating the Assumption of the Virgin. C. Fenno Hoffman, Jr., "The Source of the Words to the Music in York 46," *Modern Language Notes,* LXV (1950), 236-39, identifies the words as coming from the *Legenda Aurea* (Strasburg, 1482), published in a free translation by Caxton (1483) as the *Golden Legend.* But see John Stevens, "Music in Medieval Drama," pp. 93-94. Dr. Stevens points out that *Veni tu electa mea* is a *versus alleluiaticus* found in the *Sarum Gradual* (see the edition by W. H. Frere, p. 227) and that both this verse and *Veni de libano* are antiphons still in use today. Dr. Stevens, however, is unable to find any musical connection between music of the liturgy and music for these pieces (which he fully describes, p. 94).

See the *Liber Usualis,* pp. 1211 and 1233, where *Veni electa mea* is an antiphon for second Vespers at the Common of Virgins and Common of Holy Women.

In Miss Smith's edition of the plays, three pages of the music are reproduced in facsimile, but only one appears in color (black and red). The transcription of the music by W. H. Cummings is inaccurate. The music appears properly transcribed by John Stevens in the edition of the plays for the EETS by Arthur Brown (in preparation).

[52] Smith, *York Plays,* pp. 493 and 496.

[53] *Ibid.,* p. xxvii.

[54] Halliwell, *Ludus Coventriae,* p. 75.

[55] Harrison, *Music in Medieval Britain,* p. 65.

[56] See Halliwell, *Ludus Coventriae,* pp. 87-88, for this and the following reference.

[57] *Ibid.,* p. 386: *"Hic discendet Angelus; ludentibus citharis, et dicet Mariae."*

[58] *Ibid.,* p. 393:

"Hic dissendet Dominus cum omni celeste curia, et dicet,

Dominus. This voys of my moder ne nyhith ful ny;
I am dyssend on to here of whom I dede sede.

Hic cantabunt organa."

And p. 394: *"Hic cantabit omnis celestis curia."*

[59] *Ibid.,* p. 395: *"Hic angeli dulciter cantabunt in cœlo 'allelujah'!"*

[60] See *ibid.* for this and the next reference.

[61] *Ibid.,* p. 399.

[62] See *ibid.,* p. 400, for these last references. *"Et hic assendent in cœlum cantantibus organis, Assumpta es Maria in cœlum."*

[63] Matthews, *Chester Plays,* p. 445: "Tunc Angeli cantabunt euntes ac venientes 'Lætamini in Domino' vel 'Saluator mundi Domine': tunc omnes Salvati eos sequentur. . . ."

[64] Smith, *York Plays,* p. 505: *"Hic ad sedem iudicij cum cantu angelorum."*

[65] England and Pollard, *Towneley Plays,* p. 387:

Therfor full boldly may we syng
On oure way as we trus;
Make we all myrth and louyng
With te deum laudamus.

[66] Halliwell, *Ludus Coventriae,* p. 403.

[67] England and Pollard, *Towneley Plays,* p. 340: *"Tunc venit ihesus et cantat 'pax vobis et non tardabit, hec est dies quam fecit dominus'"*—which the *Tercius apostolus* sings in an English paraphrase ("This is the day that god maide"); and again, *"Iterum venit ihesus, et cantat, 'pax vobis et non tardabit.'"*

[68] Deimling, *Chester Plays,* p. 107, and Smith, *York Plays,* p. 101.

[69] Halliwell, *Ludus Coventriae,* p. 128.

[70] See *ibid.,* p. 130, for this closing episode.

[71] England and Pollard, *Towneley Plays,* pp. 59-61.

[72] Deimling, *Chester Plays,* p. 211: "tunc cantabit 'nunc dimitis seruum tuum, domine, in pace'"; England and Pollard, *Towneley Plays,* p. 185; and Halliwell, *Ludus Coventriae,* pp. 176-77: *"'Nunc dimittis servum tuum, Domine, et cœtera.' The psalme song ther every vers, and ther qwyle Symeon pleyeth with the child."*

[73] Wright, *Chester Plays,* I, 54. For another version, see Deimling, *Chester*

Plays, p. 58: "Tunc Noe claudet fenestram Archæ et per modicum spatium infra tectum cantent psalmum 'Save mee o God.'" These words are the beginning of an anthem popular in Renaissance times: see Stevens, "Music in Medieval Drama," p. 87.

[74] For the musical references, see Halliwell, *Ludus Coventriae,* pp. 46 and 48.

[75] Smith, *York Plays,* p. 91.

[76] Halliwell, *Ludus Coventriae,* p. 73, contains this musical service.

[77] *Ibid.,* p. 93.

[78] *Ibid.,* p. 99: *"Et hic cantent, 'Benedicta sit beata Trinitas.'"*

[79] *Ibid.,* p. 100.

[80] Matthews, *Chester Plays,* p. 257: "Tunc ibunt pueri versus Ierusalem, cum ramis palmarum in manibus; et Cives prosternent vestimenta sua in via, et cantabunt 'hosanna filio David! Benedictus, qui venit in nomine Domini! hosanna in excelcis!'"

[81] Smith, *York Plays,* p. 210.

[82] See *ibid.,* pp. 283 and 284 for the Beadle's remarks about the *Hosanna.*

[83] Halliwell, *Ludus Coventriae,* p. 256.

[84] Wright, *Chester Plays,* I, 53. Although the song is not written down in the MS edited by Deimling, it is given in the concordance, p. 57. As far as I can discover, the music for this song no longer exists.

[85] Deimling, *Chester Plays,* p. 151: "Tunc omnes pastores cum aliis adiuvantibus cantabunt hilare carmen."

[86] *Ibid.,* p. 158.

[87] Smith, *York Plays,* p. 121.

[88] *Ibid.,* p. 122.

[89] England and Pollard, *Towneley Plays,* p. 108.

[90] *Ibid.,* p. 109.

[91] *Ibid.,* p. 113.

[92] *Ibid.,* p. 116.

[93] *Ibid.,* p. 122.

[94] *Ibid.,* p. 137.

[95] *Ibid.,* p. 140.

[96] Halliwell, *Ludus Coventriae,* p. 158. The direction follows: *"Tunc pastores cantabunt* 'Stella cœli extirpavit.'" See Harrison, *Music in Medieval Britain,* p. 88, for identification of the chant.

[97] Deimling, *Chester Plays,* p. 6. Deimling notes that in one MS the word "flute" has been replaced by "harpe."

Salter prints the expense account of the Smiths who produced the play in 1554: see *Medieval Drama in Chester,* pp. 76-77:

> to the mynstrells in mane [money] ij^{s}
> we gaue to the Angells vj^{d} to ould Semond [Simeon] iij^{s} 4^{d}
> we gaue to barnes & the syngers iij^{s} 4^{d}
> [Sir Randall Barnes was a minor canon and singing master at Chester Cathedral.]
> to Randle Crane in mane [money] ij^{s}
> [Morris, p. 350, says that Randall Crane was a minstrel.]

This last is a reference to Canon Morris, *Chester in the Plantagenet and Tudor Reigns.*

[98] See Wright, *Chester Plays,* I, 23, 30, 33, 35, for the musical references in these scenes. See also the concordance in Deimling, *Chester Plays,* pp. 24, 31,

36, 37, 44. In one MS, "Minstrells playe" when God appears later in the play after Cain has killed Abel.

[99] Wright, *Chester Plays,* I, 80-81.

[100] Deimling, *Chester Plays,* p. 139.

[101] Wright, *Chester Plays,* I, 143. In one version of the play, the boy offers his "pype that soundeth so royallye": see the collation of MSS in Matthews, *Chester Plays,* pp. lii-liii.

This scene with the four boys (who call the shepherds their masters) is found in three of the existing MSS and seems to have been inserted to make use of the choir boys, since the same three MSS call for the sung *Amen* at the close of the scene.

[102] Wright, *Chester Plays,* I, 152.

[103] See Matthews, *Chester Plays,* pp. 427 and 428 for the musical references. The rubric reads: "Tunc Angeli Tubas accipient et flabunt; et Omnes mortui de Sepulchris resurgent. . . ."

[104] *York Plays,* p. 125, n.

[105] *Ibid.,* p. 499. Note, too, that four "angeli cum tubis" are carefully noted in the list of characters for the Mercers' play, the last play in the cycle, in a register of the guilds and their obligations from *ca.* 1430-1440: see p. xxvii.

[106] See England and Pollard, *Towneley Plays,* pp. 59-61, for David's lines.

[107] *Ibid.,* p. 119.

[108] *Ibid.,* pp. 184-85. One is reminded here of the same phenomenon in Chaucer's *Troilus and Criseyde* (III, 188-89)—like Simeon's bells, marking a moment of great joy and emotion. For when Pandarus has succeeded in bringing the lovers together, he notices the ringing of bells:

> Withouten hond, me semeth that in towne,
> For this merveille, ich here ech belle sowne.

[109] England and Pollard, *Towneley Plays,* pp. 367ff.

[110] Halliwell, *Ludus Coventriae,* p. 161.

[111] See *ibid.,* pp. 184 and 186 for this and the following references.

[112] *Ibid.,* pp. 386 and 393. *Organa* can mean either musical instruments in general or specifically, "the organs."

[113] For a more technical discussion of the music in the Nativity plays, see my article, "Music in the *Secunda pastorum,*" *Speculum,* XXVI (1951), 696-700.

[114] See Deimling, *Chester Plays,* pp. 147ff., for the discussion following the *Gloria.* According to Deimling's notes on the MSS, the musical notation of the angel's *Gloria in excelsis deo* is preserved in Harl. 2124: see p. x.

[115] Halliwell, *Ludus Coventriae,* p. 158. Miss Block has also noticed the similarity between the remarks of the shepherds here and in the Chester play; she believes the interpolation discussing the words of the *Gloria* to have been borrowed from the Chester cycle to replace a speech of the Third Shepherd, which is missing. See the *Ludus Coventriae,* ed. K. E. Block (London, 1922), p. 148.

[116] England and Pollard, *Towneley Plays,* pp. 110 and 113. This illuminating conversation continues as the First Shepherd comments musically:

> In fayth I trow noght / so many he throng
> On a heppe;
> Thay were gentyll and small,
> And well tonyd with all.

The Third Shepherd reacts strongly: "yee, bot I can thaym all / Now lyst I lepe." The First Shepherd encourages him, "Brek outt youre voce / let se ye yelp"; but the Third Shepherd replies, "I may not for the pose / bot I haue help." But there is a song, for the next discussion (p. 114) begins, "Now an ende haue we doyn / of oure song this tyde."

[117] *Ibid.,* p. 137.

[118] *Ibid.,* p. 370.

[119] Halliwell, *Ludus Coventriae,* p. 403.

[120] Matthews, *Chester Plays,* p. 426.

[121] Smith, *York Plays,* pp. 28, 157, 513.

[122] England and Pollard, *Towneley Plays,* p. 68.

[123] *Ibid.,* p. 270.

[124] *Ibid.,* p. 379.

[125] See *The Complete Poems of John Skelton,* ed. Philip Henderson (2nd rev. ed., London, 1948), pp. 298 ("Speak, Parrot") and 417 ("A Replication"). I cannot find that there was ever a song by this name, however.

[126] Halliwell, *Ludus Coventriae,* p. 187.

[127] *Ibid.,* p. 239.

[128] *Ibid.,* p. 402.

[129] See *The Norwich Play* in *The Non-Cycle Mystery Plays,* ed. Osborn Waterhouse (London, 1909), pp. 10-11.

[130] In his edition of the Wakefield plays, Martial Rose gives many suggestions for appropriate music in mounting the plays, on the basis of music specified definitely in the other plays: see his introduction.

[131] Hardin Craig (ed.), *Two Coventry Corpus Christi Plays* (rev. ed.; London, 1957). These are *The Shearmen and Taylors' Pageant,* re-edited from the edition of Thomas Sharp, 1825, and *The Weavers' Pageant,* re-edited from the MS of Robert Croo, 1534. The songs were printed by Thomas Sharp, *A Dissertation on the Pageants or Dramatic Mysteries Anciently Performed at Coventry* (Coventry, 1825).

[132] See n. 34 above.

[133] See Denis Stevens, *Tudor Church Music* (New York, 1955), pp. 26ff., for a discussion of Latin and English musical settings of parts of the service. At least in one instance, seventeen processional hymns were translated from Latin into English before 1333 (the date of the writer's—the friar's—death), the English verses following the Latin metrically, so that the same music could be used for both: see Rossell Hope Robbins, "Friar Herebert and the Carol," *Anglia,* LXXV (1957), 194-98.

[134] See Salter, *Medieval Drama in Chester,* pp. 76-78.

[135] It seems to have been customary before the presentation of religious drama in France in the late Middle Ages for actors and spectators to kneel and sing a hymn: see Bowles, "The Role of Musical Instruments in Medieval Sacred Drama," p. 72.

[136] Surely John Stevens is right in interpreting the rubric in the *York Plays,* p. 479, "*Et Cantant* [*angeli*] *antiphona*[*m*] *scilicet Aue regina celorum. Cum uno diabolo*" to mean that one more singer was needed (to sing a five-part antiphon) in addition to the four angels required by the play: see his "Music in Medieval Drama," p. 85.

[137] The refrain "Hey, trolly lolly lo!" is mentioned twice by John Skelton—in *Against a Comely Coistrown* and again in *Magnificence*: see his *Poems,* pp. 34 and 204. This refrain also occurs in the play *Hickscorner,* published

by Wynken de Worde *ca.* 1512, where Freewill—wishing to dance and sing—suggests this tune as the basis for discant: see the facsimile edition (London, 1906), col. Ci:

> Now wyll I synge and lustely sprynge.
>
> . . . . .
>
> now hey trolly lolly
>
> Let us se who can descaunt on this same. . . .

There are two polyphonic settings of songs with this refrain in BM Add. MS 31931 ("Henry VIII's MS"): see John Stevens, *Music and Poetry in the Early Tudor Court* (London, 1961), p. 438. All the pieces in this collection have been printed in *Music at the Court of Henry VIII,* ed. John Stevens, *Musica Britannica,* XVIII (London, 1962). This collection contains a three-part setting of "Trolly lolly" by Skelton's associate at the royal court, William Cornish.

[138] For the music, see Sharp, *Dissertation on the Pageants,* pp. 113-18. (Craig does not print the music in his edition of the plays.) For a transcription of the Shepherds' Carol, see John P. Cutts, "The Second Coventry Carol and a Note on *The Maydes Metamorphosis,*" *Renaissance News,* X (1957), 3-8. See also Richard L. Greene, "The Second Coventry Carol: a Correction," *ibid.,* X (1957), 142.

[139] E. K. Chambers, *The Medieval Stage* (Oxford, 1903), has several chapters on minstrels in England and France: see I, 42ff. Many documents cited here show the great variety of instruments played by the minstrels. The appendixes in Vol. II—extracts from account books, etc.—are filled with references to instrumentalists. See also the many references to minstrels in Appendix II, extracts from the account books of the Coventry trading companies, in Craig, *Two Coventry Plays.*

[140] Many of these ideas are discussed in Théodore Gérold, *Les Pères de l'église et la musique* (Paris, 1931). See also Nan C. Carpenter, *Music in the Medieval and Renaissance Universities* (Norman, Okla., 1958), pp. 12, 70, 299, 300. And see the references to Bowles' article in the *Musical Quarterly* cited below.

[141] For facts of this discussion, see Bowles, "The Role of Musical Instruments in Medieval Sacred Drama," pp. 74ff. See also Curt Sachs, *The History of Musical Instruments* (New York, 1940), p. 264, for indoor-outdoor grouping; Gustave Reese, *Music in the Middle Ages* (New York, 1940), pp. 385-86.

[142] The triangular psaltery with its ten strings—representing, thus, both the Trinity and the Ten Commandments—became with philosophers and poets an actual symbol for the body of Christ; and the harp, long associated with angels, had from the time of Hugo of St. Victor symbolized the Cross: "The figure of Christ on the cross is indicated mystically through the wood and the stretching of strings": see Bowles "The Role of Musical Instruments in Medieval Sacred Drama," pp. 76-77. See Reese, *Music in the Middle Ages,* p. 64, for St. Augustine on this subject. Best-known tangible portrayal of this idea is in one of the Cluny capitals: see William Fleming, *Arts and Ideas* (2nd rev. ed.; New York, 1963), pp. 208-10, which includes an illustration of the famous sculpture.

Unnoticed up to now is Skelton's reference to the idea that "Christum lyra personat," with a quotation from Jerome's letter to Paul the Priest prefixed to the Vulgate:

> For David, our poet, harped so melodiously
>
> Of our Saviour Christ in his decachord psaltry,

That at his resurrection he harped out of hell
Old patriarchs and prophets in heaven with him to dwell.

See Skelton's *Replication Against Certain Young Scholars, Poems,* p. 426. I discuss this and other musical matters in my book, *John Skelton* (Twayne English Authors Series, New York, 1968).

[143] See the many payments to organists in expense accounts cited by Craig, *Two Coventry Plays,* Appendix II. There are no references to organs in the plays themselves.

[144] For information about these outdoor instruments, see Bowles, "The Role of Musical Instruments in Medieval Sacred Drama," pp. 73ff., and "Haut and Bas," p. 125.

[145] Bowles, "The Role of Musical Instruments in Medieval Sacred Drama," pp. 82-84, gives an interesting account of the religious symbolism of bells.

[146] John Stevens, "Music in Medieval Drama," p. 82, states this idea extremely well: "This symbolic use of music to represent the divine order rests for its effect on no mere traditional stagecraft or vague emotional association. One has only to recall the traditional, Boethian view of music in its threefold division to realize how deeply ingrained in mediæval consciousness was the correspondence between the harmony of man-made music and the harmony of the Universe. Singing angels represent a higher harmony, a more complete 'order' than we can know on earth. Music is a mirror or *speculum* (to use their favorite image) of the God-created Universe." The Boethian division referred to here is *musica mundana,* the music of the spheres; *musica humana,* the harmony of the soul; and *musica instrumentalis,* sounding music, vocal or instrumental: see Carpenter, *Music in the Universities,* pp. 11-12.

I have expressed many of these conclusions about music in the plays in my article, "Music in the Chester Plays," pp. 208ff.

[147] For easy reference, see the many discussions of these treatises, *ibid.,* pp. 26ff., 123ff., etc.

[148] Deimling, *Chester Plays,* p. 158.

[149] *Ibid.,* p. 150.

[150] *Ibid.,* pp. 130-32. After an angel sings "Hec est ara Dei celi," the Emperor comments, "Ioy and blis makes my hart strong, / to hear this melodye" and says he will build a church to be called Ara Cœli "for to haue full memorye / of the angells melody." A church by this name is standing in Rome today: see L. Russell Muirhead (ed.), *The Blue Guides: Rome and Central Italy* (Chicago, 1956) for a description of Santa Maria in Aracœli ("Church of the Altar of Heaven").

[151] This idea pervades *Paradise Lost*: see, for example, II, 344ff.

THE ENTERTAINMENT AT ELVETHAM, 1591

[1] Hertford's career is fairly well known. In addition to the articles in the *Dictionary of National Biography,* the *Encyclopædia Britannica,* and Doyle's *Official Baronage,* one may find further information in George Lillie Craik, *The Romance of the Peerage* (London, 1848-1850); W. L. Rutton, "Lady Catherine Grey and Edward Seymour," *English Historical Review,* XIII (London, 1898); and Richard Davey, *The Sisters of Lady Jane Grey* (London, 1911).

See also Edith Rickert, "Political Propaganda in *A Midsummer's Night Dream,*" *Modern Philology,* XXI, 1923.

[2] E. K. Chambers, *The Elizabethan Stage* (Oxford, 1923), II, 116-17.

[3] John Nichols, *The Progresses and Public Processions of Queen Elizabeth* (new ed.; London, 1823), III, 74ff.

[4] *Ibid.,* p. 101.

[5] *The Honorable Entertainment gieuen to the Queenes Maiestie in Progresse, at Elueham in Hampshire, by the right Honorable the Earle of Hertford.* 1591. London. Printed by Iohn Wolfe.

It was sold at 6*d.* per copy. A second printing was shortly issued, a copy of which is in the University Library, Cambridge (Bb.*.50). It contains the addition of a crude woodcut, "A Description of the great Pond in Eluetham, and of the properties which it containeth." This was followed by a further edition, "Newlie corrected and amended," with a fresh and more elaborate illustration, the details of which were identified as: "A. Her Maiesties presence-seate, and traine; B. Nereus, and his followers; C. The pinnace of Neaera, and her musicke; D. The Ship-ile; E. A boate with musicke, attending on the pinnace of Neaera; F. The Fort-mount; G. The Snaile-mount; H. The Roome of Estate." All these printings appeared before the end of 1591, attesting to the popularity of the work.

[6] Nichols, pp. 101-21. This contains (opposite p. 101) an engraving of the great pond, enlarging the illustrations in *The Honorable Entertainment,* and is dated Nov. 1822.

[7] R. Warwick Bond, ed., *The Complete Works of John Lyly* (Oxford, 1902), I, 431-52.

[8] *Ibid.,* pp. 404-406.

[9] *Ibid.,* pp. 33, 398, *et passim.*

[10] E. Brennecke, "Shakespeare's Collaboration with Morley," *PMLA,* LIV (March 1939), 139-52.

[11] E. Brennecke, "Shakespeare's Singing Man of Windsor," *PMLA,* LXVI (Dec. 1951), 1188-92. Also "A Singing Man of Windsor," *Music & Letters,* XXXIII (Jan. 1952), 33-40.

[12] William Byrde, *My Ladye Nevells Booke* (1591), ed. Hilda Andrews (London, 1926). See especially p. xvi.

[13] Mark Eccles, *Christopher Marlowe in London* ("Harvard Studies in English," Vol. X [Cambridge, Mass., 1934]), pp. 9-10, 41-42.

[14] The quotations and descriptions here and in the following pages are partially from the Cambridge copy of the second quarto of *The Honorable Entertainment,* and partially from Nichols and from Bond, who collated all three quartos. The spelling in each of the originals is inconsistent, as will be observed.

[15] E. H. Fellowes (ed.), *English Madrigal Verse* (Oxford, 1929), pp. 63, 257.

[16] Transcribed by E. H. Fellowes in *The English Madrigal School,* Vol. XVI (London, 1920), pp. iv, ix, 42-48, 240-50.

[17] Fellowes, *English Madrigal Verse,* pp. 574, 626. See also Pilkington, *First Book of Songs or Airs* (1605), ed. Fellowes, in *Lutenist Song Writers,* Vol. XV, Pt. II (London, 1925), pp. 83-86.

[18] E. H. Fellowes, *The English Madrigal Composers* (Oxford, 1921), pp. 383-86. See also the article "Pilkington, Francis," in *Grove's Dictionary of Music and Musicians.*

[19] Thomas Morley, *A Plaine and Easie Introduction to Practicall Musicke*

(London, 1597), facsimile, with an Introduction by E. H. Fellowes ("Shakespeare Association Facsimiles," No. 14 [Oxford, 1937]), p. 181.

[20] Thoinot Arbeau, *Orchesography* (1588), trans. C. W. Beaumont (London, 1925), p. 56.

[21] *The First Book of Consort Lessons,* collected by Thomas Morley, 1599 and 1611, Reconstructed and ed. Sydney Beck (New York, 1959). See especially p. 17. The frontispiece reproduces the painting of the feast and pageant at the wedding of Sir Henry Unton.

An interesting photograph of six modern performers (in Elizabethan costume) holding Morley's consort instruments may be seen in Sir Frederick Bridge, *Shakespearean Music* (London, 1923), p. 17.

[22] *The Fitzwilliam Virginal Book,* ed. J. A. Fullermaitland and W. Barclay Squire (Leipzig, 1899), II, 209.

[23] *The Old Cheque-Book of the Chapel Royal,* ed. E. F. Rimbault (Westminster, 1872), p. 5.

[24] William Chappell, *Popular Music of the Olden Time* (London, 1855-1859), II, 495, 554, 585, 626, 629, 792.

[25] Morley, *A Plaine and Easie Introduction,* p. 182.

[26] Thomas Ravenscroft, *Pammelia and other Rounds and Catches* (1609-1611), ed. Peter Warlock (London, 1928), Prefaces, and p. 3.

[27] Bond, *Works of John Lyly,* p. 524.

[28] *Englands Helicon* (1600, 1614), ed. Hyder E. Rollins (Cambridge, Mass., 1935), II, 27-28, 101-103.

[29] Ed. E. H. Fellowes, *English Madrigal School,* Vol. XXIX (London, 1923), pp. 6-14.

[30] *Ibid.,* p. xiii.

[31] Add. MSS 17797.

[32] R.M.24.d.2.

[33] Add. MSS 30480-84. For a table of the full contents of this set see Augustus Hughes-Hughes, *Catalogue of Manuscript Music in the British Museum,* II (London, 1908), 139.

[34] See n. 33.

[35] *Midsummer Night's Dream,* II, i, 148-64. For spelling and punctuation the text of the First Folio has been followed.

CAMPION'S ENTERTAINMENT AT BROUGHAM CASTLE, 1617

[1] John Nichols, *The Progresses of King James I* (London, 1828), III, pp. 390-92.

[2] These songs were edited by J. Stafford Smith in his *Musica Antiqua* (London, 1812), pp. 150-65, but without the original lute part and with other deficiencies. The present writer has recently edited them for Stainer & Bell, Ltd., in *The English Lute-Songs,* 2nd Ser., Vol. XVIII (London, 1962), pp. 23-48. The words are included in Percival Vivian's edition of *Campion's Works* (Oxford, 1909), pp. 227-34, and in E. H. Fellowes' *English Madrigal Verse* (Oxford, 1920), pp. 553-58.

[3] Vivian, *Campion's Works,* p. li.

[4] T. D. Whitaker, *The History and Antiquities of the Deanery of Craven* (London, 1805), pp. 263-64. The source may possibly have been one of the

letters referred to under the date June 6, 1617, as "Copies of letters from the Earl to his son" in the appendix to *The Third Report of the Royal Commission on Historical Manuscripts* (London, 1872), p. 38, but which Mr. T. S. Wragg, the Keeper of the Duke of Devonshire's Collection at Chatsworth, informs me can no longer be traced. I am very grateful to Mr. Wragg for his kindness in answering my inquiries and for transcribing certain entries in the Bolton MSS.

[5] Bolton MSS, Vol. XCVII.

[6] Vivian, *Campion's Works,* p. 113.

[7] W. L. Woodfill, *Musicians in English Society* (Princeton, 1953), p. 257.

[8] Bodleian Library, Oxford, MS Wood, D. 19 (4), fol. 89v., and J. E. West, *Cathedral Organists Past and Present* (2nd ed.; London, 1921), p. 127.

[9] The words of an anthem by George Mason are given in James Clifford's Divine Services and Anthems (2nd ed.; 1664), p. 281, and BM Add. MS 30826-28 includes some "Pavanes" attributed to "Mr. Mason" (Nos. 3-10). It may be significant that the same MS contains an anonymous "Trinitye Colledg Pavan" (No. 17), but to draw any conclusion from this would be exceedingly hazardous. The source of West's information is obscure and does not appear to be in any likely publication prior to 1899, the date of the first edition of his *Cathedral Organists.* It may have been communicated to him privately. Eitner was able to use West's note on Mason in the *Quellen-Lexicon* (Leipzig, 1901), VI, p. 369, since when it has been repeated frequently. However, it is not impossible that Mason (who might have been a Cambridge Mus. B.,—in 1601 an unnamed candidate graduated in that degree, according to C. Abdy Williams' *Degrees in Music* [London, 1893], p. 124) left the earl's employment in 1611 (his name does not seem to occur in the accounts between then and 1617) and was commissioned to compose the Brougham Castle music while in some other employment, perhaps as organist of Trinity College. But there is no evidence of this.

[10] Bolton MSS, Vol. XCVII, dated July 18, 1617.

[11] Nichols, *The Progresses of King James I,* p. 391.

[12] See *An Inventory of the Historical Monuments in Westmoreland,* Royal Commission on Ancient and Historical Monuments, England (London, 1936) pp. 60-66, for plans and description.

[13] *The Register of the Privy Council of Scotland, 1616-1619,* ed. David Masson (Edinburgh, 1894), XI, p. 217. Nichols' dates are derived from "Coles MSS (Brit. Mus.) Vol. XLVI; transcribed by him [Coles] . . . from the original drafts found among the papers of Mr. Martin, the Suffolk Antiquary. Another copy of these Gests is among the MSS of Gonville and Caius College, Cambridge, No. 123" (Nichols, *The Progresses of King James I,* pp. 257, 389). However, these dates can be shown to be wrong in respects other than the Brougham Castle visitation.

[14] W. W. Greg, *Jonson's Masque of Gipsies* (London, 1952), pp. 2-3.

[15] In "English Cavalier Songs, 1620-1660," *Proceedings of the Royal Musical Association,* 86th session (1959/60), pp. 61-64.

[16] Article on Monson in DNB, XII (1921), p. 646.

[17] W. J. A. Jonckbloet and J. P. N. Land, *Corréspondance et ouvres musicales de Constantin Huygens* (Leyden, 1882), p. 1.

[18] Those from masques before 1609 were printed in his *Ayres* (1609), see Nos. 3, 11, 18-23; those from the masques of 1611 are in St. Michael's College, Tenbury, MS 1018, fols. 36-37v. E. H. Fellowes edited the *Ayres* in *The English*

School of Lutenist Song Writers, 2nd ser., Vol. XVI (London, 1927), and J. P. Cutts transcribed those from MS in "Le Rôle de la Musique dans les Masques de Ben Jonson," *Les Fêtes de la Renaissance,* ed. J. Jacquot (Paris, 1956), pp. 285-302. See also A. J. Sabol, *Songs and Dances for the Stuart Masque* (Providence, R.I., 1959), pp. 34-50, and the present author's edition of "Alfonso Ferrabosco II: Manuscript Songs," *The English Lute-Songs,* 2nd ser., Vol. XIX (London, 1966), pp. 14-25.

[19] The first of these songs was printed in Robert Dowland's *Musicall Banquet* (1610), No. 8; the other two in John Dowland's *A Pilgrimes Solace* (1612), Nos. 20-21. Modern editions of all three are in E. H. Fellowes, *The English Lute-Songs,* 1st Ser., Vol. XIV (London, 1925), pp. 90-108.

[20] Printed at the back of Campion's *The Description of a Maske . . . at the Mariage of . . . the Earle of Somerset* (1614) and reprinted in Stafford Smith's *Musica Antiqua,* p. 60, where it is falsely assigned to Davenant's *Luminalia* (1637). C. H. H. Parry quoted this version in "The Music of the XVIIth Century," *Oxford History of Music* (2nd ed.; London, 1938), p. 200. See also Sabol, p. 20, n. 35.

[21] The figures are from *The English Lute-Songs,* 2nd Ser., Vol. XVIII (London: Stainer & Bell, Ltd., 1962). Reproduced by permission of the publishers.

[22] But in the *Caversham House Entertainment* occurs the following direction, *"the* Robin-Hood-*men faine two Trebles"* (Vivian, *Campion's Works,* p. 80).

[23] Numerous payments to waits are recorded in the Clifford account books, see Woodfill, *Musicians in English Society,* pp. 257-58, and there are many references to household instruments. An inventory of the musical instruments in one of the houses of the late Earl of Cumberland, compiled about 1644, includes "In the great hall . . . one pair of organs, one harpsicon. . . . In the gallery . . . one viol chest with six stringed instruments," see *ibid.,* p. 279.

[24] *Ibid.,* pp. 192-93.

[25] *Tho: Campiani Epigrammatum Liber Primus* (1619), No. 188; see Vivian, *Campion's Works,* pp. li, 263, 372.

[26] See *Bishop Percy's Folio Manuscript, Ballads and Romances,* ed. J. W. Hales and F. J. Furnivall (London, 1868), III, pp. 260-62 and 499-506. Also W. Chappel, *Popular Music of the Olden Time* (London, 1859), I, pp. 370-72. I must thank Mr. David Greer for first drawing my attention to these (and other) references.

[27] Stafford Smith, *Musica Antiqua,* p. 10.

[28] Vivian, *Campion's Works,* pp. 86-87.

[29] P. Warlock, *The English Ayre* (London, 1926), p. 122.

PATTERNS OF MUSIC AND ACTION IN FLETCHERIAN DRAMA

[1] *The Works of Francis Beaumont and John Fletcher,* ed. A. Glover and A. R. Waller (10 vols.; Cambridge, 1905-1912). All references are to this edition, volume and page for poems, act and scene for plays.

[2] Cyrus Hoy, "The Shares of Fletcher and his Collaborators in the Beaumont and Fletcher Canon," *Studies in Bibliography,* VIII-XV (1956-1962). The

valuable work of Prof. Hoy in discriminating more precisely than ever before between the authors now leaves the way clearer for studies of the plays as entities and examinations of certain techniques and modes of writing that run through the canon: to his linguistic, syntactical, and metrical tests others may now be added of a less easily measurable kind. As he says in preface to his discussion of *The Two Noble Kinsmen:* "Shakespeare's presence will have to be proved on other than linguistic grounds" (XV [1962], 71). The contributions of Fletcher and his fellows must also be assessed on these other grounds. A start has been made recently: see John P. Cutts, "Shakespeare's Song and Masque Hand in 'The Two Noble Kinsmen,'" *English Miscellany,* XXIII (1967), pp. 55-85. A tentative approach to such an assessment are these present notes on musical techniques; Hoy makes clear distinctions between the contributions of Fletcher and Massinger to *The Little French Lawyer* and *The Prophetess*: music is used by each writer in his parts and yet the end product is a unified play in musical-dramatic terms. We shall never know just how collaborators went to work on a play, but it seems clear that there must have been some quite careful planning of the overall intentions of the play before each man went off to prepare his portion. The year 1964 has provided us with such an abundance of Shakespeare material that it may be allowable to hope that, if only as relief, some more concentrated attention may now be turned on his contemporaries.

[3] There are, naturally, interesting comparisons to be made between Shakespeare's handling of music as part of the structural pattern of his plays and Fletcher's; an approach to this along the same lines as those followed here will be found in R. W. Ingram, "*Hamlet, Othello* and *King Lear*: Music and Tragedy," *Shakespeare-Jahrbuch,* C (1964), 159-72.

[4] This is a favorite device of Shakespeare's—*Titus Andronicus* (V, iii), *Macbeth* (I, vii), *Coriolanus* (IV, v), *Anthony and Cleopatra* (II, vii), *Othello* (II, iii), *The Tempest* (III, iii), *Timon* (III, vi).

[5] M. S. Steele, *Plays and Masques at the Court during the Reigns of Elizabeth, James and Charles* (New Haven, Conn., 1962), p. 146.

[6] Variants of patterning an opening round a large musical effect occur in *The Two Noble Kinsmen* and *The Maid's Tragedy.*

[7] W. W. Appleton, *Beaumont and Fletcher: A Critical Study* (London, 1956), p. 59.

[8] Una Ellis-Fermor, *The Jacobean Drama* (4th ed.; London, 1961), p. 201.

MILTON ON LAWES: THE TRINITY MS REVISIONS

[1] A lecture to the English Association, London, February, 1963.

[2] "Thou taught'st our Language, first, to speak, in Tone. / Gav'st the right accents and proportion:" Wilson, *Psalterium Carolinum* (1657).

[3] *The Poetical Works of John Milton,* ed. Helen Darbishire (Oxford, 1955), II, 323.

[4] See Vincent Duckles' admirable paper, "The 'Curious' Art of John Wilson (1595-1674): An Introduction to His Songs and Lute Music," *Journal of the American Musicological Society,* VII (1954), 93-112.

[5] The reading in the third version of the Trinity MS is "theire."

[6] G. B. Doni, *Lyra Barberina* (Florence, 1763), II, 31.

[7] *Henry Lawes: Musician and Friend of Poets* (New York, 1941), pp. 167-68.

[8] Henry Lawes, *Ayres and Dialogues* (1653), sig. A^r.

[9] Henry Lawes, *Ayres, and Dialogues . . . The Third Book* (1658), sig. A2^v.

[10] Henry Lawes, *Ayres and Dialogues* (1653), sig. b^v.

[11] *Ibid.*, sig. b^r.

[12] *Facsimile of the Manuscript of Milton's Minor Poems,* ed. W. Aldis Wright (Cambridge, 1899), p. 5. The photographic reproductions in this edition are now more legible than the original MS.

[13] Darbishire, *Works of John Milton,* II, 337-38.

[14] *Ibid.,* II, 346.

[15] *Ibid.,* II, 310-11, 346, 338-39.

[16] *Ibid.,* II, 309; Wright, *Facsimile of Milton's Minor Poems,* p. 5.

CARTWRIGHT'S DEBT TO LAWES

[1] For the facts of Cartwright's life and career, see G. Blakemore Evans, *The Plays and Poems of William Cartwright* (Madison, Wis., 1951), pp. 3-21. Cartwright's first play, *The Ordinary,* for which Lawes composed at least one song, was "completed sometime before March 26, 1635," p. 259.

[2] For the facts of Lawes' career, see my book, *Henry Lawes: Musician and Friend of Poets* (New York, 1941), index under "Cartwright."

[3] G. B. Evans, *Plays and Poems of Cartwright,* p. 20.

[4] See n. 2, above.

[5] G. B. Evans, *Plays and Poems of Cartwright,* pp. 165-70, describes the several manuscript versions of the text. That which includes stage directions, Folger MS 7044, as Professor Evans kindly pointed out to me, provides the most pertinent and appropriate text for this study. My use of the word "first" does not mean that this manuscript was older than the others, but it anticipated the printed text which included the song.

[6] Discussions of the characteristics of Cavalier drama may be found in Alfred Harbage, *Cavalier Drama* (New York, 1936) and in G. B. Evans, *Plays and Poems of Cartwright,* pp. 22-32. See also Evans' bibliography on Cavalier drama.

[7] G. B. Evans, *Plays and Poems of Cartwright,* pp. 169-70, argues that the manuscript versions of the play represented the way in which it was performed at Oxford, the printed version, the way it was presented at Hampton Court. Evans admits, however, that there is no proof that Lawes did not come along the last moment before the Oxford performance and insert the final song in the ending. Insofar as this study is concerned, it is not important when the changes in the last scene were made.

[8] I have used the word "plot" arbitrarily; Cavalier drama had no plot in an Aristotelian sense.

[9] G. B. Evans, *Plays and Poems of Cartwright,* p. 173, n. 12, objects to my use of the words "tempt" or "temptation" as related to Cratander's character. Cratander "has neither passions nor weaknesses."

[10] Jackson Cope, *The Metaphoric Structure of Paradise Lost* (Baltimore, 1962), p. 68, points out that there is no real temptation in *Paradise Regained.*

[11] William Haller, *The Rise of Puritanism* (New York, 1938), p. 151: "The Puritan saga did not cherish the memory of Christ in the manger or on the cross, that is of the lamb of God sacrificed in vicarious atonement for the sins

of men." Gustaf Aulen, *Eucharist and Sacrifice,* trans. Eric Wahlstrom (Philadelphia, 1956), p. 82: "Christ's sacrifice need not and cannot be repeated in a new sacrifice." Malcolm Mackenzie Ross, *Poetry and Dogma* (New Brunswick, N.J., 1954), p. 61, explains the "spiritual Presence of Calvinism."

[12] *Plays and Poems of Cartwright,* p. 27. "All is external—on, but never under, the polite surface." And on p. 187, referring to the sacrifice of the King by proxy, Evans points out it is "shorn of all its deeper significance—almost certainly it had none for Cartwright—and appears merely as a sacrificial law supposedly indigenous to Persia."

[13] I suppose it is possible that Cartwright could have been unaware of the Puritan doctrine to which I have pointed. He may have had little interest in theology in 1636. Two years later, however, he took orders and became an Anglican clergyman. Even then, G. B. Evans, *ibid.,* p. 34, indicates that Cartwright was very liberal-minded in respect to formalism. And R. Cullis Goffin, *The Life and Poems of William Cartwright* (Cambridge, 1918), p. xxx, says that Cartwright "never took his profession seriously."

[14] Harbage, *Cavalier Drama,* pp. 142 f.

[15] James E. Ruoff, "Cartwright's Human Sacrifice Scene in *The Royal Slave,*" *Notes and Queries,* IV (1957), 295.

[16] Edward Lowe, another well-known contemporary composer who had been trained at Sarum, was an organist at Oxford; at this time, Lowe presumably kept to his post.

[17] The contributions of pagan ritual to Greek and of liturgical services to medieval drama require no discussion here. Lawes was relatively unaware of either as literary history has represented them. For bibliographical sources pertinent to such contributions, consult Mary Marshall, "Aesthetic Values of the Liturgical Drama," *English Institute Essays 1950,* ed. Alan S. Downer (New York, 1951); Una Ellis-Fermor, *The Frontiers of Drama* (2nd ed., London, 1964); O. B. Hardison, *Christian Rite and Christian Drama in the Middle Ages* (Baltimore, 1965), and the review of the last named book by George Wellwarth in *Seventeenth-Century News,* XXIV (Winter 1966), 62.

[18] G. B. Evans, *Plays and Poems of Cartwright,* opposite p. 168, prints a facsimile reproduction of a photograph of the manuscript version of this passage in the text and, on p. 249, the corresponding passage of the later (printed) version.

[19] The significance of processionals in religious ceremonial is considered in Rossell Hope Robbins, "Middle English Carols as Processional Hymns," *Studies in Philology,* LVI (1959), 559 f. Dom Gregory Dix, *The Shape of the Liturgy* (London, 1960), p. 397, points to the origin of processional in religious rites. See also his index under "Sarum" and Hardison, *Rite and Drama,* p. 49.

[20] William Empson, *Seven Types of Ambiguity* (New York, 1955), does not use Molop's Sagar as illustrative of a symbol which suggests more than one meaning. But if the number of possible interpretations is the gauge of symbolic effectiveness, Molop's Sagar deserves unique distinction.

[21] See n. 15, above.

[22] Hardison, *Rite and Drama,* p. 51, discusses the dramatic effectiveness of the tableau as the climax of the processional.

[23] Massey Hamilton Shepherd, *The Oxford American Prayer Book Commentary* (New York, 1950), pp. 67-69. The *Kyrie* was a cry or shout, "comparable to the Hebrew *Hosannah*" used by "ancient Greeks, both pagan and Christian, in sacred and secular ceremonies, and was addressed to the Emperor

or to God, as the occasion demanded." The cry was a salute, an all hail, followed by a petition for mercy or help. In the fourth century, it formed the core of the litanic response, "Lord, have mercy upon us." Its history may be traced in many different sources; one of the most comprehensive studies of the development of the liturgical *Kyrie* is that by Dom Gregory Dix, *The Shape of the Liturgy;* see index under *"Kyrie."*

[24] In manuscript, in the New York Public Library, Drexel MS 4041; I have described this manuscript in my book on Lawes, see n. 2 above.

[25] The liturgical gesture was of perhaps less significance as performed in the seventeenth century than in earlier eras. Its implementation in the service as noted in *The First and Second Prayer Books of King Edward VI* (London, 1957), p. 219, attaches less importance to bringing forth the chalice than I may have here suggested.

[26] Milton perhaps better than anyone else at the time set forth the philosophy that God's law, order, and harmony corresponded with monody; the departure from God's law—the descent into earthly confusion and bewilderment, Hell—was symbolized by discord, harsh chromatic effects, and confused meanings. See Sigmund Spaeth, *Milton's Knowledge of Music* (Princeton, N.J., 1913), who stresses the relationship between concord and God's law.

[27] I shall have more to say about this aspect of Lawes' work in a forthcoming study.

[28] To be examined in a forthcoming study.

INDEX